Socrates and the Gods

Other Titles of Interest from St. Augustine's Press

Nalin Ranasinghe, *Socrates in the Underworld*

Nalin Ranasinghe, ed., *Logos and Eros: Essays Honoring Stanley Rosen*

Plato, *The Symposium of Plato: The Shelley Translation*

Aristotle, *Aristotle – On Poetics* (trans. Seth Benardete & Michael Davis)

Aristotle, *Physics, Or Natural Hearing* (trans. Glen Coughlin)

Thomas Aquinas, *Commentary on Aristotle's Nicomachean Ethics*

Thomas Aquinas, *Commentary on Aristotle's De Anima*

Thomas Aquinas, *Commentary on Aristotle's Metaphysics*

Thomas Aquinas, *Commentary on Aristotle's Physics*

Thomas Aquinas, *Commentary on Aristotle's Posterior Analytics*

Thomas Aquinas, *Commentary on Aristotle's On Interpretation*

Josef Pieper, *Enthusiasm and Divine Madness:*
On the Platonic Dialogue Phaedrus

Josef Pieper, *The Platonic Myths*

Stanley Rosen, *Essays in Philosophy: Ancient*

Stanley Rosen, *Plato's Symposium*

Stanley Rosen, *Plato's Sophist*

Stanley Rosen, *Plato's Statesman*

Stanley Rosen, *The Ancients and the Moderns*

Seth Benardete, *Archaeology of the Soul:*
Platonic Readings in Ancient Poetry and Philosophy

Seth Benardete, *Herodotean Inquiries*

Seth Benardete, *Achilles and Hector: The Homeric Hero*

Seth Benardete, *Sacret Transgressions: A Reading of Sophocles' Antigone*

Joseph Owens, C.Ss.R., *Aristotle's Gradations of Being in Metaphysics E–Z*

Peter Kreeft, *Philosophy 101 by Socrates*

Peter Kreeft, *Socrates' Children: Ancient*

Ronna Burger, *The Phaedo: A Platonic Labyrinth*

James V. Schall, *The Classical Moment*

Roger Scruton, *Xanthippic Dialogues*

Roger Scruton, *Perictione in Colophon*

Socrates and the Gods

How to Read Plato's Euthyphro, Apology, and Crito

Nalin Ranasinghe

ST. AUGUSTINE'S PRESS
South Bend, Indiana

Manufactured in the United States of America

1 2 3 4 5   17 16 15 14 13 12

Library of Congress Cataloging in Publication Data
Ranasinghe, Nalin, 1960–
Socrates and the gods: how to read Plato's Euthyphro, Apology, and Crito
/ Nalin Ranasinghe.
p. cm.
Includes bibliographical references (p.   ) and index.
ISBN 978-1-58731-779-8 (hardcover: alk. paper) 1. Plato. Euthyphro.
2. Plato. Apology. 3. Plato. Crito. 4. Socrates. I. Title.
B370.R36 2012
184 – dc23   2012017576

∞ The paper used in this publication meets the minimum requirements of the American National Standard for Information Sciences Permanence of Paper for Printed Materials, ANSI Z39.481984.

ST. AUGUSTINE'S PRESS
www.staugustine.net

This book is dedicated
with filial gratitude to
Stanley H. Rosen,
the Father of its Logos.

Table of Contents

Footnotes to Plato

This book will argue that the *Euthyphro* offers the best way to gain access to Plato's *Apology of Socrates* in the sense of giving us Plato's own views about Socrates' trial and its truest causes. Because such an interpretation has not hitherto been undertaken, and since the *Apology* is one of the most influential works in the West's history, this suggests that if my argument holds, the fullest take on the death (and life) of Socrates has yet to be gained by the civilization that he "midwifed" out of the cultural nihilism following the horrors of the Peloponnesian War.

Accordingly this work consists of three parts devoted to the *Euthyphro*, *Apology* and *Crito*. This tripartite division will also reflect the main structure of my work. That section dealing with the *Euthyphro* will deal with the true causes and significance of the trial of Socrates as Plato understood it, the section devoted to the *Apology* proper will then go on to study what Socrates said at the trial itself, and finally my analysis of the *Crito* looks at the conclusions, literally the judgments, that Plato invites us to draw from his reflection on the pregnant meaning and kairotic reality of the trial of Socrates. This triadic structure will also be reproduced in my analysis of the *Euthyphro* itself: I first explain the significance of this dia-logue's interlocutor before proceeding to deal with its substance and then finally discussing the theological position that it implicitly points readers towards. Although both the *Euthyphro* and *Crito* debunk old myths in speech and generate new myths in deed, I will scrupulously distinguish between Plato's artful depiction of the activities that led to Socrates' trial, the actual sublime event of the trial itself, and the way by which the heroic trial and death of Socrates brings new ethical, theological and political paradigms into existence. This is why the *Euthyphro* and *Crito* must be seen to stand, like the two thieves at Calvary, on either side of the account rendered by the *Apology* of the trial itself; while taking their bearings from the central text—the true legacy of Socrates— keeping it uncontaminated by speculation or mediation, read properly they also suggest how exegesis of a Platonic text should be done. By exploring the radical implications of Socrates' life Plato makes the weak arguments of Meletus stronger. Yet, in so doing he is acting with utmost fidelity towards Socrates' legacy. Both Euthyphro and Crito represent different sets of problems pertaining to false claims to know the "known unknown" held by Socrates' enemies and friends respectively.

While this work is proudly autochthonous, in the sense of being derived from almost forty years of obsessive thought and conversation about Socrates and his world, my seemingly cavalier disregard of three and twenty centuries of Plato scholarship requires some explanation. Simply put, my book is informed by the passionate conviction that Plato's Socrates can and must speak directly to us in a time when the end of democracy begins to resemble its beginning. As such, my argument does not need to, and cannot, occupy itself with what other philosophers, from Aristotle to Heidegger, have said about Plato. Indeed if the history of Western philosophy consists of footnotes to Plato, and if, as Heidegger claims, every great thinker is fundamentally possessed by one single great thought that he must single-mindedly express, any reference that such a thinker may make to Plato will be, almost necessarily, unjust or irrelevant. My far humbler concern here is to offer a novel but internally consistent commentary on Plato's interpretation of the trial of Socrates. Any merits that this eccentric work may possess accrue from its fanatical loyalty to Socrates and Plato. I aspire only to be as impressionable and soft as Apollodorus and quite as obsessive as Aristodemus. This means that my accounts of Socrates will grow out of what my penurious soul has salvaged from the overflowing *poros* of Plato's genius. I am but single-mindedly concerned with giving birth to this love-child within my own cultural setting or cave.

Likewise, while I have read a great many books about Socrates and Plato, constant skirmishing with them will do little to advance my own argument here. I do not have time or space to explain why I don't agree with a certain scholar or way of interpretation; so Sisyphean an enterprise would only interfere with the orderly unpacking of my original reading. Although several works have offered readings of Plato's dialogues that are compatible with the account offered here, doffing my hat to all of them will only impede the task at hand. As far as I know, nobody has offered an interpretation of the *Euthyphro* that leads to the philosophical and theological conclusions about the trial of Socrates drawn here. Further, since my own preliminary reading of this dialogue was first made available on the internet over twelve years ago as an essay entitled *"Socrates and the Homeric Gods,"* any more recent scholarship drawing similar conclusions will have to acknowledge my prior discoveries. As will be seen, my argument follows a self-sustaining line of thought that connects the *Euthyphro* to the *Apology* and *Crito* in a way that displays their essential literary unity, as a post-tragic trilogy.

Another peculiarity of this work requires less explanation, apology or defense. It has to do with the materials I have preferred to swaddle my account of these three dialogues in. Rather than lose myself in digressions pertaining to other, necessarily un-impartial, readings of Plato, I have been led to go behind him and use as the background for this exegesis both the Homeric-Hesiodic accounts of gods and men that preceded Athens as well as the great Athenian works of drama and history that were pretty much contemporaneous with Socrates. By shamelessly lurking below the banqueting table, amidst these texts and reeds of Plato's cultural context, I have come to glean scraps of wisdom that birds and dogs have passed over. These literal footnotes have helped me to reconstruct the soul of Socrates and appreciate the magnitude of Plato's feat. Furthermore, while Plato's style of writing is not fearfully esoteric, it necessarily follows his own principles of logographic necessity and offers more to those who are properly prepared to beg at his banquet. Among other things this means that just as Shakespeare presupposes readers, if not an audience, familiar with the Bible and Ovid, many of Plato's most striking but least apparent insights and interpretations are couched in the form of indirect Homeric allusions and assonances.

In the bluntest terms, I also mean to suggest that even the closest readers can learn far more from the dialogues, and indeed about Socrates himself, by not assuming him to be a Proto-Islamic philosopher, suspicious of even his own shadow. Such an approach involves assuming in advance of our reading that Socrates understood himself as an atheistic wise man, as one who despised the many and cared only for the future of a very non-erotic understanding of philosophy. Even Nietzsche, who certainly knew his Homer, falls into this trap in as much as he uses the bleak "wisdom of Silenus" as the key to the Classical world. While Nietzsche's critique of the Philistine optimism of the Second Reich is well taken, his extreme reaction, itself a hybrid product of his fondness for Schopenhauer and wish to be more militaristic than the Prussians, has much to do with the elitist pessimism of Heidegger or Strauss. They too meld covert hostility to Christianity with a virulent anti-humanism that seems to hate Weimar more than German Nihilism.

By contrast, my view of Plato's Socrates runs parallel with Pope Benedict XVI's strong insistence that Greek Philosophy "rightly understood" is the indispensable ally of Christian Revelation. This work will reject the false opposition between reason and revelation that is only attractive to crypto-atheists who believe that the rabble need religion to keep them in line; to this outlook "The Philosopher" is but the shepherd of nihilism. I argue that just as philosophy, the love of wisdom, is not the same as "Reason," revelation, taken in its most fundamentalist sense, is diametrically opposed to the Christian Logos. We learn from Nietzsche that one should beware of misanthropic atheists like Zarathustra bearing gifts! It is just about as dangerous as the far more orthodox practice of robbing the Egyptians! Voluntarism, whether of the ancient or modern variety, is the oldest and most inveterate enemy of the Logos. It is hardest to detect when it masquerades as perfect piety or pyrrhic patriotism.

This is why, instead of opposing reason to revelation in an anticipatory spirit of *Schadenfreude*, I will try to show how Platonic dialogues are marked by interaction between the forces of divine grace and human eros: oracular revelation and philosophic interpretation. Such a model takes us beyond the voluntaristic extremes of fundamentalism and nihilism; it points towards the space depicted in *Gorgias* 508a, where the forces of Sky and Earth, as personified by immortals and mortals, enter into fruitful interaction. This model offers a healthy alternative to the doctrines of Divine Predestination and human depravity that emerged out of the ruins of the Roman Imperium. These ideas eventually came to be imitated by the technological forces that brought about the Death of God once he was conceived of in terms of irresistible power and unchanged perfection. While ancient poets and postmodern technologies necessarily complement the claims and aspirations of tyranny, whether divine or totalitarian, this book seeks to reveal an alternative tradition of Christian Humanism, best typified by Erasmus and Shakespeare, but originating in the confessional dimension of Homer's *Odyssey*. In other words, instead of cheerleading for vindictive gods and vengeful heroes, a close reader of the great works of our tradition could very well emerge with a far more satisfactory logos or justification of the ways in which divine grace subtly interacts with the human spirit.

Apart from depicting the triadic unity of the *Euthyphro*, *Apology* and *Crito*, this book also is also the final volume of my Socratic trilogy. Although *Socrates and the Gods* is quite capable of being read independently of the two volumes that preceded it, it is worth acknowledging the basic insight that led me to write *The Soul of Socrates*, namely the recognition that Plato wrote his dialogues out of metaphysical *penia* rather than *poros*. This suggests that the dialogues, most notably the *Republic,* are more about the diseased soul of the interlocutor than the divine wisdom of his ironic interrogator. They do not provide us with a set of transcendent doctrines that could be transferred from all-knowing teacher to perfect student.

While the *Soul of Socrates* was originally not conceived of as the first volume of a trilogy, two events caused me to write the second and third volumes, *Socrates in the Underworld* and *Socrates and the Gods*. I have already referred to the first event: Pope Benedict's *Regensburg Address*. This lapidary invocation of the essence of Christianity and the West deserves to be ranked besides Lincoln's *Gettysburg Address* and Solzhenitsyn's *Harvard Address* as one of the defining works of our Civilization. It helped me to see that the *Logos* of God had to be rescued from the virus of voluntarism that had infected both the Macworld (including its PC domain) and the Jihad. It was with this goal in mind that I penned my book on the *Gorgias*. I wanted to show how the model of the cosmos and the anti-sophistical political art set forth in the *Gorgias* was the antidote to the plague of voluntarism-based consumerism and valorized violence that afflicted the West. A strife-ridden model of reality was the direct result of a pessimistic political philosophy that justified itself by setting up a conflict between human depravity and divine perfection. Set pointedly against the backdrop of the horrific Peloponnesian War, the *Gorgias* makes a direct connection between the pandering speech of Gorgias, the inflamed desires of Polus, and the depraved soul of Callicles. I tried to show how the seemingly unlimited divine powers offered by Gorgias blind the soul and trap it in a hellish underworld, where ignorant armies clash throughout an eternal night.

The second insight, leading to the writing of the present volume and the completion of my trilogy, occurred more subtly. My beloved teacher Stanley Rosen, in connection with the editing of his *festschrift*, shared with me the story of his consternation upon discovering that his own teacher, Leo Strauss, did not possess the wisdom—final answers to the ultimate questions—Rosen believed him to have. Since my original foray into Socrates scholarship had much to do with my own realization that Rosen trained his students by refusing access to the golden apples of wisdom, this second belated recognition—that no mortal was wise—struck me like a thunderbolt. I saw that the silence of Socrates was inseparable from his ignorance and human wisdom. Just as one found out who he was by wrestling with Socrates, so gaining valuable self-knowledge rather than wisdom, Socrates himself became the wisest of men by understanding the implications of his un-wisdom. Also, by extension of this logic, God truly becomes himself by emptying himself of his capacity for absolute power and knowledge, by creating human beings he can love and be freely loved by.

While this final claim will be the subject of another book entirely, my insight into the ignorance of Socrates dovetailed perfectly with previous conclusions that I had come to concerning Socrates and his slaying of the Olympian gods. Many years ago, David Lachterman had directed my mind to Bruno Snell's brilliant insight that Homeric man lacked genuine individuality because his various organs were seen as being ruled by gods. As a result, saying "a god made me do it" with Helen seems to express the impotence of a human ruled by a divine *ananke* or perverse necessity beyond her control. Yet Socrates refutes the "bad faith" of these claims by his *daimon*-inspired display of temperance before these mighty necessities. He shows the Athenians that these gods were no more than falsely divinized desires and emotions. Before his steady gaze their many vicious gods become moderate virtues.

This theme is taken up in the first part of *Socrates and the Gods*, where I go about interpreting Plato's *Euthyphro*. I claim that this dialogue offers us Plato's best depiction of Socrates' views concerning the gods. The *Euthyphro* also takes up another theme of vital importance to the trial of Socrates, his so-called corruption of youth. My exegesis shows that any follower of the Olympian gods is inextricably trapped in an Oedipal opposition that pits fathers against sons and past against future. While Euthyphro learns not to take God's name in vain, we also see how the Socratic purging of Olympian religion sets in motion a radical re-reading of Homer that points towards the unity of the virtues and erotic monotheism. Euthyphro seems to believe that the all-powerful gods are most pleased by human flattery, but Socrates helps us to see that we best serve the gods by living virtuously and depicting the gods as transcendent embodiments of goodness.

My reading of the *Apology* argues that Socrates' real offense consists in exposing the dark gods of chthonic family values and faceless furious *ananke* to rational scrutiny. These false gods are as powerful in our day as they were in his. Yet Socrates' *daimon*-given ability to make the strong argument weaker and *vice versa* refutes belief in their divinity. Socrates' crucial distinction between inspiration and exegesis is not only the reason why it is impossible for any man to be wise, it also serves as the basis for his joyful claim that divine or metaphysical knowledge is unavailable to man. Homer, Hesiod and the tragedians can only teach us about human things. All we have is certain awareness of moral obligation and human wisdom about virtue. This suggests that human souls are only capable of moral virtue; this revelation is deeply galling to those who prefer to manipulate others' passions whilst being ruled by their own. Yet Socrates believes that he is divinely mandated to expose their vice and ignorance. He displays this power by his power to defy the fear of death as he practices virtue and even educates members of a murderous jury.

The final part of this book, devoted to the *Crito*, discusses Socrates' political legacy. While the *Apology* reveals the moral autonomy of the philosopher, the *Crito* shows us why he yet prefers to go down to the cave. We see that the virtue of the philosopher cannot be separated from his political obligations. Socrates' greatest fear is that men like Crito will fail to see that they can practice virtue in his absence. He cannot be identified with *the* "one" any more than his friend can be allowed to regress back to the undifferentiated many or *demos*. Socrates here refutes Crito's understanding of friendship and politics according to selfish economic categories derived from the family. Socrates tacitly reestablishes the polis on the basis of a new understanding of law as an ongoing conversation conducted by members of a polity concerning the just and the beautiful.

This is why my reading of the *Crito* suggests that while Socrates is a moral teacher *par excellence*, his intellectual apotheosis would be fatal to all that he stood for. Just as Christians cannot use the sacramental death of Jesus as an excuse to avoid their charitable duties, Socrates' divine mission has everything to do with reminding us that talking about morality cannot be separated from practicing virtue. At the end of the day, less intellectually gifted practitioners of virtue turn out to know more about goodness and be better at it than those of us who are only able to talk a good language game.

The Euthyphro

I. The Involuntary Prophet

Plato's *Euthyphro* occupies a conspicuous place in his literary oeuvre; both situated and dramatically set just before the trial of Socrates, it seems to deny the reader immediate access to the celebrated *Apology*. By being interrupted by Euthyphro we are also refused "Euthyphronein" literally straight thinking or direct knowledge of the prosecutorial speeches at the trial itself—which seem to be inappropriately displaced by him. This comic work also seems to introduce an inappropriate note of levity into proceedings that could justly be described as tragic and unfortunate—both for Socrates and Athens. Yet, I will argue that to appreciate the *Euthyphro*, as well as its inconvenient place in the corpus, we must read it in relation to the *Apology*, where Socrates' trial for impiety and corruption of the youth is famously depicted. This suggests that while the *Euthyphro*'s position defines it as the "antechamber" by which the court-chamber of the *Apology* and death-chamber of the *Crito* must be approached, this antechamber itself may only be seen in the light of some preliminary awareness as to where it is taking us. I am suggesting that we may be expected by Plato to question the implied relation between the *Euthyphro* and the *Apology* before we see the meaning of the *Euthyphro*, and are thus fully prepared to approach the *Apology*. Conversely, the *Phaedo* gives closure for those who—like Xanthippe—need to bid farewell to a Socrates they never really understood.[1]

As we have noted, the very title of this dialogue "Euthyphro" literally means something like "direct wisdom." In this context it is suggestive that Socrates' own approach towards wisdom is indirect and ironic. Indeed, the curious circumstances under which the dialogue occurs suggest that it stands in place of a more direct and explicit account as to what Socrates' real views concerning the gods were. To the extent that it seems to replace the probably scurrilous speeches accusing Socrates, the *Euthyphro* could be a *pons asinorum*; both making the weaker argument the stronger in revealing what was revolutionary about the Socratic invention of theology whilst by its less exoteric nature separating those who prefer dramatic sound and fury from seekers of truth. Euthyphro and the work named after him function like Socrates' interruptive *daimon*.

Some interpreters have offered close readings to suggest that Plato constructs the *Apology* in such a way as to reveal to the reader that Socrates was guilty; this patricidal perspective, which distinguishes between Socratic and Platonic irony,[2] is attractive to certain soul types for reasons that may become clearer as we turn to the *Apology* and *Crito*. However, these readings depend on prejudiced takes on the *Apology* and pay insufficient attention to the *Euthyphro* and *Crito*, works that provide all modern readers with indispensable contextual orientation concerning Socrates' religious and political dispositions. For instance it seems that Plato uses the *Euthyphro* to suggest what Meletus's real (albeit petty) motives and Socrates' religious beliefs were. In this way Plato responds to the charges against Socrates and ensures that the integrity of both the *Apology* and the great death scene of the *Phaedo* are preserved by being framed and untainted by his personal, but more comprehensive, descriptions and speculations. The spirit of Socrates is preserved at least as much by Plato's Socrates-inspired thought and art as his memory is secured by literal depiction and renderings of his life and conversations. It is vital that we bring our interpretations of Plato's sublime metaphysical suggestions into a proper relation with their pure Socratic origins. This, it turns out, is one of the chief themes of the *Euthyphro*. The experience of wrestling with Proteus can only be experienced and recollected by continual dialectical interaction between "facts" and interpretations. While Platonic indirection is a literary strategy necessitated by Socrates' silence, it must also be seen as a means of reproducing what Plato experienced. Plato shows his piety in refusing to directly discuss this virtue but instead letting it to appear before his readers' souls.

Let us then begin this study of the *Euthyphro* by identifying the dramatic context of this dialogue. As we shall see, it sets much light on the vexing question concerning what Socrates' religious beliefs actually were. This is singularly appropriate since it leads up to the theme of the *Apology*.

Socrates was accused of impiety and corrupting the youth by Meletus, Anytus and Lycon seem to have subscribed their names to the indictment later.[3] Athenian law required that the King Archon—an official chosen by lottery to exercise the ancient priestly responsibilities once performed by the long deposed Kings of Athens—conduct a preliminary investigation into the *prima facie* merits of the complaint.[4] Although it would seem that such an inquiry never took place, the *Euthyphro* does turn out to be an unofficial and informal Platonic exploration of these very issues. We are thus invited by Plato to serve as Grand Jurors before whom all the relevant materials are placed. We shall see Socrates examine the validity of Homeric accounts of the gods as they were literally understood by one who deemed himself pious. We must decide if the strange gods Socrates is accused of introducing to corrupt the youth are strange or harmful. As noted earlier, we may even directly experience piety itself as the *Euthyphro* unfolds.

In the dialogue named after him, in a conversation almost a month after the actual trial, Socrates' longtime companion Crito is sharply critical of "the way in which the lawsuit was introduced into the law court, even though it was possible for it not to be introduced" (45e). Crito means that Meletus could either have been persuaded by Socrates or his friends to withdraw his complaint before the hearing, or been ordered to do so by the King Archon himself. Crito implies that Socrates was somehow responsible for these outcomes not occurring. While the *Crito* gives some explanation of Socrates' mystifying conduct, a fuller understanding of the circumstances emerges from the dramatic action of the *Euthyphro*.

Xenophon provides evidence that Socrates was not unfamiliar with the procedure to be followed in the case of a malicious prosecution. In the *Memorabilia*, he pointedly reports a conversation that Socrates had with Crito himself when the latter was placed in just such a predicament. Socrates then advised Crito to befriend a sheep-dog or protector (Archedamus) who, in return for various courtesies and material benefits, would hound Crito's various accusers, not desisting from his unwelcome attentions until their lawsuits were dropped.[5] Bearing in mind Plato's report of Crito's reproachful words to Socrates in prison, it is clearly suggested by Xenophon that similar methods could have been employed against Meletus with every assurance of success. Xenophon, who was on campaign in Central Asia at the time of the trial, is clearly searching for reasons why Socrates did not defend himself in this manner. For himself, the stolid ex-cavalryman is content to accept Hermogenes' explanation that

Socrates merely sought to die while still retaining his faculties.[6] But it is necessary to attend to the objection that since the pious Meletus was more zealous than a mere sycophant, he could not so easily have been bought off or threatened. We must turn to the *Euthyphro* and search for hints as to what the truest motives of Socrates' accuser were.

Did Meletus prosecute Socrates out of patriotism, religious fanaticism or opportunism? Though Socrates discusses Meletus briefly in the *Euthyphro*, very little of what he says explicitly concerning his chief accuser sheds light on the younger man's motives. Meletus is described as a young man of obscure origins; he claims to know how, and by whom, the young were corrupted (2b-c). Socrates sets Meletus's wisdom in ironic contrast to his own ignorance, thus suggesting the possibility of a conversation that never took place—a dialogue that should have been called the *"Meletus,"* literally "On Care." Such a conversation could not have taken place in a formal legal setting. As we know, Socrates' actual exchanges during his trial were far more direct and acerbic since he was not really afforded the opportunity of questioning his accuser in his accustomed manner. However, even in this unhelpful situation, Socrates succeeds in exposing Meletus's stupidly contradictory opinions concerning his alleged atheism. Although the *"Meletus"* would doubtless have featured a more complete version of such a revelation, it would have reached its conclusion in a more comic and far less confrontational fashion. Such a dialogue could only have taken place before formal legal proceedings commenced, and it would doubtless have ended—like so many other dialogues—in Meletus being deftly relieved of his pretensions towards wisdom. Socrates would have conducted himself with his customary combination of humility and irony, allowing Meletus to reflect privately on the extent of his ignorance. The result would have been very similar to that of the *Euthyphro*: Meletus would suddenly have been reminded of other more urgent cares he had to attend to, thus cutting short his conversation with Socrates.

This, then, must be our own revised and improved version of Crito's reproachful question. Why did this conversation with Meletus never take place? Instead of answering us directly, Plato substitutes another dialogue, the *Euthyphro*, literally "the direct knowledge" dealing with a conversation regarding piety to replace the *"Meletus."* It also is noteworthy that while the name Meletus means care, the culminating question of the *Euthyphro* has to deal with the care or tending of the gods! Bearing in mind Socrates' reputation for non-punctuality, it is strongly suggested that this interruption led him to miss the hearing before the King Archon, thus ensuring (in his seeming contempt for the law) that the unopposed indictment present-ed by Meletus had to go to trial. We may even playfully suggest that this dialogue stands in for the speeches of Socrates' accusers (made many days later) that the *Apology* does not provide.

But if this was indeed what happened, was his absence intentional? Also is his lack of respect for the laws of Athens—which required his pres-ence—impious? We recall that on certain other occasions when Socrates did not act or was delayed, his *daimon* (or divine sign) prevented him from doing what he would normally have done. The *daimon* is not just a mental phenomenon that could be explained away as a form of internalized pru-dence; these daimonic interventions could often take the physical form of interruptions by others all but begging to be relieved of their false wisdom, thus causing an emergence/emergency that forced a midwife to step into the breach.

The *daimon* announces its presence by forcing Socrates to act in a dai-monic manner. His belated and reluctant arrivals on the scenes of the *Gorgias*, *Protagoras* and even the *Republic* come to mind. Xenophon seems to provide grounds for our inferring that this is what happened here also. While, in Plato's *Apology*, Socrates says that his *daimon* did not inter-fere with his leaving home for his trial (40 a-b), Xenophon's *Apology* has Socrates state that it twice stopped him when trying to consider *a defense* for himself before his trial. The *daimon* "prevented me from working on my speech when we thought we ought to find some way to secure my acquittal, whatever it took."[7] We may infer that these two interruptions hap-pened prior to the hearing before the King Archon and before the trial itself. Plato seems to illustrate how this *daimon* protects Socrates from the corrosive effects of long speeches. This is also reflected in its preventing us from hearing the fiery speeches of Socrates' accusers!

Plato seems to provide accounts of both of these occasions by writing dialogues concerning the related topics of ignorance and piety. The *Theaetetus* sets out to discuss the implications of Socrates' seemingly skeptical position regarding the subject of knowledge, and leads eventual-ly to a confrontation with the alternative viewpoint of Eleatic Monism. Meanwhile, the *Euthyphro* attends to the question of how we could deal with the divine things amidst the conditions of uncertainty that Socrates attested to through his constant professions of ignorance. It is entirely appropriate that it should also indirectly address the issue of inspiration, the human faculty that must compensate for our lack of certain knowledge concerning the highest things.

Consistent with the theory that this dialogue represents a daimonic interruption of Socrates' natural concern with self-preservation, in his thoughtful essay on this dialogue Leo Strauss convincingly argues that: "Socrates did not seek that conversation" with Euthyphro, "the conversation was forced on him."[8] At the outset, when they meet accidentally before the *Basileus Stoa* of the King Archon, it is Euthyphro who questions and Socrates who answers. Strauss notes that the normally urbane Socrates "does not gladly talk to Euthyphron" at the beginning of this dialogue.[9] Could it be that he was preoccupied with matters of seemingly greater importance? It is only after the self-styled prophet Euthyphro advises him in that instead of giving "thought to his enemies he should confront them" (3c), that Socrates starts to take the conversation more seriously. This, it seems, is the daimonic sign to Socrates that he should not take any extraordinary measures to prepare a defense but instead converse in his accustomed manner with the jurors.

We are thus warned in a playful manner to pay attention to Euthyphro's words when he claims to have been ridiculed whenever he spoke, even though everything that he said did actually come to pass (3c). As Socrates makes clear in the *Apology*, he does not question the possibility of inspired knowledge; his only contention is that the human medium of such revelation is frequently ignorant as to the meaning of his oracular utterances (22b). Although Socrates is not generally given credit for having understood this fact, and is notoriously regarded as a bitter enemy of poetry, it is a truism that the distinct powers of poetry and criticism seldom inhere in the same person. This is also why Socrates often drew attention to his own spiritually barren condition when he was functioning in a maieutic or exegetical mode. The Platonic Socrates' more poetic utterances are pointedly attributed to an external source before then being un-egotistically offered up for interpretation to the reader.

That Euthyphro is inspired seems to be confirmed when he goes on to assure Socrates in a positively oracular manner that "the lawsuit will proceed as he will wish it to" just as Euthyphro *thinks* his will (3e). The alternation from prophecy to thinking is highly suggestive. These words are in response to Socrates' preference for a friendly conversation at his meeting with the Archon; Socrates went on to express much uncertainty as to what would happen if events took a more serious turn. Euthyphro's winged words mean that Socrates has ultimate responsibility for his fate. As we shall see, Delphi's answers don't free us from responsibility; rather, they demand even greater efforts on our part. This is a very Socratic theme; the existence of gods does not allow us to substitute generic ritualized piety for soul-based acts of individual virtue. Socrates must also be struck by the uncanny inaccuracy of Euthyphro's earlier assertion that Meletus is attacking the city at its hearth (3a). While it is *Socrates* who takes on the chthonic furies poisoning the sacred fire, dim-witted Euthyphro has yet identified the real cause of his offense.

How we react to an oracle says a great deal about who we are. In other words our self-understanding is enhanced in equal measure by the oracle's utterance and by our own existential response to this challenge. It is also striking that by depicting Euthyphro, a man who is in every other respect ridiculous, serving as an inspired oracle here, Plato is tacitly granting the reality of oracular inspiration—even as he gently mocks the exegetical pretensions of an oracle lacking self-knowledge! Euthyphro is least oracular when trying to further his personal interests. *His* lawsuit does not go as he wishes it to. Perhaps this is why prophets are not respected in their own towns.

Concerning his own case, Euthyphro's answer that his opponent is quite old and cannot fly away from him (4a) also corresponds to Socrates' appraisal of his own situation. We recall that he described himself in the *Apology* as one too old to flee from death (39a-b) and also smile at the implied comparison to Daedalus—who was able to fly on waxen wings or Platonic tablets; there is also a playful gesture towards the *Meno,* where Socrates spoke about tying Daedalus's statues down (97d-e). It does not matter too much whether Euthyphro inspired or echoed this Socratic self-characterization, the connection is all too evident. Socrates seems to be told in no uncertain terms by the gods through Euthyphro, a very ignorant man, that if he stands his ground and fights, the best possible result will ensue. He must not engage in sophistic legal maneuvers that would discredit both his life and his divine mission. It follows also, although this deduction will only be made in the *Crito*, that Meletus himself will turn out to be Socrates' unwitting benefactor.

Furthermore, once he finds out about the truly outrageous nature of Euthyphro's lawsuit, Socrates finds himself bound by piety, a literal experience of religious obligation, to dissuade him from prosecuting his father. This chance encounter with Euthyphro thus functions in many ways as a daimonic sign to Socrates that he should not attempt to quash Meletus's indictment. Though Socrates was accused falsely of impiety, both Euthyphro's oracle and his own principles would lead him to conclude that a worse man could not harm a man better than himself (30d). However,

Euthyphro's lawsuit was truly impious. By refusing to relieve Euthyphro of his blasphemous opinions concerning the gods and instead concerning himself with the survival of his material aspect (since Meletus could do his better soul no real harm) Socrates stands in far greater danger of being "polluted" by Euthyphro's impiety. The internal voices of duty, piety and gratitude all dictate that Socrates purify Euthyphro, instead of caring for his own aging body. Like Odysseus on the feast of Apollo,[10] he is required by his Delphic mandate to tear off his beggarly robes and play the role of the King Archon—the "ruling" beginning for our investigation. In doing so, he will be inspired to reveal some of his own views about the gods. Socrates might even learn a great deal more about himself and the gods through this involuntarily pious action.

But this revelation must wait its proper time. For the present we should return to our place in the dialogue and observe that the substitution of Euthyphro for Meletus seems to represent very much more than a compelling reason for Socrates to desist from confronting his accuser. There is also a very strong *positive* parallel between the two young men. This is first suggested by Euthyphro's first words to Socrates "*ti neoteron*","or "this is new" (2a) in their evocation of the charge that Socrates brought new divinities into the city. When we try to study the soul of Euthyphro, we see that his true reasons for prosecuting his father are startlingly similar to those impelling Meletus to prefer his "*graphe*," literally "writing," against Socrates' habits of speech. The deadly letter of the law is opposed to the spirit of justice.

While we do not know whether or not Euthyphro is a real person or whether the dialogue is a substantially accurate report of an actual conversation, Diogenes Laertius writing over five hundred years later reports that Socrates dissuaded Euthyphro from his purpose when he indicted his father for manslaughter.[11] However, this could merely be a paraphrase of the *Euthyphro*; as such it is about as significant as Xenophon's understated report in his *Memorabilia* that Socrates convinced Glaucon not to enter politics.[12] The only Platonic references to Euthyphro occur in the later *Cratylus* where Socrates claims to have been inspired by a Euthyphro who seems to pay inordinate attention to the literal meaning of names.[13] There is an evident likeness between the meaning of Euthyphro's name and his area of expertise that once again draws attention to the question of whether or not he truly exists. The truly remarkable parallels between Euthyphro and Meletus also indicate that just like the Eleatic Stranger of the *Sophist* and *Statesman*, "Euthyphro" is more fictional than real. This entitles us to pay very close attention to every detail of his conversation with Socrates. Otherwise put, Plato's account of Socrates' chat with Euthyphro is likely not a literally accurate tale of an actual Socratic encounter. It occurs in a perfected cosmos micromanaged by its imperfect creator—a place where accidents never occur and every detail has meaning. While Socrates cannot define piety, he still feels its authority in a specific case requiring human prudence rather than divine wisdom.

Unlike many Socratic interlocutors, especially those after whom dialogues are named, Euthyphro's character and motivation lack psychic depth and plausibility. Yet unlike another kind of literary character, he is not a certain ideal type. He is not the stereotypical lovesick youth, wily slave or greedy old man who populate the comedies of Aristophanes. But although he is unique Euthyphro is yet not his own man; he exists specifically for the purpose of this dialogue and functions like an exaggerated caricature that points beyond itself. And, as we shall soon see, he is also not his own man because he lives under the large shadows of Zeus and his own father.

Let us take another careful look at Meletus. We saw that Crito was certain that he could have been persuaded to back off at several points in the trial, thus suggesting that his piety and/or patriotic fervor was not as absolute as it seemed. Socrates will soon show that he is neither pious nor public-spirited. Moreover, since Socrates was manifestly not a rich man, Meletus's interest does not appear to be primarily financial. It is far more likely that his prosecution is connected to his political ambitions. In the bluntest terms, it seems that his plan was to gain cheap political *kudos* by an easy public triumph over a well-known and relatively defenseless public figure.

In keeping with the image of Odysseus disguised as a beggar in his own palace in Ithaca, Meletus seems to be playing the role of Iras—the rash young parasite (so named by the suitors after Iris, the gods' messenger) who hoped to gain the favor of the suitors by expelling an ugly pest .[14] Like Odysseus in his own home taken over by furies and parasites, or Christ in the Temple, pious Socrates must consider the best response to this challenge. Having endured worse challenges over his long career as Delphi's *daimon*, he will not succumb to his emotions and act irrationally; in so doing he would only betray himself at this critical juncture in his life. Instead, he must focus on the best outcome and ignore every other provocation.

We find further confirmation in this appraisal of Meletus's motives in the fact that Athens did not have official public prosecutors.[15] Public-spirited citizens were expected to gain prominence through exposing and replacing corrupt older leaders. This tradition endured into Roman times. The youthful Julius Caesar (prior to being named Supreme Pontiff—the Roman equivalent of the King Archon) made his first foray into public affairs by unsuccessfully prosecuting the ex-consul Dolabella when he was about twenty years old.[16] The scarcely bearded Meletus was affiliated with the poets, (23e) and we recall that the poet Aristophanes first made his name by attacking the prominent demagogue Cleon in his *Knights* when he was in his twenties; when Cleon struck back, Aristophanes turned to a safer target—Socrates.[17] We must also bear in mind that it was not unusual for a poet to play a prominent role in Athenian politics. The tragedian Sophocles was elected general at least twice; he also served as imperial treasurer and was finally named as a special commissioner following the disastrous Sicilian expedition.[18]

It is worth noting that since Greek religion was ultimately based on the poetry of Homer and Hesiod, Athens could not have anything like a doctrine of the separation of church and state. Poets necessarily played an important role in both public and religious affairs through state-sponsored dramatic productions that were eagerly viewed by almost every adult Athenian. Poets may not have exercised priestly functions but they effectively functioned as political theologians: they re-created and updated stories about the gods and thereby conducted officially sanctioned dramatic revelations of the contemporary meaning of Athenian tradition and Olympian religion.

We might conclude then, with deceptive frivolity, that Socrates is accused of corrupting the youth of Athens by operating without a poetic license; he is conducting rational inquiries into supra-rational matters that were traditionally addressed through the rhetorical means of irrational poetic inspiration. Plays like Aristophanes' *Frogs* and *Birds*, which deal quite irreverently and explicitly with the gods and matters beyond the clouds and beneath the earth, were apparently not regarded as being impious and corruptive by the guardians of orthodoxy. This presumably is because dramatic works primarily engaged the desires and senses; they were not regarded as serious and cold-blooded individual investigations into forbidden areas. Differently put, their objective was common catharsis rather than actual theo-logy; everyday injustice is allowed to persist after taking the edge off any bitterness that could lead to real change. The feminine equivalent of this is the Bacchic rites of Dionysus; we are also reminded of the Roman Saturnalia. While it is arguable that the Socratic dialogue, a genre that Aristotle compared to the mimes of Sophron,[19] also results in a comic catharsis, the fact remains that these Platonic works relieve us of conventional wisdom and leave us with perplexity. By contrast, a comedy ultimately vindicates conventional wisdom and purges us of intellectual misgivings. Likewise Euripidean tragedy only seems to confirm our worst suspicions concerning the gods—thus providing wretched mortals with knowledge, albeit of a very pessimistic kind, of the true nature of reality. Neither genre takes a very optimistic view of the rationally examined life. Socrates is thus far more confident than the poets about a thoughtful individual's capacity to live amidst uncertainty. As such, he presents a deeper challenge to the manipulative authority exercised on and through the unschooled emotions by politicians and poets. The basic content of this revelation pertains to the dangerous power and irrational passions of the true hidden gods. While mortal hubris entertains by unsuccessfully engaging the Olympians, it must never give offence to these undying and darker chthonic forces.

It follows that Socrates was in many ways the perfect target for a malicious prosecution by a jealous and ambitious poet. There was also the well-known precedent set by Aristophanes himself over twenty years earlier. That poet's cheap attack on Socrates in the *Clouds* resulted in the play coming last in the Greater Dionysia.[20] It follows then that Meletus, a bad poet, could prove himself to be the superior of Aristophanes, succeeding whilst the latter had failed by directly prosecuting Socrates in the more congenial setting of the courts of justice. Since most of Socrates' anti-democratic friends and companions had died in the ugly years after the Peloponnesian War, he could be blamed vicariously for their sins, just as Aristophanes had projected many of Chaerephon's enthusiasms and excesses on Socrates. The depleted citizenry of Athens was less inclined to tolerate intellectual speculation in these austere times. Rather than turning to philosophy to become aware of their mistakes, it was more convenient to outlaw such speculation by deeming that this kind of profane investigation caused their plight. Prompted and pandered to by the disguised elitism of the poets, they preferred to celebrate their autochthonous common sense—as it was revealed to them by the city. Like the playwrights (and Penelope's suitors) the *demos* did not want Socrates (Odysseus as beggar) to disrupt their irresponsible play.

As a sophist might present the choice, Meletus was in a "no-lose" situation. Either he would win his case and gain fame, or by losing he would earn even greater glory by forcing Socrates to abandon his infuriatingly ironic contempt towards democratic politics and rhetoric. Indeed the desired comic result would have Socrates fall down from the "Clouds" and grovel before the jurors to save his life. Meletus would gain the gratitude and respect of the many worthies who had been humbled by Socrates over the years. Socrates would be exposed as just another coward who would compromise his lofty principles in the face of death. Like Thales falling into the well,[21] the philosopher would be forced to "recollect" his origins in the cave.

In the simplest terms, Meletus's purpose was to frighten and humiliate Socrates by taking him on in a game of "Chicken." Youth have the advantage over their elders in circumstances where they have so much less to lose and that much more to gain. He confidently expected the old man to blink first and concede victory at least in the name of his wife and their very young children. Then, as we shall see, intoxicated by the exuberance of his own verbosity and maddened by Socrates' contempt, Meletus went against his own best interests in proposing the death penalty when he could have triumphed in his chosen genre of comedy by advocating exile—the fate that Socrates actually feared most. The comic poet thus succumbed to tragic hubris and unwittingly contributed towards the immortalizing of the very man he sought to humiliate. He should never have thrown Brer Rabbit into the briar patch!

We see how Euthyphro and Meletus, ridiculed prophet and failed poet, both turn to the left-leaning Politically Correct law courts for redress. Socrates obligingly helps them by giving equal offense to the Political Theology of the right. It is implied that Euthyphro is prompted by the same ambitions as Meletus. He is tired of being ridiculed by his family and the Athenians for his prophetic excesses: "whenever I speak to the Assembly concerning the divine things and predicting for them what will happen, they laugh at me as if I were mad" (3c). We must note that Euthyphro could well be mad in the sense in which Plato discusses poetic inspiration. As we have just seen, he could on occasion speak truly without being able to give a proper account or explanation of his words. Even when inspired, Euthyphro seems to be incapable of understanding or explaining oracular inspiration itself.

Euthyphro however would reject such a distinction between winged words and the more pedestrian task of exegesis.[22] He sees himself as one who is learned in divine things and thus entirely competent to interpret the meaning of his own oracles. Unfortunately when his drunken day laborer murdered a family slave on Naxos, it did not occur to his father to seek the advice of Euthyphro, the family theologian, who also had a personal interest in this matter. Instead, his nameless sire dispatched a man all the way to Athens to ascertain from the official exegete the fate of the homicide. In the intervening time Euthyphro's man died of neglect and exposure.

Euthyphro had to suffer the humiliation of being disregarded by his father, in his self-professed area of competence. This, rather than the democratic piety that one life is as good as another, is what moves him. He decides to demonstrate to his scoffing kinsmen the true power possessed by one familiar with divine affairs. Through his dramatic accusation of homicide and impiety, Euthyphro intends to compel both his father and the Athenians to accord him the respect he had hitherto been denied. Euthyphro is almost as young as Meletus since Socrates makes ironic reference to his wisdom being almost as great as his youth (12a). By dramatically pointing to the letter of the law, both young men will proceed to accuse their communities with impiety if they do not find against their respective defendants. It is far easier for the drowsy *Demos* to condemn an innocent man than for it to collectively perform the near-impossible task of re-examining the dark origins of Athenian religious tradition in a few hours.[23]

Euthyphro's allegations are so wild and implausible that we are forced to dig deeper to find any basis at all for his case. Did he really want to accuse his father of homicide? His lawsuit is made stranger yet by the realization that he is prosecuting his father for events that must have taken place at least five years earlier; Athens lost possession of the island of Naxos in 404, at the conclusion of the Peloponnesian War. Socrates was tried in 399.[24] Also, pollution has to do with the physical contagion stemming from the murder of a family member. Given the absence of familial or spatial contiguity with the polluting event, it is hard to escape the inference that something else led Euthyphro to open this can of worms. By this device Plato invites us to study the evidence and find the true causes of Euthyphro's actions. Surely his real goal is to humiliate his sire and gain face in the zero-sum household economy: now *he* will be the man of the home! Hegel's remark that only one man is free in an Oriental despotism applies here too.[25]

Just as Euthyphro points us towards Meletus, in the sense of suggesting what the latter man's motivation was, Meletus concomitantly helps us to understand Euthyphro better. Euthyphro's belated concern about pollution parallels Meletus's implicit exploitation of older unspoken accusations against Socrates. These had to do with his connection to Critias and

Charmides, members of an infamous group of brutal Oligarchs—the Thirty—who were installed by the victorious Spartans as rulers five years ago.[26] Though Socrates does not mind referring to the accusations of Aristophanes, it seems that Athenian law forbids him from referring to these other matters since the Athenians had prudently decreed an amnesty on such prosecutions based on old enmities.[27] Nevertheless, Meletus will make these various unspoken connections the real basis for his malicious indictment (18a–e). The parallel suggests Euthyphro, like Meletus, is literally digging up grave old matters from the past for selfish advantage. We have seen that Meletus was not very pious or patriotic and really sought to humiliate Socrates and/or drive him into literal or political exile to gain *kudos* and a place in the sun. Euthyphro seems to be similarly driven.

Just as Euthyphro's day laborer had been deceased for several years, genuine piety seems to be long dead in Athens; only blind fury and spite remain. Euthyphro's ambitious literalism is a dangerous religious development closely related to the political mood of democratic chauvinism. Both Meletus and he will proceed to exploit this thoughtless piety by subjecting it to emotional blackmail. As is still done today, they sought to turn dumb prejudice into official policy: Hitler used anti-Semitism in this way. Either Socrates and Euthyphro's father are guilty, or the Athenians and their fathers have been guilty of religious hypocrisy over many generations. In a situation where many men would otherwise be compelled to jettison their certainties and be left with nothing, it is better that one man should die. Rather than peering into the abyss that opened up before Euthyphro when his dogmas were subjected to rational scrutiny, the jurors are urged to cloak themselves in cheap patriotic piety and find an innocent man guilty of blasphemy. Anyone exposing their collective righteousness to the disquieting experience of uncertainty is a disruptive influence and must be dealt with accordingly.

Euthyphro deflects any objections concerning the propriety of a son prosecuting a father for the polluting murder of a non-relative on foreign soil by appealing to divine precedent. His decisive proof is the conduct of the gods themselves. "While human beings agree that Zeus is the best and most just of the gods, at the same time they agree that he bound his own father because he gulped down his sons without their consent, and that the latter in turn castrated his own father because of other such things" (5e–6a). It follows by this logic that because Euthyphro, by virtue of his superior knowledge of divine matters, is more pious and thus a better and more just man than his father; he is fully justified in prosecuting and supplanting him. It was in this spirit that Pheidippides chastised Strepsiades in *The Clouds*,[28] and although Aristophanes accused Socrates of inspiring this crime, Plato suggests that we take a good hard look at Meletus's poetic precedent. While one who prosecutes his father is probably corrupt, it does not follow that his father is necessarily responsible for this corruption. Indeed, Socrates consistently drew attention to the embarrassing fact that even the best Athenians were unable to impart virtue to their sons. The *Meno* reveals that while Socrates did not blame them for this, and indeed tried to show why this was not possible for virtue to be transferred in this way, his very drawing attention to this state of affairs offended the "family values" of fathers like Anytus.[29]

It is *Aristophanes* who is obsessed with the possibility and justification of pious father-beating. His first play that we know of, the *Banqueters*, contains a variation on this theme and his *Wasps*, which was written immediately after *The Clouds*, features a clash between a dissolute old father and his conventionally moral son.[30] Aristophanes gleefully portrayed himself as a self-made young conservative who vainly criticized the corruption of his elders in the name of piety and traditional values. Although Aristophanes claims to chastise Socrates for irresponsible conduct that could easily be emulated by the unscrupulous, we must see that it is Aristophanes who is being copied in the *Apology*. While Euthyphro represents Meletus in the dialogue we are presently studying, we must not forget that Meletus self-consciously stands in for Aristophanes in the *Apology*. The author of *The Clouds* certainly bears responsibility for the consequences of Meletus's ambitious imitation of his self-promotion. The problem with *mimesis* is that it is almost necessarily unaware of the truest motives animating the creator of the imitated object. Sadly in a situation where reasoned appraisal of religious matters is invariably difficult and disapproved of, self-serving hypocrisy is implicitly encouraged to take its place. If Socrates is to be blamed for the irresponsible actions of his imitators, so should Aristophanes.

When Euthyphro invokes hallowed Olympian precedent he is conveniently ignoring the fact that both Zeus and Kronos could have claimed to act according to the natural law of self-defense when they bound and imprisoned their fathers. Uranos had already imprisoned all of his children in the Earth, and Kronos had every intention of swallowing up baby Zeus.[31] Euthyphro's case hardly falls under this category. Moreover Zeus, like Orestes, was in a situation where both victim and culprit were relatives. By tying up Kronos, he could be said to have avenged Uranos, his grandfather,

who was castrated by his son. Euthyphro is certainly not avenging an innocent victim of crime. Why then does he act so strangely after so many
years? We note that unlike a slave who belongs to a family—and has job
security—day laborers are not even worth enslaving. It is not coincidental
that Achilles used this lowliest of stations to illustrate his great desire to
live.[32]

As Plato presents them, the facts compel us to conclude that
Euthyphro's motives and precedents are pre-political rather than ethical.
Euthyphro, we must recall, is concerned with piety not with justice. Like
many a tyrant, he will feign outrage in order to perform a worse atrocity:
we are reminded of Mussolini's claim that he invaded Abyssinia to protect
the rights of its Muslims! Euthyphro is not really anxious to avenge his
dead servant; indeed he even calls him a murderer (4d). Though he intends
to please the gods through his act of extreme and unjust piety, this piety is
essentially selfish. Even when not primarily motivated by fear of punishment, many religious persons act charitably for the sake of going to heav-
en—not out of a truly virtuous desire to do what is good for its own sake.
Kronos and Zeus likewise expected to gain rule over Gaia by deposing
their sires. Not content merely to supplant their unjust fathers, the sons
"naturally" replaced them as tyrants. Like Clytemnestra's subsequent
tyranny over Argos, and transformation into the ancient fury of the house
of Atreus,[33] the tyrannical results of this deed exposed the hypocrisy of any
claim to have acted out of pious regard for justice.[34] Both Kronos and Zeus
overthrew fathers who buried or swallowed their children out of the not-
unjustified fear of being overthrown by them. By insisting that he is following the precedents set by the two divine rulers, Euthyphro is unwittingly suggesting that he too is driven by their truest motives rather than by
their most plausible pretexts.

It seems then that Euthyphro's real fear or grievance has to do with not
having been accorded his proper "place in the sun" by his father; in other
words he is afraid of being eclipsed by his sire. This was already suggested in his father's unwillingness to acknowledge Euthyphro's authority in
matters having to do with piety and justice. In this sense, it is Euthyphro
himself, not his hired man, who claims to have been swallowed up by his
father (or buried in the ground) and denied nutriment on the grounds that
he is a potential parricide. The more salient fact of his being a crackpot in
religious matters is conveniently ignored.

The very fact that Euthyphro's father is never referred to by name here
is also significant. It is as though we are expected to think of him only in

terms of his fatherhood. For the purposes of the dialogue, it is this relation that determines his essence. He is not a "who" but an impersonal "what"— it's nothing personal! More generally, it is in this tragic Oedipal spirit that each new generation represents a threat to the one that preceded it; in order for the young to realize their own individuality, it is inevitable that they should trespass on the jealously guarded prerogatives of their fathers and elders. It is striking that both Kronos and Zeus are often depicted as their fathers' youngest sons, thus underscoring that this conflict is between youth and old age. The triumph of the son ensures that the father's days of procreation are over. The fact that it is always the *youngest* son who slays the dragon or giant in a fairy tale suggests that the monster in question is none other than his own father. While we can only develop this theme later, Plato's treatment of Socrates, his philosophic progenitor, stands in striking contrast to the general rule depicted in this dialogue. The goal of the Platonic dialogues is to make Socrates younger and also more beautiful and loquacious than usual. Far from castrating his sire, as Kronos did to Uranos, Plato's poetry makes Socrates posthumously prolific. This is Plato's performative virtue; the equivalent of Socrates' existential demonstration that a good man can face death with grace and courage.

In a situation where past and future are at cross-purposes, religious traditions inevitably break down. Both sides use religion as a weapon in this struggle, disguising their real selfish motives from others and even themselves. The fathers claim to be defending time-honored custom against the rude innovations of their sons, while the sons profess to rescue true religion from the corrupt and cynical practices of their fathers. The father's recollections of the hostility he felt towards his own father will only make him more suspicious and hostile towards his son. The son, in turn, will find it natural to show his own son the hostility that his father displayed towards him and claim that he is teaching his son to be a man. Sadistic initiation rituals are a fine example of the socially approved manner in which this veiled aggression is passed down from old to young. Aristotle gives the striking example of the son who claimed, in his defense for beating his father, that just as his father beat his father, as did his grandfather, his own son would do the same to him because it ran in the family.[35]

In the field of culture also, the insecure youth of a community soon realize that they can only gain honor by overturning the laboriously built artificial worlds by which their fathers seek to be remembered after *their* deaths. In other words, while the young desperately seek immortal fame and glory by rescuing original nature from their corrupt sires, the old

defend the *status quo* as nature and demand blind allegiance to their unacknowledged mistakes. Both sides are trapped in a situation where the very
forms of violence struggled against are unwittingly reproduced by the
struggle itself. As the history of the *polis* shows, destructive cycles of
mimetic violence cannot be sustained for very long. Worlds are never
wholly natural or entirely artificial and both reactionaries and revolution-
aries fail to distinguish the created from the natural.

It was in the previously described youthful spirit of piety that
Euthyphro used the flimsy pretext of an unlikely pollution, involving the
long-forgotten slaying of a family member (the slave) by a non-relative on
land no longer possessed by the family. It is embarrassingly obvious to
everyone but himself that his real purpose is to supplant his father: the only
thing worse than deceiving another is deceiving oneself. Here again attention is being drawn to the prophet being the worst exegete of his own
words. It is also striking that Euthyphro did not mention the actual answer
of the exegete from whom his father sought advice; it is not likely that
clemency for the landless homicide would have been advised. Neither
would the providential death of a murderer have scandalized Athenian
piety.[36] Such an indirect and non-contagious disposal of a murderer was
the preferred method of execution in Athens. Likewise, in the unlikely
event of Euthyphro's sire being found guilty, he would have been either
compelled or encouraged to go into exile.

We can also see how Meletus's charges against Socrates are artfully
reflected in Euthyphro's case. Socrates could be said to have accused the
Olympian gods of many crimes and vices unbecoming to their divine status (6b). As such, he effectively bound and castrated these personifications
of the divine by demanding logically consistent and virtuous conduct of
them. Then again, just as Euthyphro's unnamed father and Kronos were
accused of casting their victims beneath the earth, Socrates has emulated
Orestes and followed Aeschylus who in his treatment of the Furies in the
Eumenides depicted the sacred powers of the underworld as chthonic (literally earthly) powers that must be recognized but not worshipped unconditionally. Unlike Aeschylus's Athena, who sought to turn the energy of the
Furies on the enemies of Athens at the *Oresteia*'s end,[37] Socrates sets out
to expose and discredit these perverse forces with the fervor of his Delphic
patron Apollo—their original foe in the *Eumenides*. While Athena represents the link between thought and winning that typified Pericles' Athens,
Apollo looks more towards harmony.

By denying the self-evident virtue of the Olympian gods, and through casting scorn on the Homeric and Hesiodic accounts of their efficient causality, it could be said that Socrates has irreverently punished the old gods for their sins. More specifically, he has bound them in ties of rationality that have caused them to weaken, if not die, from neglect when torn down from the heavens and reduced to merely chthonic status. While Meletus is outraged at Socrates' temerity in condemning gods, and rendering them impotent or incredible through his dialectical arts, he sees nothing wrong in the behavior of the original offenders—the gods. We could perhaps say that he does not know what they were like in their prime, viewing them just as we see Socrates today. Euthyphro likewise blithely overlooks the far more heinous action of his day laborer. We may even go so far as to say that Euthyphro's treatment of the gods is not unlike the way in which he uses his hired hand; utility rather than piety governs his actions. The gods do him a service, albeit one that he cannot afford to mention or acknowledge, even as he aspires to seem magnanimous.

Socrates' attitude towards the gods is very different; like Euthyphro's father he has forsaken prompt and literal obedience in favor of a detached non-contiguous process that relies on rational exegesis. Socrates believes in gods because of his faith in *daimons*, semi-divine intermediaries between gods and men.[38] As we saw, Euthyphro's sire also relied on exegetical mediation. The cryptic utterances of the Delphic Oracle exemplify this process by which human interpretation links together divine principles and human folly. Conversely, Euthyphro and Meletus believe in literal and direct, irrationally mediated, contact between selfish blameless gods and shamelessly scheming sycophantic men. This is inevitable given their wish to see the divine purely in terms of power; they are both day laborers trying to become house-slaves. Yet the master-slave model is hardly adequate to describe the relation of gods to men.

We must see that it is *Zeus* who performed the action (binding his father and throwing him into a pit to die of neglect) for which Euthyphro now wants Socrates chained and executed. In other words it is Zeus who is being both imitated and punished by Euthyphro. Here it is noteworthy that Euthyphro is like Dionysus—literally son of god—in hailing from Naxos. Also his drunken temporary servant has partaken of wine, the gift of Dionysus. Euthyphro also resembles Dionysus in seeking revenge and recognition from those of his own blood who had previously ridiculed his divine powers.[39] In this he reflects the hubris of democratic men who believe in their own manifest destiny under the intoxication of demagogic pandering. This parallel continues into the *Apology* where Meletus stirs up the drunken votaries of democratic anti-intellectualism to scapegoat Socrates—who rejects their blasphemies—for his elitist impiety. "The People United" *are* Dionysus for one gaudy night before they tear themselves to pieces. Meletus likewise is drunk with power when he commands his jury of aged male maenads to destroy Socrates. Yet Socrates' eponymous "enduring power" preserves his integrity.

Euthyphro's resemblance to Meletus is also implied in Socrates' description of his young accuser "going before the city, as if before his mother, to accuse me" (2c). Zeus and Kronos, his divine role models, acted with the support of Gaia, the Earth Mother;[40] and of course Dionysus's maenads were feminine. Gaia supports the efforts of the new crops to displace the old withered plants and gain their place in the sun. Similarly, in Aristophanes' *Clouds*, Strepsiades' real fear is not of being beaten by his son; it is rather that he suspects Pheidippides of having designs on his mother that could possibly be reciprocated.[41] The Oedipal motif is plain; by suspecting their sons of harboring the very incestuous desires they were accused of in their youth, the fathers unwittingly provoke their sons to depose them. In Machiavellian terms, *Fortuna* is not just a woman or whore,[42] she is a mother who turns to *her sons* for virile qualities lacking in their sires. Ironically both fathers and sons bewail their own impotence while fearing the evil virility of the other. Just as Thucydides depicted the Spartan fear of the wanton fickleness and proud irrationality of the democratic Athenians,[43] Euripides' *Bacchae* suggests that Dionysus is the democratic god *par excellence*. Half god and half son of a bitch, he incites the hysterical demos to perform actions they will later regret bitterly in the light of day.

The time of the *Euthyphro*, 399 B.C., is well suited to discussing the radical questions concerning the relationship between the human and the divine that this dialogue brings up. While it could be objected that we have given too little attention to the prevalent religious practices at this time, we may contend by claiming that the terrifying events of the end of the Peloponnesian War and the years following it changed everything. Thucydides famously claimed that the Peloponnesian War was the greatest action in history.[44] This was because it revealed the ugly truth about gods and men—thus unseating the Trojan War as the main source of knowledge about the nature and care of the gods. Events like the Melian dialogue and the Corcyrean revolution[45] suggest that just as the gods were identical with power and disregarded justice, contrary to Aristotle's claim that virtue is more stable than scientific knowledge,[46] even the sacred bonds between father and son were at the mercy of Fortune. Tragedies like Euripides' *Heracles* or *Hippolytus* warn us that divine madness or jealousy could overtake any hero anytime. Likewise, to Euthyphro's eyes, the war's catastrophic end had restored the Homeric and Hesiodic gods as primal barbaric forces acting with compelling necessity on the human spirit. These events led to the death of classical Attic tragedy—which mediated between the gods of the *Iliad* and the sort of human virtuosity that Odysseus represented. In the last years of the Peloponnesian war, Euripides—the last tragedian—could only flee Athens and, like Job's wife, curse God and die.[47] Plays like his *Bacchae* and *Heracles* suggest that if the gods exist, they are far more cruel and wanton than the merely jealous beings worshipped by tragedy and cultic religious practice. Maybe the best parallel is with our own times; the triumph of increasingly inhumane apocalyptic technological power has led many dim-witted theists to view the gods in equally savage and violent terms. To them rational and divine interests are forever opposed.

Human morals were similarly tainted by the total defeat and humiliation of Athens. Only this blighted post-war context can explain Euthyphro's outrageous accusation of his father. While victory has a hundred fathers, defeat is a bastard. Defeated fathers can no longer be admired or emulated. In an age without viable virtue or credible role models, most forms of violence and opportunism are justified or naturalized. Thucydides says that in the earliest (Homeric) times, it was not insulting to ask a stranger whether he was a pirate.[48] The wheel has now turned full circle. We must distinguish between the old gods of the tragic city, the literally conceived Homeric gods of Euthyphro, and the strange new gods Socrates was accused of introducing.

II. Fathers and Sons, Gods and Mortals

Returning to the dialogue, we see that while Euthyphro does not have a Gaia-like mother to whom he could complain he fortunately meets Socrates, who had just introduced himself to Theaetetus as a midwife (149a). The *Euthyphro* reveals the subtly amusing way by which Socrates makes our emulator of Zeus abort his misguided schemes. Once they are exposed to light, the ideas that Socrates deftly midwifes out of Euthyphro duly turn on their progenitor. Socrates is also like Gaia (or the Eternal Feminine) in always demanding better and more adequate conceptions of the divine. These aspirations are not appreciated by those with a vested interest in defending a status quo held together by thumotic fury. They are not wholly unjustified in viewing the self-styled midwife as a potential abortionist of their incestuous offspring.

When Socrates ironically describes the youthful Meletus's accusation against him as the act of a child running to his mother, we are reminded of that fledgling poet's role model: Aristophanes, who approvingly, albeit for demagogic reasons, contrasts feminine or populist common sense to rational hubris.[49] But as apt as the comparison is, we cannot forget to ask a more important question: if Athens is Meletus's mother, who then is his father? The suggestion seems to be that he has run to his mother to complain about his father because, otherwise, his father would be the appropriate authority in matters having to do with the state. The parallel with Euthyphro and Kronos/Zeus also entitles us to conclude that if we follow this father-hating analogy to its conclusion, *Socrates* is his father. This is why Plato has slyly left Euthyphro's father nameless. It is equally absurd for him or Socrates to flee prosecution at their age (4a). We recall Socrates' claim to have conducted his moral mission like a father or older brother (31b).

The deeper significance of this theme of fathers and sons is brought out when Socrates states approvingly of Meletus that "he alone of the politicians proceeds correctly. It is correct to take care of the young first . . . just as a good farmer properly first takes care of the young plants . . . by cleaning out their corrupters" (2e–3a). Meletus was thus later contrasted by Plato to Socrates—who claimed in the *Gorgias* to be the only living practitioner of the true political art (521a). Though in reality instilling human virtue could scarcely be compared to the cultivation of plants, this program is similar to the *Republic* where men were told that they had sprung up from the earth (414d-e). Here Socrates developed the absurd consequences of the political ambitions of another foolish youth: Glaucon.[50] That scheme involved expelling those over the age of ten to protect the young from corrupting influences (540e–541a). We could even say that while Euthyphro unconsciously sought to depose his father by accusing him of polluting homicide, Meletus designates Socrates as his father by the very act of seeking to humiliate or kill him. Socrates' reputation as an irresponsible father accords with this charge. Conversely, Meletus believes that "he don't need no education"; the unconditional love he professes for—and expects from—his mother is sufficient. This view overstates the role of the maternal or sacred, and denies the value of divine transcendent grace; the latter is both personal in the sense of only responding to individuals as well as impersonal to the extent of not granting undeserved happiness.

If the city is Meletus's mother, the extended analogy confirms our identification of her as Gaia: the Great Mother or Hera: the goddess of jealousy. The Athenians prided themselves on their autochthony; they claimed that they alone were native to their motherland and not descended from invaders who had raped the soil and killed its original inhabitants like all the other Greeks.[51] It is through being rooted in their Athenian mother-soil that the young plants grow and receive all of the nourishment that they need to flourish. Foreign innovations like rationalism and sophistry, and strange gods like those introduced by Socratic rationalism, threaten to destroy the ancient and sacred link that Athenians have with their mother-land. In other words, since virtue is present in the soil, a teeming chthonic womb of good virtuous democrats, no external fertilizer is required. Virtue is natural to the Athenians; they do not need, and must not receive, any education beyond exposure to their self-evidently (Euthy-phro) good traditions and the care (Melete) of their elders.

The string of misfortunes that Athens has had since the last years of the Peloponnesian War can only be attributed to the malefic influence of these unnatural influences reminiscent of the beginning of *Oedipus Tyrannos*. The mother soil has had a series of bad harvests; the scanty beard, doubtful antecedents, and unimpressive appearance of Meletus himself is a mark of this sad state of affairs. Indeed, the most valuable crop of the Athenians, their young, are corrupt and disrespectful. Curiously enough the extreme courses of action that both Meletus and Euthyphro have chosen to follow are in themselves evidence of the very decadence they deplore. As was the case with Oedipus and Thebes, or Orestes and Argos, the fathers and the *arche*—the "true" origins of the sacred polity— have been lost. They may only be recovered by a sacrificial act of unusual violence and power. It was in a like spirit that Nietzsche—himself a self-identified decadent—announced and enacted the "Death of God." The terrible despotic ways of an Agamemnon or Laius are forgotten or forgiven amidst the chaos following their loss. We are reminded of how the chorus in the *Oresteia* mourned Agamemnon as the "kindest of kings."[52]

In the vein of *Oedipus Tyrannos*, which itself describes a far older tradition of scapegoating and sacrificial violence, the people are led to believe that some act of pollution (*miasma*) must have separated the chosen people of Athena from their historical destiny. To appease the anger of the gods or goddess, a suitable culprit must be found and brought to justice. It seems that Socrates, who never leaves the polity while yet avoiding the game of politics, is an appropriate scapegoat. This is why he plays the role of unjust father in Meletus's Oedipal drama. It is also fitting that the Delphic Oracle—Orestes' instigator—is his only witness. Though himself a child of the Attic motherland, he has unnaturally polluted her by his blasphemous midwifery, unnatural fathering of other men's sons, and rational hubris. Likewise, Euthyphro blames his father for an ancient crime committed on Naxos, where Theseus abandoned Ariadne to Dionysus. This suggests both that he is Dionysus and that he has a key to wisdom that has been lost by the Athenians. While Theseus was famed as a monster-slayer and myth-debunker, Euthyphro seeks to re-found Athens by restoring the old superstitions in a newer guise, as brazen flattery of the gods.

We have already noted that while scantily bearded Euthyphro claims to be emulating Zeus in his punishment of the unjust Kronos, he is actually blaming his father for doing what he says that Zeus did justly, i.e., for binding a wrongdoer and casting him into a pit. It follows then that although Euthyphro claims that he is following the precedent of Zeus, in supplanting his father who did what Zeus did, Euthyphro is in effect unconsciously accusing *Zeus* of impiety and seeking to depose the reigning god. While this act of founding murder is impious before the fact, it is divinely sanctioned and made sacred after the event. While we shall examine this question in greater detail later, we should note that by imitating Zeus, Euthyphro is overturning the very basis of traditional piety, the basic class distinction between gods and men, and crossing the divide between divine signs and human facts. Yet, in fairness, it must also be conceded that Euthyphro is also holding Zeus to a higher, transcendental standard of justice: the principle of the rule of law, which holds that the law applies equally to all. Yet by making himself the content of revelation, Euthyphro seems to affirm that all claims to horizontal justice, and indeed "the rule of law itself, are wholly superseded by an unconditional obligations towards the gods that he has revealed. In this sense, only an archetypal structure can truly provide the authority that various mimetic mortal authority figures tragically fail to embody.[53]

The oracle is *unwittingly* giving expression to inspired truths even as he interprets them, blindly, to justify his own petty ambitions and passions. We recall the asymmetrical connection between Hesiod's domestic troubles and the sublime poetry that it occasioned. The absurdity of Euthyphro—who explicitly believes that justice consists in all men blindly pleasing the gods through imitation—invoking this contrary principle (that law applies equally to all) out of selfish expediency ironically serves to highlight the involuntary origins of divine revelation. Both Zeus and

Kronos piously invoked the transcendent idea of justice; its use as a weapon against their enemies is testimony only against the bad intentions of the signifier, not against the universal validity of the signified itself. The fact that even a tyrant must use the concept of justice shows that this idea cannot be dispensed with—even as it awaits a more suitable existential embodiment.

Although we have claimed that Socrates is interested in developing a more adequate appreciation of these divine things, we must also note that he is not at all interested in tearing them down from the heavens and making them subject to human manipulation.[54] It is crucial that we recall that Socrates' quarrel was with the poets, not with the gods themselves—whoever they were. His complaint was that when the poets boldly claimed to provide literal or journalistic accounts of the gods out of the unacknowledged fertility of their imaginations, they brought truly divine things into dangerous discredit.[55] Like Euthyphro, the poets are guilty of hubris when they lay claim to positive knowledge above and beyond their area of expertise; further, they professed that this knowledge could be imparted by them to all of the people, all of the time and for all time.

Just as democracy demands an educated electorate, both religion and poetry require performers and audiences who neither confuse letter with spirit nor take the profane signifier for the sublime signified. In other words Socrates is demanding that inspiration, exegetical skill and self-knowledge have to be combined in the polis for humans to enjoy a proper connection with the divine things. While egotistical conduct makes both self-knowledge and inspiration impossible, Socrates' conduct attests that the true heroic selflessness—which self-knowledge brings—can exist alongside genuine inspiration by the mediation of thoughtful exegesis. Such a synthesis is far preferable over the frenzy of a dervish, the fury of a fanatic or the corrosive judgment of an uninspired man of prudence. Beauty, goodness and truth cannot be mutually exclusive concepts. This anticipates one of the central ideas of this rich dialogue; the principle of the unity of the virtues emerges out of a repudiation of Homeric and Hesiodic polytheism.

When Socrates attacked the Homeric and Hesiodic portrayals of the gods, he did so on the grounds of their crude "mis-anthropomorphism." But while that reputed blasphemer, Socrates, verbally rejects the poet's all-too-human images of divine beings on the grounds of their injurious influence on human virtue,[56] pious Euthyphro's deeds unwittingly bear out the truth of these complaints. He moves blithely from poetry to practice and tears down these extreme exaggerations of human qualities from the sky to reenact them on the earth itself.

In other words where the poets, those natural allies of tyrannical rulers, turned the ancient vices of old kings and aristocrats into awesome heavenly punishments that could be inflicted by the gods upon men, they did so in order to render these patterns of behavior taboo on earth. Seeking to both flatter the powers that be and also to gain additional rewards through protecting the prerogatives of the noble, the poets derived their descriptions of the gods out of their everyday experience as flatterers and sycophants in the courts of tyrants.[57] Because the jealous gods could overwhelmingly trump any human vices, ignoble men like Thersites, or Hesiod's foolish brother Perses, were well advised to stick to the straight and narrow path of uncritical ritual obedience. It is suggested strongly by the sycophantic poets that there is one pattern of behavior appropriate for the gods and their kingly descendants, and another for ordinary god-fearing mankind.

The poets warned puny mortals against trying to demand justice from the gods. Both Euthyphro and Socrates violate this prohibition, albeit in diametrically different ways. While Euthyphro implicitly dethroned Zeus for injustice as he sought to piously imitate the gods, Socrates seems to demand in the name of both justice and piety that the highest aspirations of human virtue (rather than the worst vices of the rich and powerful) become the basis for any poetic conceptions of the gods: the gods *must* be generous and erotic rather than selfish and violent. It is this genuinely pious hermeneutic principle that Socrates uses to counteract the various blasphemous excesses of overweening (and self-serving) divine flattery. While the revelations of an oracle are of necessity ambiguous, thereby recognizing human freedom, pious Socrates insists that these enigmatic words are best understood by being given the most virtuous—albeit vulnerable— of all possible responses and interpretations. As we shall see, the *pankalon ergon* (13e) accomplished by serving the ideas of the gods is revolutionary; all-gracious eros overthrows static perfection.

By pitting Euthyphro against his complementary twin Meletus, Socrates hopes to help Euthyphro to see his own hubristic impiety reflected in another man's folly. This is a common Socratic pedagogic strategy. Even if we hold on like Menelaus, Plato's dialogues are notorious for revealing the nature of the interlocutor rather than that of Socrates himself. We are reminded of this protean aspect by Euthyphro's boastful but unwittingly prophetic claim were he to meet Meletus: "I would discover where he is rotten and our speech would turn out to be much more about him than about me" (5b-c). Contrariwise, an encounter with Meletus would lead Euthyphro to see himself! Long before the escapee from the Cave described in the *Republic* will be able to look in, at or towards the Sun, he must deal with the vertiginous experience of seeing himself reflected in the un-blinding light of truth. As Glaucon learned in the *Republic*, self-knowledge must precede any legitimate claim to authority over others. Since Euthyphro has complained, implicitly, of having been buried by his father's pre-eminence, the analogy is quite appropriate.

In an important sense, although largely an imagined character, Euthyphro also represents generic humanity itself in combining elements both sublime and ridiculous. He embodies the *Poros* of inspiration alongside the *Penia* of insecure egotism. Although open to divine insight, he is also all too vulnerable to unworthy temptations. For our purposes, however, once we find out more about the views of Euthyphro our ultimate objective will be to reverse this process and seek to find out more about Socrates' views concerning the gods by their negation of his dialectical foil. Only by this procedure of "negative theology" will it be possible for us to understand Plato's take on the position held by Socrates concerning these matters. This dialogue constantly draws our attention to the importance of the careful reader being very much aware of the many interpretative choices and temptations surrounding him. If, as we have suggested, Euthyphro is a fictional construction, this quality suggests that his emergent nature is totally subject to Plato's purposes and is the Ariadne's string to our reconstruction of his outline of a Socratic theology.

Although Socrates in the *Cratylus* said that Euthyphro was given to engage in prodigious etymologies (396d), a surface reading of the *Euthyphro* suggests that he is also an eccentric collector of Olympian trivia. Rather, Euthyphro seems to have made it his business to swallow and commit to memory every "astonishing story" about the gods (6b-d). As his name's etymology suggests, his reading of these stories is proudly literal and invincibly unreflective. Like any prophet, Euthyphro is blindest in any interpretation that involves himself. Thus, as we see him intent on a self-serving mission in the dialogue named after him, he necessarily appears at his worst. An oracle's statements thus occur at the expense of his self-knowledge. In foretelling the future to Socrates, Euthyphro unconsciously vindicates the name his father gave him, even as he challenges his authority by virtue of the very name that, in the spirit of the *Cratylus*, he identifies with his essence. To be true to his name and see straight, Euthyphro must see through himself! An inspired oracle is an imperfect medium of revelation, and not an infallible maker of truth.

In his role as a blindly intemperate Oedipal oracle, Euthyphro naively believes that the space between sign and signified is Euclidean. Believing that he can undertake a giant leap for mankind through one short step of interpretation, Euthyphro is unprepared for the hermeneutic odyssey ahead of him. His fundamentalist attitude leads him to disregard any impious question as to the consistency of the various stories that he has swallowed whole—like Kronos—as evidence of his unswerving faith. His basic position -that it is not ours to "make reply or reason why"—has been affirmed by orthodox monotheistic theologians for millennia. Combining piety and flattery, they say that as gods are beyond human limitations, all things are possible to them. Euthyphro's gods are not subject to the laws of logic or the principle of non-contradiction. He would shun Ockham's razor but despite routine denials (10d) would avidly swallow his voluntarism.

In such a situation, we can use the language of the *Gorgias* and claim consistently that while justice is the advantage of the strongest, piety is the flattery of the strongest beings: the gods. In this context the relationship between justice and piety becomes far more nuanced. On the one hand it seems as if lowly mortals can only marvel and wonder at the incredible reported deeds of their masters; they cannot hope to understand the ways of the gods, especially as their actions seem to be based on arbitrary hyperbolic power rather than action concerning which a logos must be rendered. But this could also mean that flattering piety may be said to swallow up all the other virtues, just as Kronos swallowed up so many of his children. Zeus, likewise, who claimed to be more powerful than all the Olympians in the *Iliad*, is thus the source of justice.[58] But, as Nietzsche saw, this also could be a way by which priests outwit physically stronger warriors by superior cunning and mastery of both guilt and flattery.[59]

Seemingly untroubled by moral or hermeneutic considerations, Euthyphro regards the hoary old myths as exact factual accounts of the history of Olympus. It is not accidental that this heady diet of fantastic nonsense, neither seasoned by any appreciation of poetic interpretation nor accompanied by any semblance of self-knowledge, leads him to aspire to perform stupidly hubristic deeds. It is in this context that Socrates' emetic therapy will prove to be particularly effectual. Before self-knowledge can come, unappreciative Euthyphro must be forced, like the defeated Kronos, to disgorge the divine trivia that he has unreflectively swallowed. It is out of this unformed *hyle* that we may discover the origins of a Socratic theology.

All of this lies in the future however. As yet, we only have before us Euthyphro's absurd claims that he has precise knowledge about how divine things are disposed (5e) and even more wondrous and astounding things that he wishes to impart to Socrates (6b-c). Socrates' initial response to Euthyphro's grandiose pretensions is characteristically muted. Though it is Socrates who feels called on by his *daimon* to perform the role of the King Archon in reviewing and dismissing this preposterous lawsuit, he implies that Euthyphro has arrived providentially, as a kind of visiting god, to admonish and educate Socrates. By becoming Euthyphro's pupil, Socrates madly suggests, he could compel Meletus to prosecute his master rather than himself (5a). As was the case with Euthyphro's prosecution, the disparity between offense and scapegoat is suggestive. Also, deftly but silently caricatured here is Strepsiades' blaming of weird Socrates for his common cupidity. Private shame is more effective than violent exposure; while the latter only makes the culprit defensive, forcing him to see the likeness, complete the syllogism and make the inference—thus involuntarily accusing himself—is more effective. Education matters more than victory.[60]

We also see that Socrates remains consistent with the principles that he set forth in the *Gorgias* in advocating education rather than punishment as the remedy for wrongdoing (478b-e). As he sets about the task of rehabilitating Euthyphro, Socrates hints that studying under Euthyphro would be a worse punishment than the death penalty demanded by Meletus. Instead of persisting in his alleged corruption of the youth, he humbly offers to be corrupted by Euthyphro's wisdom. By subjecting himself to this terrifying ordeal, Socrates will surely purge himself of ignorance and atone for his seeming agnosticism about divine things. This squares with his remark to Meletus in the *Apology* that were he guilty of corrupting the youth it could only be inadvertent, and the most appropriate punishment would be for Meletus to teach and admonish him in private (26a). Here again, Plato uses the *Euthyphro* to indicate the probable form of that unperformed comic dialogue, the "*Meletus;*" in doing so he also pays off his teacher's debt to Apollo by providing suggestions about the shape that Socratic theology should assume.

However, unlike Plato, both Meletus and Euthyphro prove to be quite incapable of undertaking the task of rehabilitating their fathers. Just as Euthyphro accused his father of murder for his honest perplexity over the fate of the murderous manservant, Meletus avoids Socrates and treats him as one polluted by contagious ignorance on account of his candid skepticism towards poetic theology. True belief is an act, or better yet a decision, of loyalty. Indeed we seem to be urged to rejoice over the scandalous irrationality of our faith. An irrational leap of faith must precede initiation into the mysteries that Euthyphro will reveal to Socrates. This will prove to be very much in keeping with the arbitrary power of the jealous gods he voluntarily believes in.

Socrates' inquiry concerning the various scandalous stories told by Homer and Hesiod concerning the gods, "Shall we assert that these things are true, Euthyphro?" (6c), implies that by becoming Euthyphro's student, he would also enter into the client relationship with his master that the gods seemingly have with favored mortals. This relationship is one of unquestioning belief and literal obedience. This, it is worth interjecting here, is one reason why Socrates could never set himself up as a teacher. In his behavior towards Euthyphro, Socrates accepts that he must blindly imitate his master's posture of cringing devotion towards the gods. By the very act of questioning Euthyphro and asking the gods to explain their ways to man, Socrates breaks this contract and places himself in the ranks of those who do not enjoy a "Most Favored Mortal" relationship with the gods. Socrates called the mimetic irrationality of this relationship into question when he asks his "master" to identify the essential form of holiness that makes all holy actions holy. Euthyphro's prompt response reveals that he has not given the matter any thought: "What is dear to the gods is pious and what is not dear is impious" (7a). In other words, it is ultimately the arbitrary will of the gods that makes something holy, not some secret underlying law; god is higher than the concept of goodness. By justifying his ways to man, a god ceases to be god. Likewise, a prophet can only tell us what god wants, not why he wants it. What his god (and his prophet) wants most from man is our unquestioning obedience and absolute submission.

Socrates points out one of the more obvious difficulties with this position when he asks Euthyphro about its application in a polytheistic context. The very same act could be loved by some of the gods and loved by others. Where does this leave piety? Further, by insisting on the arbitrary caprice of a god, the very real possibility also remains that the same god could like one action at one time and find it quite distasteful at another. Surely we cannot possess knowledge of a divine essence that could bind a god to be what he or she must be? In the absence of any direct "hot-line" between Heaven and Earth we seem to be left in a quite untenable position. Socrates is subtly pushing Euthyphro towards admitting that what will always please his anthropomorphic gods, at any time or place, is the human desire to curry favor with them, in other words, flattery.

Yet, before this admission is made, and its implications are made fully manifest, another important aspect of polytheism is addressed by Socrates. Disagreements amongst the gods, according to him, could only pertain to matters that cannot be resolved by objective, quantitative standards; if Hera, Athena, and Aphrodite all agreed that one of them was the most beautiful, they would not have wrangled over the Golden Apple of Eris.[61] In other words, the winged word "beauty" was the golden apple! Lacking definitive knowledge of these matters, subjective preferences hold sway; yet these very desires are caused by objective but ill-defined ideas. This is consistent with the Socratic dictum that *human* evil is caused by ignorance.[62] Without knowing what is transcendent, the only appropriate inscription on Eris's Apple is "To the Strongest."

If there is no access or awareness of transcendent truth, brute strength ultimately resolves qualitative disputes between the gods and men by reducing them to quantifiable matters of power. None will question Hera's right to possess the apple if she is stronger than the other goddesses—and has the power to maim or destroy her rivals. This was why Aphrodite surrendered her girdle to Hera with good grace in the *Iliad* when it was merely a question of acknowledging Olympian hierarchy.[63] Ultimately, Zeus's will prevails only through the other gods' recognition of *force majeure*. Once enthroned, absolute power may only be addressed (or controlled) by flattery. Zeus is called just, just because he is the principle of order. Since any order is better than chaos, Zeus's might is the only right. Under these wartime conditions, the transcendent category of justice is reductively defined as order. The rule of order-imposing power demands that transcendent ideas be reduced to predicable shadows of their true natures. The subterranean polity of the *Republic* is constructed following this reductive interpretation of justice. But here too, erotic faith in a future higher order of justice may prove stronger than the brute realism of new power in the now.

As swiftly as Meno's slave gave assent to geometrical axioms,[64] Euthyphro accepts Socrates' brilliant suggestion that it is over matters of quality (good and evil, right and wrong, noble and base) that even the gods wrangle. The real question has to do with the existence of transcendent standards that the gods themselves turn out to acknowledge and pay homage to in their very wrangling. These very quarrels in Olympus over matters of quality suggest that there are some matters that even the gods find to be beyond them and worthy of mighty disputation and battle. Even if the gods disagree over what is good or noble or beautiful, they are all agreed that these nebulous qualities are superior to the bad or ignoble or ugly. The bitterness of the battle and the continuing prevalence of the polytheistic system—which had not been rendered redundant by Zeus's power—derives from the three goddesses' recognition that there is something truer, more beautiful, and better than raw power. The power of flattery over raw power is proof of this. Zeus derives his power by playing off the various unformed transcendental principles against each other. He can only exercise his dictatorial powers in an age of strife where the choice is between unjust order and chaos; the moment the other gods find they can co-exist without him, he loses his authority. Zeus uneasily senses, like Herod, that he only rules in the interim before these principles are properly synthesized. Gaia's "teeming womb of kings" will, like Goethe's Eternal Feminine, continually generate better approximations towards this blindly sensed perfection.

Although Socrates is trying to direct Euthyphro's attention in this higher direction, towards unifying transcendent qualities higher than the Olympian gods themselves, his "master" remains fixated at the literal level. While Euthyphro's science of piety amounts to the belief that the gods are best pleased by human efforts to honor them through imitative acts, a sort of instinctual knowledge of the power of flattery, he would not simply spew forth his store of Olympian trivia and appear as a mere rhapsode. Like Thrasymachus in the *Republic*, he wants both total power and a reputation for wisdom.[65] As a good "value-free" theosophist, he deems any judgmental questioning of gods, or critical evaluation of their deeds to be both improper and impious. Piety, to Euthyphro's way of thought, is unilateral: it does not oblige the gods in any way, yet in adhering to this position, he hopes to win their favor through a blind devotion that conveniently denies that the gods require anything more than this, and gains great power over humans looking to him for religious guidance concerning what is holy in specific cases. In these cases he can deploy his vast body of mythic trivia in a way that serves his own interests. As with Prometheus, the gods only gain flattery while their pious prophet receives power and profit. For this Ponzi scheme to work, the prophet must spread his gospel of divine voluntarism widely while prudently hiding the miraculous convergence of divine will and priestly or poetic interests

Euthyphro would claim that mankind's failure to respect the gods' prerogatives provokes the jealous wrath of heaven. In this respect, Euthyphro is very much of the same mind as Meletus and other religious men of the time. But he goes beyond Meletus in his "straight thinking" desire to transcend the mediating tradition and link up directly with the gods themselves. While the religious traditions of a community unquestioningly worship the gods, they only ritually emulate certain of their deeds; these traditions mediate between divine and human things and preserve the ontological distinction between gods and men. Euthyphro's desire that things be done on earth as they are in heaven overturns this distinction and threatens to incite the jealousy of the very gods he is so anxious to flatter. In other words, while Meletus represents tradition without reflection, a premeditated hypocrisy in the name of the time-honored ways that lets business as usual go on, Euthyphro's direct imitation of Olympian conduct on earth is hubristic. As Strauss observes, piety is imitating ancestral worship of the gods, not in mortals imitating the very acts of the gods.[66]

Socrates, Euthyphro and Meletus are all obviously in a situation where the continuity and vitality of the religious tradition, connecting their time to that of the Olympian gods, has broken down. This sad predicament could be attributed to the Sophistical Enlightenment and the tragic conclusion of the Peloponnesian War. Flattery of the Olympians and indirect imitation of their ways has been manifestly shown to lead only to disaster and chaos. Either Protagoras was right to hold that the gods are indifferent to human concerns or pessimistic Euripides's depiction of jealous and sadistic deities was correct. However they looked at it, the war-chastened Athenians were no longer conscious of dwelling in a god-hallowed cosmos. All-consuming time swallowed the claims to undying glory made by violence-crowned Periclean Athens—the School of Hellas.[67]

While we shall suggest that Socrates' solution to this *impasse* is to realize the potentiality latent in Homeric religion, both Euthyphro and Meletus would disagree with this approach. Even Aristophanes' follower, Meletus, only wants to return to the traditional unquestioning ways. Yet Euthyphro hopes to radically uncover, possess, and revive the very origins of piety. He would do so by literal re-invocation and recreation of the deeds of the gods, thus restoring their presence and favor. He hopes to "shock and awe" the Athenians by giving them a rare example of piety.

The difference between the two prosecutors is expressed succinctly by saying that while Meletus is a knave who acts foolishly in accusing Socrates, Euthyphro is a fool involuntarily acting like a knave. Meletus cynically chose to scapegoat Socrates for illicitly exceeding the limits imposed by the polity concerning speculation into transcendent matters; by this act he expects to purify the polis and gain the reputation of being a prudent and pious man. He certainly does not expect that the gods will pay attention to his subterranean housekeeping; his purposes are political, not theological. By contrast, Euthyphro stupidly scapegoats his father as part of a naive attempt to replace politics with revelation. By the extreme fervor of this act, he hopes to convince the gods and Athenians of his total single-minded devotion to their greater glory and receive kudos as his just reward. While Meletus does not really "care" about the gods, Euthyphro is just as shameless in not being even remotely concerned with equity.

In his zealous fundamentalism, Euthyphro refuses to acknowledge that the myths of Homer and Hesiod are anything but the literal truth; it is this very belief—become infallible knowledge—that makes him the gods' prophet and champion. Through his inspired oracles and wise exegeses, Euthyphro offers to re-create meaning in a god-impoverished world. He is unwilling to acknowledge the far weaker pragmatic effective position of Meletus that telling stories about the gods and performing public sacrifices revives and unifies the polity. If either Meletus or Euthyphro is correct, politics and revelation cannot exist together. It is Socrates who will tacitly suggest a manner in which mankind's sacred and secular obligations, God and Caesar, may be reconciled to each other by a gift of the gods: the Hermes-given faculty of judgment.

In their pious claim to return to the divine origins themselves both Euthyphro and Meletus deny history, which as Marx noted may only be recreated as a farce.[68] By resolutely directing Athens's attention towards a mythic original condition, one where revelation, whether traditional or immediate, wholly supersedes the vain and profane speculations of reason, they are willing to deny the value and significance of all that has been learned since mankind's fall into secular time. It seems that Euthyphro is very willing to sacrifice to all-devouring Kronos all that culture and civilization have erected since his deposition. We recall that while Euthyphro emulated Zeus in punishing his father for injustice, the act of pollution itself resembles a deed performed by Zeus himself. This striking variance between the content and form of piety suggests that Euthyphro could be seen as appeasing the furies of Kronos in a situation where the hegemony of Zeus seems to have been overthrown. This contradiction draws further attention to the problems involved in attempting to please several different gods and mad masters at the same time.

The theme of the *Apology* is anticipated here; we see that Socrates is the wisest of men because he realizes that knowledge of the sort that is desired by Euthyphro is neither possible nor desirable. Paradoxically, Euthyphro's tautological position that whatever is dear-to-the-gods (*theophiles*) is pious has already committed him to a crude monotheistic perspective. By accepting that the holy is whatever all the gods love, he has conceded that Zeus, the strongest of the gods, could impose his "love" on the weaker deities in much the same spirit in which he would impregnate a lowly female or animal. If there is no higher standard than the arbitrary preference of the gods, given that one god is stronger than the others it follows that there is only one true god and his will is holy. Still, we don't see why things on Earth won't follow the rule of omnipotent Zeus. While Euthyphro is necessarily committed to the absolute sovereignty of Zeus, or the principle that power should rule, Socrates has already raised the possibility of an objective standard that the most powerful of the gods must conform. Socrates also exposes an obscene gap between the ideal and the real that is now either bridged by voluntarism or concealed by flattery.

Meanwhile, Socrates has directly put the question to Euthyphro: is the pious whatever is dear to the gods (or god), or is something dear to the gods because it is holy? (10a). In other words, is there some transcendent necessity or authority that even the gods must acknowledge and try to serve through their various powers? Is it not this quality, rather than the raw and divisive power of Zeus, which ultimately unifies the gods themselves? If, as we shall see, power is all that is necessary, all of the other Olympians cease to be divine once the *force majeure* of Zeus is asserted. If, however, power is not the only principle of sovereignty, if might is not *ipso facto* right, then—as we have noted—Zeus is merely an uneasy tyrant. In his helpful commentary on this dialogue, Thomas West notes that "the substantial point between Socrates' dry logic-chopping seems to be that the gods' love or will must be directed by that which really is good, noble and just, or else the meaning of human life must be dependent on the arbitrary will of mysterious beings who may not even be friendly to men and—given the multitude of willful authorities . . . the life of men and gods alike must be a tale of ignorant armies clashing by night. . . ."[69]

Once Euthyphro has the full meaning of this question explained to him by Socrates, the self-proclaimed prophet of Zeus is plunged into a vortex; the primeval chaos has opened up before him. Although he claimed to be pious, Euthyphro is forced to recognize that he was only using religion to serve profane and egotistical ends. Suddenly, Socrates has brought religion to life and asserted the authority of the truly divine—the ideal—over the real. Frustrated as Tantalus, Euthyphro cannot deploy his fragments of lifeless trivia to suit his will, as a fundamentalist quotes scripture out of context. Like the statues of Daedalus, the long-frozen images of the gods spring to life as potent and accusing archetypes. Euthyphro sees that Socrates, his erstwhile student, has wrought this revolution. For the first time he senses the true awe-inspiring power of the ideas. Like hapless Phaethon, driving the chariot of his divine father, he comes face to face with the sheer unconditional reality of the "things themselves," the heavenly constellations that have timeless authority and power over all human undertakings and Olympian designs.

Yet, Socrates continues to torture Euthyphro. Combining the roles of Daedalus and Phaenarete, stonemason and midwife, he plans to take "an eager part" in showing Euthyphro how to teach him about the pious (11e). The next question is deceptively simple. Euthyphro is asked whether it is not necessary *to him* that all that is pious is just (11e). When Euthyphro agrees, he is then asked whether all of the just is pious (12a). Are the two qualities identical, or is one merely a part of the other? Socrates, with seeming irrelevance, trots out an obscure quote "where fear is, there too is reverence " (12b) only to disagree with it and argue that fear is a broader category than awe. When Euthyphro says "that part of the just concerning the tending of the gods is reverence, while that concerning humans is what remains" (12e), Socrates raises several analogies of animal tending and asks him how humans tend to the gods to their (the gods') benefit.

Euthyphro emphatically denies that humans improve the gods through piety as animal tenders improve their flocks. He claims that piety is more like the service servants perform for their masters (13d). Nevertheless, Socrates points out that even this must produce some tangible benefit, and Euthyphro cannot identify it. He shares the inability of many pious theologians to acknowledge that there are inherent limitations placed upon idealized divine power by the self-evident reality of human freedom. By viewing the power of the gods purely according to efficient causality, will and selfish material advantage, one becomes tone-deaf to the subtly non-physical manner in which divine inspiration operates. When Euthyphro repeats his claim that prayer and sacrifice are the pious things that preserve families and cities (14b), Socrates leads him to admit that prayer and sacrifice are knowledge of giving gifts to the gods and making requests of them. Piety, in Euthyphro's own words, is "a sort of commerce between gods and human beings" (14e).

Given his view of the divine, Euthyphro must admit that his perfect gods do not receive any tangible benefit from this trade: only honor, respect and gratitude.[70] He must concede that piety is simply the art of pleasing the gods. This brings him around in another circle since he cannot explain why the gods are *necessarily* pleased by the piety that he, Euthyphro, found so certain and important that he is even willing to accuse his father of murder, just as Meletus tries to please the chthonic powers by prosecuting Socrates. One way out of this is to admit openly that it is through conspicuous and absurd acts of flattery that men please the gods, but we saw that in so doing he would lose the public reputation for theosophic wisdom that he craves. If, more reasonably, he says that it is virtue that the gods want, he would be hard pressed to explain how his father's involuntary negligence could constitute vice in merely human or civic terms. If, in the last resort, Euthyphro claimed to be inspired, he would need to provide some demonstration of his power. Yet, we have seen his gods' impotence before Socrates, whose hierarchically inferior demi-god or *daimon* demands that he strip both himself and other men of all self-professed wisdom.

Euthyphro's defeat is confirmed when he declines to continue educating Socrates. He claims to have other pressing business to attend to; through our contact with him, we may presume to prophesize that he will not come back to press charges against his father.[71] It is our task to linger by the Protean figure of Socrates and seek clarification of the oracular words and images that his *daimon* inspired. In trying to understand the cryptic images contained in a dialogue we surely participate in the task of tending and cultivating its long-neglected and overgrown surface. While many readers over the intervening twenty-four centuries have used this uncultivated terrain to display their cleverness and ambush their opponents, we must examine the dialogues, Platonic equivalents of the statues of Daedalus, in the hope of recalling the spirit of Socrates. In Socrates' absence, only a one-sided investigation of Meletus's case took place at the King Archon's Stoa. The real trial occurred elsewhere. We, likewise, must go beyond the comic surface of the dialogue and analyze the suggestive data that Plato has put before us.

III. The Homeric Inheritance

Abandoned like Ariadne on Naxos, let us begin this "second sailing" by reexamining the main theme of the *Euthyphro* and hope that some god will come to our assistance. Is what is holy discovered or created (willed) by the gods? Our previous study of this question revealed strong reasons for believing that Socrates adheres to the first position. If the holy is discovered by the gods, and ultimately served by them, it is much easier to hold that far from being jealous of human strivings, they are pleased by Eros and even sustain it. Indeed, it seems that the truest purpose of divine inspiration, itself a form of Eros, is to encourage *virtuous* human striving on earth. In other words, the gods are most pleased by human virtue since their very purpose is to mediate, in a tangible manner, between the flux of the human world and the intangible domain of the holy. The "gods" may be likened to the *daimons* described by Diotima in the *Symposium*; their task is to mediate between the human realm and transcendent divinity (202d–203a). They dwell in the high non-adversarial levels of reality, far beyond the thumotic jealousy, resentment and strife that pervade the earthly regions and make short-lived human erotic virtue all the more precious.

If ultimate reality is represented in a fragmented manner by the gods, each one of them must represent a different quality. The chaos on Olympus represents the poetic belief that these aspects of reality are incompatible with each other. As we observed earlier, the justice of Zeus is nothing more than order; his Hobbesian sovereignty derives from the recognition that order under any conditions is preferable to chaos. Like the despots and tyrants, in whose image he is rendered, Zeus rules through violence. Only he could impose order over those fractious Olympian deities. Yet it is this very discord that requires such a ruler. Zeus is both the origin and the remedy for this disorderly of affairs. Just as Agamemnon rejoiced in the quarrel between Achilles and Odysseus,[72] Zeus lives through the manipulation and maintenance of discord. It was for this reason that Heraclitus, the philosopher of flux, famously referred to Zeus as a child at play.[73] More accurately, we must see Zeus as a childish representation of divinity, a primitive symbol that must be refined and improved if the consequences of blasphemy are to be averted.

By his continual emphasis on the unity (or ultimate harmony) of the virtues Socrates presents the possibility of a mature alternative to Zeus and polytheism. Erotic harmony would replace the selfish antagonistic virtuosity of a Zeus. We noted how, like Kronos swallowing up his divine offspring, in a sense imprisoning them in a second womb, Zeus's insecurity kept these various potentialities for virtue in wrangling variance. A better ruler could overcome these oppositions. While the promise of Prometheus to mankind in Aeschylus' *Prometheus Bound* was that eventually justice would triumph over the tyranny of arbitrary order,[74] the final stage in this evolution must surely take us beyond justice itself. As Plato points out in both the *Republic* and the *Laws*, the very category of justice becomes redundant when true harmony prevails.[75]

While arbitrary order was necessary in a situation where the desires were stronger than reason, and justice prevails in a state of continence where reason is stronger than the desires, both are conditions of suspicion. If chaos is a state of total war of all against all, then order is no more than a state of martial law, and justice is a state of civil armistice—a City of Man with a draconian criminal code. The true goal is surely a state of temperance or trusting self-knowledge where reason and the desires, fathers and sons, Sky Gods and Furies, are all reconciled to each other.

Accordingly Socrates proposes to actualize a truer idea of justice out of the disparate fragments of myth that Euthyphro has obligingly vomited out before him. Just as passages like 7d point towards a theory of forms, this program is contained, albeit in inchoate form, in Socrates asking how piety and justice were related to each other. According to Euthyphro, piety was that part of justice dedicated to the tending of the gods. It is readily apparent that Euthyphro does not care a whit for human justice, the lesser division of the two. His piety entirely supersedes any concerns with human equity. By his willingness to sacrifice his father, Euthyphro hopes to be the religious leader of a rejuvenated polity. He does not see that history turns tragedy into farce when it is forced to repeat itself. Those who misuse religious texts to serve their selfish interests are condemned for their offence by being left only with literal meanings that they continually and ruinously try to control like the damned in Hades. It is surely true that "the letter killeth."

Euthyphro's eccentric views on the subject of piety are hardly unique. A straight reading of *Genesis* suggests that Isaac has no rights before his father Abraham's desire to retain the favor of his personal protector-god.[76] As the result of his proven willingness to sacrifice Isaac, the pious Abraham is told that his god will reward him with offspring as numerous as the stars of the sky and the sands of the beach. For himself, Isaac is merely Abraham's "seed money." This hapless youth whose names ironically means "laughter" is no more than his father's speculative investment in a sort of Pascal's wager by which Abraham expects to live eternally through his offspring. It is surely no wonder that Abraham's god is also referred to in *Genesis* as the "Terror of Isaac." The patriarchal Abraham is as innocently cold-blooded and single-minded as Zeus and his forefathers; there is also a striking similarity to the amoral "great design" of William Faulkner's great tragic hero, Colonel Sutpen in *Absalom, Absalom*. Despite his many offenses against human dignity, there was nothing particularly cruel or vindictive about Sutpen; his towering ambitions merely made him morally indifferent to the feelings of others.[77]

When Socrates asked Euthyphro whether piety was part of justice or vice versa, Euthyphro's reply that piety was a part of justice led to the unsatisfactory results we have just examined, ultimately amounting to a kind of political theology. The converse, that justice is a part of piety, suggests that we act justly only for the sake of the gods, that everything is permitted when god is dead. Since this is equally unacceptable, we should now examine the possibility that piety and justice are related to each other in a genetic manner, consistent with the leitmotif of this dialogue, as father to son. Such a reading would also reflect Socrates' constant demand that poetic piety should stand before the bar of human justice.

Let us return to the passage from Stasinus quoted by Socrates: "Zeus the lover, him who made all things you will not name for where fear is there is also reverence (12a-b)." While it is curious to read this Socratic equivalent of the Third Commandment to not use the name of God in vain, advice Euthyphro would do well to heed, we must also attend to the implication teased out by Socrates that all fear is reverential. Socrates opposes this idea, pointing out that there are many other forms of fear that have nothing to do with awe or reverence (12b). The fullest implication of his interpretation is that fear, while serving as the origin of the feeling of awe, could just as easily stifle its child and lead to impiety and vice. Instead, just as blind lust was educated to become the awesome vision of cosmic love in the *Symposium,* the sublime experience of awe must outgrow its fearful antecedents and lead us to virtue; Zeus, the promiscuous lover, undergoes a similar transformation by Socrates, allegedly through the influence of literally god-honoring Diotima.

This is why Socrates said in the *Republic* that scandalous stories about Zeus (the lover) must be suppressed for fear of blasphemy. "The young cannot distinguish between literal and allegorical accounts" (378d). Socrates' hostility is not towards Homer; he is concerned about the blasphemous effects of fundamentalism and literal-minded piety. Indeed, this is also why Socrates said in the *Apology* that it was all but impossible to gainsay the conventional opinion, which many jurors heard as children, that he was an atheist (18b-d). Since they clung to the literal sense of stories they learned as children, he could not converse with the many about divine matters. It was for this reason also that Aristotle remarked that political education was wasted on those still under the rule of passion.[78] Part of Plato's achievement seems to consist in translating Socrates' sublime insights and oracular inspirations into a musical language more comprehensible to the desires of those less gifted individuals who tirelessly scour the marketplace of ideas.

Socrates says that he is prosecuted because of his refusal to accept scandalous stories about the wrangling gods (6b). Swearing by the god of friendship, he wonders aloud why he is prosecuted when Euthyphro is not (6a-b). Although Zeus is nominally the god of friendship, the inner meaning of Socrates' words seems to be that the highest divine principle must surely be able to reconcile the various divine qualities that Zeus himself is only able to direct against each other. The idea of the god of hospitality should be able to reconcile the estranged virtues; the gods and/or the powers they represent must be united to each other in friendship.

What is most awe-inspiring is not the fearful, selfishly wielded, power of Zeus, but the capacity of ideals like friendship to lead us to behave in ways that go against our selfish interests. Stated differently, instead of worshipping, imitating, or ridiculing the antediluvian nakedness of the father, this problem should be overcome through his progeny being realized/dressed in more appropriate attributes. This is how the relation of part to whole and ground to origin could be formulated; an approach which is singularly appropriate since, as we have seen, the subject matter of the dialogue deals with the primal tension between fathers and sons. We could see piety as the raw unformed potential from which the idea of justice emerges, like Athena from Zeus's head.

The *Euthyphro* suggests in many different ways that the relation between fathers and sons should be viewed in terms of potentiality and actuality, not as the previously prescribed Oedipal conflict between jealous rivals charging each other with hubris. It is only in such a manner that a tradition may be revitalized. The past and future cannot be set at cross-purposes; the fulfillment of the past must be the task of the future. Piety, originally merely a superstitious fear of powerful and hostile divine forces, becomes progressively refined (and turned around) into an awareness that the gods only require unselfish enlightened conduct of man that rebounds also to their greater glory. The divine potential of Zeus could only be expressed in promiscuously indiscriminate acts of procreation and violence; only after this power-obsessed paranoia is transcended, a process that begins in Homer, is it freed to realize the vision of virtue, affirmed for its own sake and performed for the greater good of the cosmos, that Diotima paints.[79]

The *Euthyphro* thus represents a theological counterpart to the civil doctrines of *Gorgias*: the recognition that punishment, whether divine or human, must be for rehabilitation rather than retribution.[80] The position that humans please the gods best by acting virtuously is strengthened by seeing that our capacity for virtuous actions increases when our conception of the divine is improved. Instead of the "many mad masters" of Sophocles, the fear-governed notions of piety represented by the Olympians, Socrates pushes the discussion in a monotheistic direction by advocating a unified non-alienating model of virtue. The seemingly absurd question of how human beings could render service to the gods acquires new dignity and meaning.

Instead of flattering the gods, in a way that runs the grave risk of blasphemy by imputing all manner of vice and cruelty to them, Socrates suggests to Euthyphro that we serve the gods best by properly depicting piety and practicing virtue. Tantalus, referred to earlier as one whose riches would be renounced by Socrates in exchange for accurate knowledge about the gods (11e), is a prime example of such blasphemous flattery. To gain divine favor Tantalus (who claimed great familiarity with the gods) chopped up his child and served him to the gods when they dined with him.[81] This infanticide gained Tantalus a place in Tartarus. Yet the poets also chopped up the Idea of the Good into god-sized fragments to be deployed in the Cave for power and profit. Conversely, but with similar intent, Euthyphro refuses to separate one accident from his sire's essence and offers him up to the gods, demanding divine punishment for pollution on all of him!

Unlike Tantalus, Socrates sets out to serve the gods by suggesting that mankind should refine poetry until it expresses the best of all possible ideas. Such an approach stands in contrast to rhetorical poetry that exaggerates an idea out of all proportion out of a desire to flatter the gods and covertly gain power over man. This monotheistic line of speculation indicated in the *Euthyphro* leads towards Christianity and the argument that God is the sum of all perfection. However, we must also see that Plato's distinction between the domains of the ideal and the real may be the best way of avoiding the pitfalls that the ontological argument otherwise leads to. Instead of a frozen divine perfection opposed to flawed humanity in a relationship of scarcely concealed *ressentiment*, alienation, and unhappy consciousness, the *Euthyphro* suggests that any picture we have of the divine is ultimately an ideal which humanity must refine and tend through its own moral progress and self-knowledge. This is surely a worthy act of piety.

It is too easy to say that the ideas replace the gods.[82] Such a view, tacitly affirming contemplative wisdom and unrequited desire, rather than the wisdom of love, is Aristotelian, self-divinizing and ultimately atheistic.

Works like the *Gorgias* suggest instead that Socrates would affirm the possibility of genuine interaction between the divine and human realms: setting up a space where human eros and divine grace could meet fruitfully.[83] Likewise, instead of uprooting genuine piety from the chthonic realm of unthinking custom and blind loyalty, Socrates sets out, in the spirit of the *Eumenides*, to enlighten and liberate these ancient forces. Socratic humanism is not corrosive or proud. It is rooted in awe, filled with temperance, and crowned with wonder.

Socrates' ancestors, stonemasons and sculptors, paid homage to gods through graven images; with even greater piety, their descendant liberates the sublime potential slumbering inside the statues. Like prisoners long hidden in a deep dungeon, the various divine attributes are freed from their bondage to blind custom. Differently put, both the prisoners and the images are led out of their underground cave. They are reconciled and unified in a sunlit vision of the Good. Overcoming both the divisive totems of fundamentalism and the moral chaos born of liberal positivism, the *Euthyphro* points towards the possibility of a universal religion—one based on the idea of Goodness, the practice of virtue, and the finding of grace and beauty in the cosmos. While humans are necessarily born in the cave of the body and must live, for the most part, far from the sublime vision of the Good, there is yet a sense that we are not just worms but glow-worms.

Although, in the remainder of this book, we shall go on to apply the lessons learned from the *Euthyphro* to cast much needed light on the *Apology* and *Crito*, let us continue in an appropriately speculative vein by examining the historical influence and the contemporary spiritual relevance of this dialogue. I shall claim first that the *Euthyphro* contains the first expression of some of the most valuable ideas in Christianity. Then, I will argue that our own materialistic world, where the "Death of God" is a *fait accompli*, is actually polytheistic through and through. As such, the simultaneously superstitious and sophisticated Third Millennium seems to be ready for a thorough Socratic purification from its cynical and self-destructive ways.

We referred earlier to the Mosaic Third Commandment, and Socrates' insistence that man should not invoke God's name to flatter the powers that be. Yet it should also be noted that the basis of Biblical religion, the truly pious insistence on the loving goodness of God, is also contained in this dialogue; the Trinitarian refinements of divine love responding to human eros and carnally (re)entering the cave is anticipated in the *Republic* and

Symposium. To put the matter simply, when Socrates rejected the poets' empirically derived portraits of the gods he did so in the name of a firmly held idea of God's objective goodness. It is fitting that this Abraham of Philosophy, this theological Don Quixote, the patriarch and irresponsible father of idealism, must be asked to justify his novel conception of divine goodness in the face of overwhelming psychological and historical experiences pointing towards a violent and irrational ontological substratum.

We should remember that the itinerant Greek poets were certainly not "children at play." While we do not know anything about Homer's life, it is certain that Hesiod derived his somber teachings concerning the gods, and what man could expect of them, from his own arduous works and days in the bleak Dark Ages preceding Classical times. Polytheism is more natural in a world fraught with irrationality and deficient in meaning. When one's experience seems to lack unity or satisfying meaning, and life itself appears to be strife-ridden and perverse, it is natural to agree with Hesiod that there are many jealous gods who "keep livelihood hidden from men."[84] When Zeus himself maintains ascendancy over the other Olympians through his sheer power, it is futile for mere mortals to expect any greater consideration. When power-based order rules in heaven, it is surely the utmost folly to expect the more liberal principle of justice to hold sway on earth.

The poets' own precarious position is well depicted by Hesiod in his story of the hawk and the nightingale. When the hawk's cruel talons "skewered" the nightingale, she raised a pitiful cry, only to be told by the hawk in a "lordly" tone that all her screaming was in vain. She was the prey of her better, and even though she was a great singer he would decide whether to have her for dinner or to let her go. "Only fools defy the stronger, for they suffer both defeat and humiliation."[85] Yet, though the indirect meaning of this passage clearly has to do with the poet, and his obligation to bend his eloquence to serve the purposes of the tyrant, we cannot ignore the direct sense of these lines, which apply to humankind in general. While man's eloquence and nobility in suffering may evoke the involuntary admiration of the careless gods, Hesiod suggests that at the end of the day our fate will depend on their thoughtless caprice.

Hesiod's final word to us seems to be that we have no right to expect justice. We should indeed be grateful that some semblance of order is maintained on earth as it is in heaven. Even if our lives are short and miserable, at least our graves will be treated with reverence by our equally slavish offspring. By having high expectations of piety for our children, we only ensure that our own ways will not be remembered when we have passed away. It is appropriate that each generation should distrust both fathers and sons according to the patterns just described. Hard work is its own reward in the sense that it leaves little time for us to dream up exaggerated ideals of how things ought to be; vain fantasies will only call down swift punishment from the gods.

Hesiod suggests that human affairs are best ordered by the cosmic force of strife—which governs matters on earth, as it does in heaven. Divine strife ensures that men will always compete against each other for the scarce means of livelihood. Humanity will thus never have the mutual trust or leisure time to earn the wrath of the gods by plotting against them. We could note that Plato's Aristophanes replaces Eris/strife with Eros with the same explicit goal.[86] Likewise, inevitable human strife and the envy that long-suffering peasants feel towards arrogant princes will always be tempered by the recognition that mortals do not retain the favor of the jealous and capricious gods for too long. Vengeance however is best left to the gods. In the absence of easy livelihood, which the jealous gods have hidden from man, the mute acceptance of an inequitable hierarchy of power turns out to be an indispensable means to survival in an inhospitable cosmos.

According to this bleak reading of Hesiod, even Achilles is ultimately a plaything of the gods. The tragedy of the mortal hero is that no matter how noble and beautiful, he is unable to maintain his dignity before the comic laughter of the childlike gods. How then may Thersites, Socrates, or some other commonplace clown, demand to live and be ruled according to standards that even the kings themselves can expect to be judged and condemned by? Even the gods themselves can ultimately expect nothing better from remorseless necessity of time and *ananke*.

The polytheistic system also follows directly from the basic irrationality of existence. It is a truism that neither Zeus nor any of his predecessors was a creator *ex nihilo*. Their task was to make temporary order out of chaos. Their ascendancy was contingent on their ability to preserve order: the psyche, polis and cosmos are all fields of strife. As we noted, Gaia, like Machiavelli's insatiable pagan goddess *Fortuna*, would turn her attention to any virile youth who could out-perform his father. The chaotic flux of brute reality demanded constant, violent, order-imposing virility, a task that would sooner or later drain the potency of any master. It would be inevitable that insatiable sadism rather than love would serve as the principle of order in a situation where there seemed to be little or no propensity towards harmony in the godhead itself.[87] The pleasure of inflicting the agony of defeat would soon replace the empty thrill of victory.

In isolation from each other, the Olympian gods are inverted cripples or splendid pagan vices. For the idea of the Good to be re-collected, these qualities must somehow be reconciled to each other. It is noteworthy that each of the primal passions governing existence, the very forces that are worshipped as Olympian gods and recognized as sufficient causes for human actions, functions as a vice when left to its own devices. Each of these qualities is only capable of enjoying a short and glorious life before the ghastly vision of the many contradictions and injustices to which it gave rise will cause it to self-destruct. Self-knowledge, like the Owl of Minerva, comes to idols at their twilight.

The *Iliad* illustrates the terrible extent to which the various Olympians exemplify disorder and vice in their antagonism to each other. Hera, the mother of heaven, is the embodiment of jealousy; she is most ardent in her desire to sack and ravage sacred Ilium, perhaps in revenge for the choice of love over resentful fidelity. Athena, the goddess of wisdom, is little better than polytropic Odysseus in her Machiavellian scheming for victory through any means. Aphrodite, the goddess of love, is similarly turned inside out and exposed as a whorish spreader of legs, licentiousness and lust. Her lover, Ares, who should remind us of courage, is a drug-dealer in rage and insatiable bloodlust. Apollo, the serene force of music, limit and healing, is but a partisan sniper spreading plague and discord. Even in the kinder and gentler world of the *Odyssey*, Poseidon vindictively stalks Odysseus for ten years, seeking satisfaction for an act of self-defense performed against his savage and murderous son.

Yet perhaps the most revealing of all of Homer's flashing images is the uncanny glimpse he provides of the rival gods, Athena and Apollo, disguised as vultures, sitting on the branch of a tree and watching the duel between those two unlucky heroes (and blood relatives) Ajax and Hector.[88] Like a patient bird-watcher, the reader somehow senses that he has been granted the rare privilege of seeing these most sublime of gods in their true colors and natural habitat.

We have already paid some attention to the atrocities committed by the successive holders of the title "Father of the Gods." Far from representing any improvement over the brutal tyranny of his father and grandfather, Zeus himself could be accused of the heinous crime of planning the Trojan War from start to finish to rid the earth of the heroes. This "Father of the Gods" is particularly interested in killing Achilles, since Thetis was supposed to bear the god who would overthrow the son of Kronos.[89] What Homer euphemistically termed the "Plan of Zeus" turns out to be little better than a cold-blooded "Final Solution" to the vexing problem of man, a being with whom the gods share a common descent.[90] In keeping with the worst tendencies of the Old Testament, Genocide is arrived at as the only completely satisfactory response to Genesis.

Once it is viewed through the theological categories that Socrates has provided us with in the *Euthyphro*, Homer's *Iliad* may be interpreted as if it harbored within itself an account of the rise and fall of Zeus. We must recall that Homer's scandalous stories concerning the gods only serve to explain the deeds knowable to man—the strivings of the Greek and Trojans before the deadly gates of Ilium—that demand to be both remembered and explained. It is therefore not illegitimate to replace one account of the causal mechanism sustaining these deeds with another—equally consistent with the human action of the story. Shakespeare's bitter comedy *Troilus and Cressida* may be read as a reductive account of the Trojan War, one where the very Olympians are swept away and replaced with the basest human passions.[91] Avoiding an atheistic response to Plato's pious criticism of Homeric immorality, we will look for a theological superstructure to the story of Achilles that will be more consistent with the concerns of Socrates and Plato.

The celebrated "Plan of Zeus" is really quite simple. Since it is imperative that Achilles—the one destined to supplant him—should die, Zeus will exploit his god-like victim's immortal yearnings after glory at any price, which quite exceeds the capacities of his mortal frame. This inability of the finite to express his infinite desires will drive the son of Thetis mad and lead to his assured destruction. Zeus surely rejoiced when this desire for glory leads Achilles to quarrel with Agamemnon and withdraw from the fray. Now separated by his hubris from friend and foe alike, Achilles prays to Zeus that the Greeks suffer terribly until Agamemnon apologizes to him.[92]

Although Homer's *Iliad* is often viewed as the most eloquent description of a polytheistic world order, one could with great plausibility argue that only the first seven books of the *Iliad* are truly polytheistic; Achilles' departure from the Greek ranks allows all the other champions, both Greek and Trojan, to display their claims to be first among equals. With the sole exception of Great Ajax, each hero's Olympian protector sustains his *aristeia*. Each enjoys his brief moment of glory before being brought down by the power of an opposing god. But as soon as Zeus asserts his overwhelming power in Book VIII, the other gods diminish.[93] Even the famous night raid of Odysseus and Diomedes merely illustrates the dark recognition that just as the other heroes could only shine as the planets in the night when the sun-like splendor of Achilles was withheld, once he asserts his authority Zeus reigns supreme. Then, as the epic draws to its end, Zeus curiously recedes into the background as Achilles reasserts his mastery over the theatre of action.

Throughout the middle of the *Iliad* however, the plans of Zeus proceed with perfect mechanical smoothness. Aided by Zeus, Hector will dominate the battle as the other gods and heroes cower before his evidently invincible prowess. Meanwhile the desperate Greek plight draws the beloved friend of Achilles, Patroclus, into the battle; both Hector and Patroclus are men of considerable decency even though this quality is contemptuously brushed aside by the coercive *ananke* of divine intoxication. After a few moments of giddy triumph, wearing armor that is far too big for him, blinded Patroclus is ambushed by Apollo and killed by Hector. In the final third of the *Iliad*, we see Achilles maddened by the consequences of his blind pride. Ignoring the assured certainty of his own death if he rejoins the fray. Achilles duly kills Hector and the *Iliad* ends with his ritual preparation for death.

A subtle change in fortunes is signaled to us by Homer when suddenly, in Book XVI, even Zeus must shed tears of blood, not divine ichor, and accept the will of the fates that Sarpedon, his son, should die.[94] It is arguable of course that Zeus is cynically sacrificing his best beloved Sarpedon in the same spirit in which Abraham was willing to murder Isaac; his paramount objective is the preservation of his hegemony. It is only this supreme desire that makes the sacrifice of Sarpedon become necessary. Yet this loose strand can also be seen to be the means through which the artful and self-serving machinations of Zeus could be deconstructed. It seems that even Zeus cannot predict or calculate the effect that his artfully choreographed production will have on his captive audience or himself.

If one were to read Homer through the reverent yet virtue-loving eyes of a philosophical poet like Plato, a very different picture of the destiny of gods and man could be seen to emerge. One would see clearly that in the final third of the *Iliad* events proceed with such awesome necessity that Zeus, the omnipotent and omniscient manipulator of the middle of the epic, is reduced to the status of a spectator. While he knows everything that is supposed to take place before the doomed towers of Troy, even he must watch spellbound as the tragedy of Achilles unfolds. This sublime spectacle leads the war-traumatized human spirit to magically bear fruit again. We come to see that mortal courage may triumph against even the most remorseless divine hostility. The *Odyssey* thus serves to reinforce the lesson provided by the *Iliad* regarding the human spirit's capacity to endure raging blasts of Olympian caprice. This understanding leads to a wisdom that may be imparted to future generations.

Paradoxically Zeus, through his very anxiousness to destroy Achilles, by ensuring that Thetis—the destined mother of his successor—be married to a mortal, has carried out the plans of destiny. Although Zeus gladly acceded to the desire of Thetis that her mortal son should die gloriously,[95] seemingly ensuring the continuance of his own tyranny, he did not realize that his joint design with Thetis engenders the apotheosis of Achilles: precisely the development that he tried to thwart. Zeus's manipulative ways are suddenly made to seem contemptuous before Achilles' acceptance of death. The genuine love Achilles has for Patroclus, whose name means glory of the father, displaces his titanic pride and dims his father Zeus's glory. According to this subversive interpretation, Zeus's downfall begins when the once mighty potentate Priam, who fathered almost as many children as Zeus himself, visits Achilles' tent and begs humbly for his son's body before the final battles, which will culminate in his utter ruin, are joined. This act of true courage, born of love, forces Achilles to see his own pettiness and dissipates the impending explosion of rage that would otherwise have led to destruction of everything—ideals, souls and institutions— that mortals held sacred and maintained Zeus's ascendancy over the wretched human spirit. Even though, after Achilles' death, Neoptolemus will brutally slay him over his desecrated altars, Priam has somehow inspired a human decency in Achilles that allows the son of Thetis to renounce his nihilistic wrath and die as a magnanimous hero.[96]

As Socrates pointed out to Euthyphro much earlier, even the gods themselves are compelled to quarrel in involuntary recognition of the transcendental destiny of the qualities that they presently represent—however inadequately. Although Paris told the three wrangling queens that Aphrodite was the most beautiful, the matter could be decided by a trial of strength. Though only two of the gods watched the duel between Hector and Ajax, all of them will be compelled by truth to acclaim Achilles, the greatest threat to Zeus's continued sovereignty, as the strongest and most beautiful. Even gods like Apollo, Ares, and Aphrodite, who bitterly opposed the Greeks on and off the battlefield, must recognize what has been demonstrated before their very eyes.

The human spirit proves to be greater than anything that the selfish Olympians could imagine. This means that Zeus must watch his successor arise out of the very gruesome carnage before Troy that ironically, was intended to crush the presumptuous human spirit once and for all. Zeus himself did not realize that the scripted death of Achilles, which he was destined to craftily cobble together, could be so moving. The play rises out of the script, not with the shambling strength of a Frankenstein, but with the supple grace and unity of a young god, to confound its producer. The jealous father must involuntarily salute the triumphant apotheosis of his successor.

In a sudden flash of hindsight, the prophetic vision only granted before death, Zeus ruefully realizes the arrant futility of his best-laid plans. By his ability to accept guilt and be reconciled with his comrades, Achilles has shown himself to be a greater man than his maker. He embraces his mortality and will no longer haggle for glory in exchange for the lives of others. The curse of Uranos (and the hope of Gaia) that each generation should surpass its predecessor, has once again renewed itself through him, Zeus has betrayed himself through the very power of scheming that enabled him to overthrow *his* father. Of course, the Greeks were very familiar with this process, their dramatists had to produce several new plays each year based on a very limited canon of old myths that very well known to their audience. Yet, year after year, they made the Athenians aware that neither age could wither or custom stale the infinite variety of the tradition. The spectators were unfailingly treated to novel and imaginative renderings of the ancient myths, revealing hitherto undiscovered treasures in the *mythos*. Somehow, miraculously, heroic performance possesses the ability to take the jaded omniscience of the critic by surprise.

The actual death of Achilles only occurs after the conclusion of the *Iliad*, in keeping with the later conventions of the Greek theater that its most sublime moments can only be enacted within that dark-browed circle within the human imagination. But this very tradition of open-ended incompleteness, echoed in the Platonic dialogues, also makes its possible for the torch of Prometheus to always be passed on to the next generation of thinkers and dreamers. Infinitely better than Euthyphro and Meletus, and even out-surpassing proud Aristophanes himself, we must realize that Socrates and Plato are the truest guardians of the Greek literary tradition.

It was surely in this bold humanistic spirit that Homer transformed a short and brutal account of a cattle raid into a saga of undying power and beauty. The original Achilles, who was probably a brutal young ruffian, is magically metamorphosed through the divine Homer's poetic genius into an eternal symbol of heroic youth, doomed by cruel fate to lead a short but glorious life. It only remains for Plato to make Socrates the hero of a drama by which the long reified sediment of Greek religion is magically made to rejuvenate itself.

While all of this is very well, how may we be assured that ultimate reality itself will reflect and cooperate with the short-lived heroism that we have seen on the stage? In other words, Dionysus only flashes into being momentarily, before being torn to shreds by his ravening maenads.[97] Doesn't this indicate that any truer reconciliation of the divine attributes, the ideal pointed to by Socrates, will necessarily be short-lived because it depends on incorrigible human beings? What do the short and glorious careers of the likes of Achilles and Dionysus have to do with the urgent desire of less favored mortals for minimal horizons of meaning under which they may live, suffer, and die? Regardless of whether or not we believe in the Homeric gods, do they not (especially in the latter case) provide politico-religious frameworks that allow human affairs to be conducted with about as much order as the brutal conditions of our existence permit? Isn't the gravity created by pious lies preferable to the chaos unleashed by the stark unvarnished truth?

In the absence of gods of the sort that Euthyphro believes in (deities who could account for the strange mixture of order and chaos in the world) would not the belief in such gods championed by Meletus still provide a sound basis for a pragmatic political regime? In other words, if we cannot flatter the arbitrary gods, we must at least please the *demos* and pander to the irrational popular fears and prejudices that constitute the bedrock of reality. Irresponsibly idealistic standards of human excellence will only serve to undermine a tradition that took many generations to erect, and leave nothing in its place.

In response to this very plausible accusation, which ultimately must serve as the truest basis for the charges of impiety leveled against him, Socrates (our hero in this narrative) would claim that the ideas themselves demand to be unified. The Socratic doctrine of the unity of the virtues is derived from the empirical recognition that in isolation from its fellows, a virtue becomes a vice. This parallels our not-unrelated observation concerning the Greek gods as epitomizing splendid vices in their isolation or division from each other. The fundamental challenge posed to us by Socrates' life and Plato's dialogues concerns the possibility of educating the desires, which all throughout human history have been depicted as insatiable and irrational vices and even made divine in one way or another. The *Euthyphro* suggests that this goal may only be accomplished through the heroic task of unifying and integrating the various virtues, both on earth and in heaven. Only then will it be truly possible to claim that the gods that Socrates was accused of worshipping and bringing into the city are not strange and alien but innate and natural. Born and bred in our dreams, and worshipped in inchoate form in the cave, we must grow accustomed to seeing them in the light of cosmic reality.

While the question of the unity of the virtues was perhaps dealt with most fully in the *Protagoras*,[98] the *Euthyphro* draws attention to the disastrous consequences that ensue when the gods are opposed to each other. We have already noted how the wisdom of Athena becomes Machiavellian cunning, while the courage of Ares is merely bloodthirsty rage. Likewise, no human virtue may truly realize its potential when it is isolated from the others. For example, justice without courage is pusillanimous, while courage without justice is reckless folly. Love without temperance is blind lustful folly, while temperance without love is selfishness. The other virtues serve as reference points by which an individual virtue may be able to "know itself."

While each quality may exist independently of the others, albeit in a raw and unrealized state, on Olympus or in the animal kingdom, they can only truly exist in the human world when they are combined with—and speak to—the other virtues. A courageous human will thus use his courage to serve just causes although the idea of courage may be intuited without reference to the concept of justice. While a lion may remind us of courage, the human virtue of courage exists in conjunction with other virtuous qualities like love, justice, and thoughtfulness. The *Phaedrus*'s treatment of beauty illustrates this point even better since a beautiful object or creature points beyond itself—reminding us, and perhaps even the gods, of higher and more universal harmonies and ideals.[99] The true *telos* is an erotic polyphony of virtues rather than a simple monistic unity.

The *Euthyphro* also suggests what is called "the sovereignty of the object" over and against arbitrary voluntarism—whether human or divine. This means that even the gods, and perhaps only the gods, must recognize something for what it truly is when that quality is indelibly "dyed" into a soul by its life and death. This also means that by seeing beings *sans illusion* they must recognize essential qualities where these are present and so cannot view mortals as leaves or flux to be manipulated with total impunity. Humans are thus of infinite interest to the gods because they have moral and erotic freedom; Zeus could seal the fate of Achilles but he could not know the spirit in which Achilles would die and thus did not see how this interference would bring about his own downfall. It follows that there are limits to divine power that correspond to the soul's capacity to choose virtue or vice. A virtuous man can be happy to the extent of knowing he has done nothing unworthy of himself even as he is tortured by acts that indelibly stain his torturer. Conversely his omnipotent torturer cannot erase his own awareness of having being shamefully unjust. Job was not around when the world was created, but Satan cannot forget —for he *was* around—his sadistic treatment of Job and the murder of his irreplaceable children.[100]

By their absurd and petty conduct, Meletus and Euthyphro also serve to remind us that piety and justice cannot exist in an abstract form; piety becomes pharisaic while justice turns retributive and materialistic when it is deprived of a transcendent dimension. When one quality becomes separated from its fellows, it becomes all too prone to turn vicious and self-serving. In other words, isolation causes a potential virtue to become insecure and "idiotic" as it loses self-knowledge (temperance) and ceases to "be-in-a-world." An unsecured virtue or "loose cannon" will frequently cause more damage than good, since the consequences of its alienated folly serve only to bring into discredit the very virtue that it originally represented. The *Odyssey* displays what happens when Odysseus, the favorite of Athena, is alienated from Poseidon: god of earth and sea. By the implacable hostility of the chthonic powers, the wily son of Laertes is reduced to a rootless and ruthless vagrant huckster, ruled by his incorrigible belly and insatiate appetite for trouble.[101]

While we have dealt with the predicament of the isolated virtues, it is also necessary to consider the opposite vice: the consequences ensuing from "too perfect a union" between the virtues. In such an instance there is the risk that the individual virtues may also be stifled by an excessively rigid order imposed over them by self-righteous piety. Such an "over-continent" approach imposes stringent restraints on erotic virtuosity in the name of piety. Once again, order will strive to deny the claims of justice and friendship. We learn from the *Euthyphro* that the flattering rhetoric of divine omniscience and omnipotence must not be allowed to negate god's most amazing miracle of all: the human soul. Creative interaction between many diverse souls and unique virtues cannot be stifled by those using God's name in vain; each spiritual monad must reflect the beauty of the cosmos in its own way; the erotic potentialities in man cannot be expected to sing in perfect univocal harmony before the end of history. Even the Olympians craved spectacles of human virtuosity wherein they saw their ruling passions refined and realized.

By regarding the individual virtues only as disruptive desires and potential vices, the friendship that characterizes true temperance is speedily transformed into a relation of suspicion and mistrust that divides the souls and pits man against the gods. Despite a distinction he draws between its two forms, something that Plato parodies when he has Pausanias separate heavenly and earthly Eros in the *Symposium*, Hesiod identifies strife as the governing principle of the cosmos in his *Works and Days*,[102] and we have seen ample reason to suggest that Homeric Zeus also rules by dividing and conquering through strife. Aristotle exemplifies this problem at the psychic level in his separation of the moral and intellectual virtues in the *Nicomachean Ethics*.[103] His moral virtues do not have a positive function; their role is to curb the disorderly desires of the many so that the contemplative activity of the divine intellect may proceed uninterrupted. This also means that morality is an essentially demotic mimetic virtue that can make no claim on higher powers. Such an over-intellectual reading will lead us to read the *Apology* as a paean to *Cloud*-based intellectual solipsism and, by concluding irresistibly that Socrates really wanted to be Aristotle, sin a second time against philosophy. By his intellectualist emphasis on certainty and changelessness as attributes of divine perfection, ideas that would later be taken into Christian theology by Augustine, via neo-Platonism, Aristotle prefers orderly mores or habits against the suspiciously untidy ways of Eros. Yet Socrates steadfastly held, even when threatened with death, that mimetic custom is a poor substitute for the truly catholic way of giving thoughtful attention to the messy whole; the Socratic cosmos is held together by erotic/daimonic mediation between divine and human realms. This clash between the needs of order seeking contemplation and Eros, the White and Black horses, may be the very basis of the quarrel between Plato and Aristotle.

Though Aristotle downplays the loftier significance of Eros, the dialogues clearly suggest that Socrates placed great emphasis on the importance of the relationship between the idea of the Good and Eros. While the idea of goodness is too abstract, alienating, and judgmental to be left to its own devices, Eros cannot function properly without some clear destination towards which its activity could be directed. Goodness and Eros must be related to each other as noun to verb; the content of the former will give meaning and value to the otherwise indiscriminately promiscuous strivings of the latter. While Eros ceaselessly encourages the universal potential for and towards goodness, the distinction between Good and Evil must not be set aside. While abstract goodness itself becomes evil in its lack of generosity towards wayward and grubby potential, pure charity would unwittingly enable and empower Evil by obstinately refusing to swerve from its blind covenant to love everything unconditionally, believing that everything is divinely preordained.

The capacity of the various virtues to dwell harmoniously with each other must also be mirrored in our dim understanding or appreciation of the divine nature. By emphasizing the unity of the virtues, Socrates seems to strike a mighty blow in favor of monotheism, but the fullest implications of his reasoning are as complex as they are suggestive. While it is impossible to posit anything about either the number or nature of the gods, if we take Socrates' devout ignorance concerning theological matters at all seriously, we can draw the negative conclusion that whatever the gods are, they do not jealously pit the various virtues against each other in the same humor that Penelope's suitors showed in arranging a bum fight. Socrates may be viewed as refining the ideal of polytheism away from the deadening effects that result from their being subsumed under one actual being, and thereby denied to humans by a jealous deity. Virtue, as Socrates and Plato understand it, may be seen to derive only from the lively interaction of these several transcendental principles with humanity. The vexing question of the divine nature is found to be utterly beyond the capacity of the human intellect. Indeed, this condition of ignorance is even welcomed since it ensures that virtuous actions rather than sophistic wisdom or technical expertise are the best way to please the gods. To this extent, the revelation of common metaphysical ignorance is the necessary complement to democratic equality; the axiom that all humans must have an equal chance to gain virtue and find happiness makes little sense if *eudaimonia* is gained by divine favor or undeserved inheritance

Once the compulsive desire for *total* order at *any* cost over what is viewed as the chaotic and objectively (or originally) sinful human substratum is removed, there is no longer any need for the various divine qualities to be cynically kept at wrangling variance from each other for fear of human emulation. Christianity exploited Socrates' emphasis on the unity of goodness to serve its own interests when God was defined as the sum of all conceivable perfections. Yet, by substituting the static category of Aristotelian perfection for the living presence of the God of Abraham, Isaac and Jacob,[104] *this* immaculate conception of the divine nature denigrates its erotic and living aspects under the pretext of paying higher praise to God. In other words, as a result of its origins in fear and need (rather than love and goodness) pious flattery becomes unreceptive to the erotic origins of genuine piety. Piety cannot be defined in terms of the body, by invoking pleasure and pain; it can only be understood by the spiritual categories of virtue and vice.

Conversely, by regarding the divine as an erotic paradigm of human virtue, instead of a perfect transcendent *telos* beyond the human sphere, the "Platonic" take on what is godly in terms of "goodness" allows for erotic mediation between the divine and human realms. By this shift in emphasis from probing or praising the divine essence to doing what is good, the point is made that virtuous action is more pleasing to the gods than metaphysical speculation or base flattery. Indeed while the impulse leading us out of the cave is seldom un-mixed with pride, the reasons that cause man to return to the cave and body can be erotic and not merely concupiscent. While Aristotle's emphasis on the unmoved mover's changeless intellectual perfection closes off any possibility of divine concern with the matter of the cosmos, even hamstringing the doctrine of the Trinity, Plato's approach to this issue holds open the possibility of our participation in an on-going process of cosmic becoming. The accounts of transcendent reality given in the *Symposium, Gorgias* and *Phaedrus* all describe a cosmos constructed along these erotic and interactive lines.

While the *Euthyphro* urges its readers to speculate beyond the rather threadbare theology that Meletus and Euthyphro more or less unquestioningly inherited, it also prepares us, when we turn to the *Apology*, to investigate the origins of the furious hatred that Socrates seemed to have evoked in his jurors. The inescapable recognition that Socrates consciously stoked these flames cannot but prompt us to probe the origins of the powers that he so tragically took on. More ambitiously, while the *Euthyphro* inspired us to investigate the strange gods that Socrates was accused of having introduced, a careful analysis of the *Apology* will provoke a radical analysis of the familiar gods that he allegedly sought to displace. As a result, we are impelled to inquire as to how Socrates' self-evident ethical categories have come to be so strange, foreign and uncanny to most orthodox theologians and other professedly god-fearing individuals. How could they have been supplanted? What dire powers possess the capacity to uproot these divine precepts from their rightful place and sentence them to perpetual exile as unrealistic and blasphemous ideals?

The answer to this question would surely have to take into

consideration the perverse combination of pessimism and selfishness that we have found in both Meletus and Euthyphro; these forces have long been found to exert an influence over man that is far in excess of their moral authority. We may temporarily describe these powers as being inherent to the famous cave of the *Republic*; the spiritually impoverished subterranean original condition man is born into. Since they prevent him from receiving an education that open him up to those transcendental influences sustaining his erotic ascent upwards and towards the Good, incarnate man is born enslaved to these dark forces by powerful bonds of social convention and religious tradition.

While it would be simpler to postulate an eternal dualistic opposition between these two different kinds of ontological principles, the bright sky-gods and the dark chthonic furies, the *Euthyphro* suggests that darkness becomes light through a process of evolution—a historical tragedy in which man plays a crucial role. The aloofly abstract authority of the ideas should be reconciled to the immediate pathos of reality. While this connection between dark furious origins and enlightened erotic destiny—the *alpha* and the *omega* of the cosmos—cannot be proven, intelligent and daring speculation along these lines is hardly at variance with the path indicated by the greatest works of Greek literature. We have seen that the *Euthyphro* could be read as a continuation of the theogonies of Homer and Hesiod. While a more explicit but less substantial argument in favor of such a process is explicitly laid out in the *Oresteia* of Aeschylus where the once implacable furies are welcomed into the pale of civilization, Plato's Socrates performs this integration better than blood-stained Orestes. He thus proves to be a better reader of Homer. Such a line of interpretation may also be a welcome consequence of taking Socrates and Plato seriously—both as wise teachers and seers in their own right, and also as blessed exegetes of inspired poets.

We cannot conclude without remembering that clownish Euthyphro is used by Plato to represent the problem of revelation itself. He affirms the literal authority of the command of god, an unconditional imperative that may require the auditor to override the basic experiences of thought and conscience. While revelation is usually encased in a sacred tradition and an orthodox interpretation, thus affirming one god, one text, one interpretation and one practice; so seamless a façade usually conceals a multitude of ambiguities, pragmatic accommodations and sacred secrets. The fate of any perfect divine revelation ultimately depends greatly on the actions of the pious chorus of human relay runners bearing it through time. But does this mean that there are some things that even god cannot do? Further, if some things are beyond god's power, before we co-operate with him are we not entitled to speculate concerning the nature of virtue and god's intentions towards us? This is not unrelated to the question of how and why we should serve god.

All of these speculations, which have taken us far beyond our brief, must now be set aside temporarily in order to prepare for the *Apology* itself. We must see if Socrates' own words can provide a mandate for the revolutionary re-reading of Homer that Plato's works seem to point us towards. If not, all we have said is only a flighty interpretation of an obscure text that may or may not show us how to decode the cagey words of one of the most enigmatic men who ever lived.

Plato's *Apology of Socrates*

I. The Witness of Clouds

Socrates begins his *Apology* by observing that he hardly recognized himself as he was depicted in the speeches made by his accusers (17a). This may be Plato's way of telling us that we're already in Hades, the Cave-like underworld of collective prejudice where people have no idea (a-ides) of who they really are outside of public opinion. But before we go any further into Socrates' speech we should attend to a very relevant and valid issue that his statement implicitly raises. Why does Plato fail to record the accusers' speeches? As it stands, the *Apology of Socrates* is an incomplete and one-sided account of the events that it purports to chronicle. We must ask why Plato, who is usually even-handed to the point of constructing dialogues that often appear to favor Socrates' opponent, does not follow such a procedure here. But doesn't this uncharacteristic omission of relevant information seriously compromise his objectivity as a witness?

One possible reason could have to do with when the *Apology* was written; the youthful Plato, it could be said, was most under the influence of Socrates here and least likely to be objective in so poignant a context. As such, he would angrily refuse to repeat the slanderous accusations made against his beloved master and friend. Yet many attempts to construct reliable chronologies collapse if we are to take seriously the evidence of Dionysius of Halicarnassus who said that Plato continually played around with the texts of his dialogues for many years after they were written.[1] This suggests that we should seek to understand Plato's unique narrative strategy with respect to the *Apology* as if we were responding to a challenging question that he confronts us with, instead of conveniently assuming that he lacked either sufficient objectivity or the hermeneutic sophistication to be conscious of such considerations.

But it is best to only make assumptions regarding subtle authorial intention after we are sure that simpler explanations are not sufficient to account for the problem in question. A more plausible scenario would have Plato choosing not to report the speeches of Socrates' opponents because they were too weak in their original form. Nor could he represent them in his customary value-added manner because this would necessitate that he follow the same procedure with the speech of Socrates; given the historical importance of this occasion, we can see why he would prefer not to do this.[2] If posterity and accuracy mattered as much to Plato then surely it would be easy to provide both the accusations and the *Apology* without embellishment?

Can we assume that the speeches of Socrates' accusers were too weak to be reported? The fact remains that these weak arguments were strong enough to gain his conviction. Could we not at least be allowed to make up our own minds, or is it that the aristocratic Plato is so afraid of the impressionable rabble that he cannot place Socrates in double jeopardy? The obvious response to this last contention is that were Plato that cynical, he would not have chosen the vulnerable dialogue form of writing in the first place. As we shall soon observe through detailed analysis of the *Apology*, the Socratic mission was founded on the assumption that the truth had to be imparted to all, even though it could only be discerned on an individual basis. As with the banquet in Matthew's Gospel, all were invited—but they were still required to be properly clad.[3]

This is why we prefer to assume that Plato's reasons for reporting the trial of Socrates the way he does are ultimately pedagogic. We shall explore the consequences of the assumption that it is solely for the sake of the reader that Plato chooses to report the *Apology* as he does. This is underscored by the unprecedented fact that Plato informs us, repeatedly, that he was a witness to these proceedings. Unlike the subtly satirical *Phaedo*, that mockingly metaphysical dead-bed dialogue that Plato disassociates himself from as an eye-witness (59b), he is willing to vouch for the almost literal accuracy of what is represented in the *Apology*. Just as Plato was willing to offer thirty minae to supplement Socrates' one mina, the thirty dialogues he composed all line up—as a chorus would—behind the old gadfly's voice, as it speaks directly to us in the *Apology*. All of the other works in the Platonic corpus, despite being unmatched literary and philosophic masterpieces, only illustrate the primal experience conveyed in the

Apology. Unlike these other dialogues, which reveal the souls of the inter-locutors/readers to themselves, the *Apology* is as close as Plato could get to re-creating the uncanny experience of Socrates.

Plato's oft-repeated assertion from the *Second Letter* that he made Socrates appear "young and idealized" is of relevance here.[4] Socrates did not practice the art of demotic music. His abrasive dialectical strategies were not calculated to flatter or reassure his interlocutors; indeed they had quite the contrary effect. It is Plato who makes the harsh tones of Socrates more palatable to the reader by obeying Apollo's command and working at setting his master's voice to music (60e). By the sublime experience of wit-nessing these artfully staged dialogues, we may come to see for ourselves what lies behind Socrates' ironic silences and Plato's irenic myths. The ultimate touchstone of reliability, the gold standard guaranteeing the other dialogues and securing the ground from which Plato's muse takes flight, must remain the uncannily personal experience of the *Apology* itself. Even if Socrates could not recognize himself, rejuvenated and beautified, in the other Platonic dialogues, we could surely expect that the father of his off-spring would not have any difficulty seeing himself as he is depicted in the *Apology*.

We recall also that the prepared speeches of his various accusers were readily available in the years immediately following the trial of Socrates, presumably the time Plato wrote down the *Apology*. However these speeches would only have detracted from the effect that Plato wished to create. While all of the Athenian *Agora* would have resounded with pas-sionate opinions, both pro and con, concerning the guilt or innocence of Socrates for years after his execution—the question even remains hotly debated today—we must understand that this question is only of peripher-al importance to the *Apology*. This is why Plato will not allow the casual reader to approach the *Apology* objectively as a judge or juror, to pass ver-dict on long-forgotten events of doubtful relevance to the present day. Socrates respected the ideal of justice more than the sacred rituals of judi-cial procedure. He turned the tables on his jurors and judges. Addressing his judges as if they were the accused he urged them to judge themselves, to ask themselves whether they were in a position to cast the first stone. Just as he felt co-opted to serve as the King Archon in the case of Euthyphro, Socrates involuntarily functions as the prosecutor in the *Apology*; he accuses both his prosecutors and jurors of impiety and corrup-tion. His conduct resembles that of Jesus in the temple.

This is why the reader of the *Apology* must also recognize that he or she stands accused by Socrates. To understand this seminal work properly, the so-called "fourth wall" separating the audience from the players must come down. *His* "defense" must be seen to have the disconcerting effect of putting *us* on the spot. We cannot approach this twenty-four-hundred-year-old text with the attitude of a visitor to a museum or theme park; we tend to read the *Apology* today with every expectation of passing tolerant judgment in favor of Socrates. "What a pity" we say to ourselves; if Socrates were alive we would surely gain his praise and un-ironic admiration for our erudition and heightened sense of justice. Indeed, we could even chide the old dinosaur gently for the unenlightened way in which he constructed his draconian *Republic*.

It is easy to read the *Apology* approvingly after the event. Socrates died a Christ-like death for the sake of freedom. He was killed by the prejudice of the Athenians. His blood is not on our hands. We know that since he redeemed us by his death and exposed the bankruptcy of Athenian culture, we do not have to struggle against superstition and prejudice, or even read the Classics, anymore. Just as Christ's crucifixion created the Church, Socrates' execution endowed the university; the sacramental character of both deaths brought into being corporate bodies that are redeemed by their founder. "Well done, old chap!" is all that needs to be said before moving on to the next exhibit. But far from being in the Classical Athenian exhibit in Disney World, we are in Jurassic Park. Differently put, that quaint old dinosaur, Socrates, never really died and we are now unexpectedly being mauled by him. Socrates will demand that we jointly and severally defend *our* own unexamined presuppositions. He must be seen to subvert some of *our* most cherished inherited values and sacred beliefs. He is needed now more than ever before because today, in the words of Aeschylus' *Libation Bearers*, "the dead are killing the living."[5]

Plato wishes his readers to experience very much the same complex mixture of emotions, fury coupled with bewilderment and outrage, that Socrates' conduct provoked. If he were in our midst today, would we not also vote to sentence Socrates to death? We must see that we're much like his jurors. Socrates' words must be seen to fly in the face of our own values and practices. Plato uses the technique that Dostoevsky employed in his *Legend of the Grand Inquisitor* to ask us if we would not sentence Jesus to death all over again. By his art Plato brings Socrates back to life so that we may be challenged, to the very depths of our being, by his uncanny lived presence; this is what is most dialogic about his *Apology*. Just as Jesus would not survive in Christendom, Socrates' attitude towards his colleagues' venal sophistication would render him *persona non grata* in the academy. The battles fought by Socrates have timeless import. Just as the *Euthyphro* explores the possibility of recovering primal origins, the *Apology* redirects us, as individuals, to the surface of a timelessly present site, a shining city outside the cave, both sustaining and challenging our humanity. In each case the validity of a sacred mediating process is denied.

Returning to our earlier complaints we can now see that Plato has been even-handed after all. Not content with merely providing an intellectual account of the trial, he has represented the case against Socrates in its strongest light by having the old gadfly inspire in us the very passions that the Athenian jury experienced. To truly understand the case against Socrates we cannot be cold-bloodedly scientific and dispassionate; we need to personally experience the deep-seated visceral fury that welled up in the guts of his jurors. At the end of the day Socrates and Plato are more interested in our souls than our minds. This is why many philosophers, classicists and close readers of texts secretly hate Socrates. While most philosophers see little difference between a dialogue and a crossword puzzle, just as classicists enjoy the consolations of philology, and other "close readers" try to prove that every deep thinker is an amoral atheist, the *Apology* is all about the urgent moral and spiritual demands a philosopher must make on his life, family and polity.

We are now ready to deal with Socrates' ironic complaint that he almost forgot himself after hearing himself described by his accusers. He suggests that the fabric of lies woven around him was so convincing that it almost persuaded him to succumb to anger—the natural element of the courtroom. His accusers almost made forget himself, to cease to be Socrates. We are reminded of the terrible sweetness of anger; according to the *Iliad* this power delivers many men to the birds and dogs.[6] Socrates must be guided by his *daimon* to resist the mellifluous—literally honeyed—tones of Meletus and overcome the tempting furies he must expose and denounce.

According to Socrates, the most remarkable among the many lies uttered against him was the shameless allegation that he was a dangerously clever (*deinos*) speaker (17b). His accusers are shameless because they must realize that he will immediately refute this canard by his very speech. This is why they preemptively warn the jurors against heeding his words. It is also why they must infect the jurors with their own shamelessness— drenched in fulsome flattery and rancid righteousness. It is all too easy to be dragged into a *thumos*-saturated world of accusations and false outrage.

Here, in the cave's sacred darkness, we are stripped of individual judgment and truth as a terrible collective identity is born. Intoxicated by self-righteous indignation, this monster swallows men and consumes souls; we are reminded of Odysseus's battle with the shameless Cyclops, perhaps in this very cave.[7]

In the *Protagoras* Socrates contrasted the impotent but bold rhetoric of the Athenians to the terrible but laconically understated deeds of the Spartans (342e). Here in the *Apology*, Socrates claims that he is not a clever speaker because he refuses to construct his speeches carefully and shamelessly as his accusers did. However a truthful speaker could speak in a way that is unexpected and unsettling if he addresses an audience habitually accustomed to lies and flattery. What is most "terrible" about Socrates' manner of speaking is that he will not deviate from his accustomed everyday language. By using ordinary words he will stress the continuity between speech and deeds that usually ensures that a prophet will never be respected by his own people: those who know that he seldom practiced what he preaches. This is the reason Moses could not physically enter his promised land; it also explains Socrates' death and way of dying.

Thanks to the unity of his well-governed soul, Socrates will speak simply and truthfully in a context where truth is most praised and least expected: a court of law. Likewise, as he transmits these words, Plato also seems to assure us that he will not allow his own strong feelings, his own terribly righteous and honey-sweet anger, to stand in the way of accurately conveying Socrates' words and deeds to us. We are headed to a primal scene as fearful as any we faced in the *Euthyphro*, a moral crossroads on the way to Delphi where our own anger is liable to erupt as spontaneously as Oedipus's. Yet Plato must also hope that this naked exposure of the spirit of Socrates will test the mettle of our souls.

Truth is least expected in a context where we are overpowered by desires and fears. Socrates is not supposed to speak truthfully because, as Thucydides and Hobbes assert, the fear of death must override any sworn obligation to speak honestly. Decency matters more than truth and since all decent men fear death it is hubristic of Socrates to mock their fears by speaking truthfully. Standing at the gates of Hades, men are expected to follow necessity and say anything that will deliver them from its dreadful maw. Like the plague itself, which was far more terrible because all the residents of Attica were huddled together within the city walls,[8] this contagion—a mixture of anger and fear—afflicts all those crowded within the cavernous courtroom. This plague infects the body with false knowledge;

it overwhelms our minds with the fear of death and floods our bodies with self-righteous anger. Only Socrates, acting like Tiresias, the one man possessed of his wits in Hades, could resist this mad necessity.[9] We are reminded of the only man knowing the art of navigation, or the *Gorgias*'s true art of politics, in the *Republic's* ship of state analogy.[10]

Lisping Alcibiades anticipated Socrates' enemies when he slyly compared his erstwhile lover to a Siren in the *Symposium* (216a). We recall from the *Odyssey* that the Sirens promised to tell Odysseus who he was whilst calling him to his death.[11] Socrates is like a Siren in that he offers the men of Athens a dangerous self-knowledge that could place their carnal interests and sacred values in grave jeopardy. This paralleled the physical ugliness that disguised the dazzling spiritual beauty of Socrates. On both counts we must admit that he is attractive to certain parts of the soul and "terribly" ugly to those aspects of the soul that are linked to the cravings and fears of the cave-like body. This very psychic division was described in *Republic V*, where we hear of Leontias's morbid desire to gaze upon certain dead bodies. Leontias eventually gave in, telling his concupiscent eyes: "Have your fill you wretches and feast upon this beautiful sight" (440a). Simply put, Socrates threatens to overthrow the hegemony of the body by restoring self-knowledge to the soul. He trusts that this self-knowledge will not lead us to put our eyes out like Oedipus. Far from corrupting Athens, Socrates serves Athena and Apollo; he angers his fellow citizens by exposing the emptiness of the glittering phantoms offered by Hera and Aphrodite.

Socrates also promises that he will speak the "whole truth" (17b). His speech will not consist of an artfully chosen potpourri of falsities and half-truths woven together for maximal rhetorical effect. Reversing Callicles' jibe in the *Gorgias* that he spoke with a childish naïveté unbecoming in one of his mature age (485b), Socrates says that it would be more ridiculous for him to deviate from the distinctive ways of speech and conduct he practiced all of his life (17d). Only then would his enemies succeed in causing him to lose his self-possession and forget himself—he will not let seven times as many evil spirits flow back into his long-cleansed soul by allowing it to be used in vain.[12] He will not permit his reputation be used to corrupt the young.

By promising to reveal the whole truth concerning himself, Socrates also undertakes that he will not conceal from the jurors material facts that will make it harder for him to win his case. He conducts himself in a manner inimical to his best legal interests. It will become increasingly clear that his concern is with revealing causes rather than manipulating the direction of the trial with a view to influencing its results. By contrast to the victory-crazed Athenians, who were blind to anything but winning and destroying their enemies, he is quite willing to place his entire life on trial. He lets them see that he has already won a battle over his own fears and passions. Thus he will enter the court as a real man who rules himself, not as one flattened into a shadow or caricature of himself by his fear of death and the vain desire to gain a pyrrhic victory over his accusers. Yet by doing so, he first implicitly and then explicitly accuses the Athenians of impiety and corruption, since they have refused willy-nilly to govern their lives by moral axioms said to be naturally evident to all humans. The tragedy of the *Apology* pits the soul against the cave. The soul must detach itself from the cave before returning to it in glory as its ruler and judge. The enlightened prisoner's behavior is both odious and arousing to the slumbering furies of the cave.

Socrates reverses the customary opposition between truth and rhetoric, the respective values of the soul and the cave, to preserve the utmost consistency between words and deeds. He warns the Athenians that his defense speech, like his life itself, will be truthful and ugly rather than beautiful and untrue. This also means that his speech is not an artfully contrived creation; we recall from the *Euthyphro* and Xenophon's *Apology* that his *daimon* twice prevented him from considering how he would speak at his trial.[13] The reason for this is clear to him; Plato's *Apology* represents the public consummation of the revelatory process of self-discovery that began with Chaerephon's visit to the oracle at Delphi. As Socrates' life flashes before his eyes, the man about to be sentenced to death comes to see the divine pattern woven through its coarse fabric.

By choosing "to speak at random, through the words I happen upon" (17c), Socrates refuses to cut and measure his words to please his audience as a clever speaker would. He will not be clever in artfully subordinating means to ends. His words will not passively follow his fears and desires as a poet tags behind a tyrant. Rather, he must conduct himself and speak as one who is inspired or mad. Only by doing this will he, in Heidegger's winged words, "stand in the pure draft of truth."[14] He will allow his *daimon* or character to speak through him and to him. Plato will interpret these inspired words in many dialogues in a way that will yet continually direct our attention back to this timeless event.

In a more secular idiom we may say that Socrates can speak spontaneously because his character has been long established by the purifying power of honesty. Socrates can be present to himself because he has not permitted his consciousness to become a polluted stream of fears and desires. Since he already knows himself, he cannot, and will not, fabricate or assume a generic mask to pander to the many. He has reasons for believing that this false persona would be more corrosive or deadly than any penalty a jury could impose upon him. While randomly put together men—wayward children of chance and desire—must choose their words carefully, fearing that their past lies will conflict with present exigencies, a temperate man can say what spontaneously comes to his mind; his thoughts and character are already consistent.

By refusing to speak in the "dialect" of the courtroom, Socrates is also clearly rejecting the seemingly pious but actually nihilistic values upon which this judicial "language game" is based. According to the theogony of strife that was revealed in the *Euthyphro*, reality is too complex and heterogeneous to be governed by any single set of humanly comprehensible principles; it consists of a set of mutually incompatible language games that reflect the polymorphous perversity of the soul and its many mad masters. But underlying this all is a sacred order of Gaia that exceeds the rational grasp of language; it is held as an axiom that existence and its preservation matter more than any of the other essences expressed in the form of virtues. Yet while Socrates refuses to give a dogmatic account of a transcendent superstructure that he opposed to this raging Will to Life, he does not believe that man lives by life (or rage) alone. He rejects the sovereignty of the values of life and reproduction. For this he will feel the wrath of Hera—the furious goddess of the family and its chthonic satellites: the body and the cave. Socrates is seen as the last survivor of the generation of reckless heroes who waged the ruinous Peloponnesian War and, seeking glory at the cost of life itself, all but destroyed Athens.

To his pessimistic opponents it follows that a prudent man must swallow his pride, forget his principles, and worship the *genius loci*—the regnant cultural values or local theology of the particular cave or context into which he finds himself thrown. But since Socrates does not believe that morality is merely a function of time, place, bodily necessity and material exigency, he will continue to be himself and ask the same irreverent and unsettling questions of the men of Athens. The Athenians find this posture of seeming moral autonomy deeply offensive since it called into question both their religious tradition and the implicit reasoning underlying their choice of such a religiosity. These matters had traditionally been regarded as sacred precisely because they could not be rationally justified, least of all by fearful humans. Indeed our common stifled anger at the injustice and irrationality of life creates a mystic bond of memory leading back to Achilles himself! This very irrationality had the effect of making legal proceedings of any kind, but particularly those about piety, adversarial and violent. Athenian common sense believed that a greater degree of rationality and liberality could not be expected in human affairs than what was immanent in a fundamentally chaotic reality. While justice cannot be expected at all from the irrational gods, any justice gained at the horizontal level is only secured at the expense of other less powerful mortals. This amounts to saying that justice is proportionate to the will to power.

In a sense the most basic question of all here has to do with whether or not it is decent for a temperate soul to fear death. This is similar to asking whether God's love or the promise of bodily resurrection is the essential tenet of Christianity. As we suggested, the fear of death is ultimately made into the basis for a theology that places the heteronomous value of placating the gods or powers that be far above the ethical conduct demanded by conscience and the moral archetypes. The more irrational these gods or fundamental principles are, the harder it is for our virtues to make any headway against the bleak reality revealed by the poets. Indeed one who stresses the unconditional obligation to practice virtue frequently incurs the charge of Pelagianism to the extent that he seems to not offer due deference to sacramental grace and sanctifying rituals. To Socrates these virtues and vices are but ruses by which men vainly hope to manipulate these irrational powers though all the while trying to maximize pleasure and minimize pain: the true gods of the body and the cave. Those who live selfishly project their psychic disorder on the gods and reality itself. Plato's take on the conditions for the possibility of Socrates' life, as stated in the *Gorgias*, seems to be that the ultimate reality is a cosmos—literally beautified by co-operation between benevolent gods and erotic mortals, neither trespassing their limits (508a).

Reiterating the primacy of ethics over fear-based piety developed in the *Euthyphro*, a priority consistent with his belief that the soul should rule the body, Socrates demonstrates in the *Apology* that the knowledge and practice of virtue makes a human being autonomous in the sense of not being ruled by external fears and inner compulsions. Death is the greatest among these powers since it can bring an end to all of them. We could even say that the fear of death and corruption is the cause of psychic corruption and spiritual death, to the extent that it causes mortals to become alienated from their capacity for moral autonomy and virtue—the very means through which they gain some measure of immortality and thereby triumph over death.

Hades has the last word when it invades the body and reduces it to a cavity infected by fear and anger. Death thus defines life itself; it also makes the polis deny itself and become a cave populated by so many forgetful "bats." Buckling under the fears of the body, the soul loses its ability to see or live in the fullness of reality; as a result life becomes nasty, brutal and Hobbesian. This also is why the physical threat of mortality and the psychic awareness of morality cannot be seen as opposing principles. Indeed as Achilles and Pericles saw, awareness of mortality should spur us to perform noble deeds and thus leave an indelible mark on the collective memory of the political community. Socrates, who believes that this immortal desire could be led beyond the cave, and its dual preoccupation with death and reproduction, suggests that only clear-eyed awareness of the human condition allows its best possibilities to be lived out. The fear-ridden theology of the body is the origin of corruption. Even the model of Homer and Pericles privileges being celebrated by others—as opposed to having the opportunity to realize oneself. In other words, a true polis would have allowed Hector to realize his more human virtues rather than being remembered for tragic and vain acts of heroism performed in defense of a doomed city. He is remembered for *what* he did, not for *who* he really was. Achilles dismissed this possibility as a long life without glory[15] because he was destined to be—or knew—nothing better. For him, reality is a zero-sum game. Conversely Socrates, emulating Odysseus, can sing a better song about the possibility of a long glorious life realizing the fullest possibilities of reality. To him, reality offers more generous choices than the tragic tantrums or sad soliloquies of an Achilles or Hamlet. Humans can bring out the best in each other by bringing words and deeds together in a true polis.[16] This setting allows for the evolution of the dialogue out of the more oppositional genre of tragedy. The *Apology* is the transitional work between the genre of tragedy and the comic Platonic dialogues.

When we reflect on Plato's evenhandedness in setting up a dialogue, we cannot forget that he was educated by the conduct of his silent teacher in an extremely agonistic situation. Yet Socrates' own sense of justice dictates that he makes his prosecutors case stronger by exposing the chthonic origins of their complaint. It would otherwise have been a relatively simple matter for Socrates to refute his accusers at the level of rhetoric; he deals with Meletus's explicit charges quite effectively. When we consider the slenderness of the margin by which he was convicted, there can be no doubt that if he had confined his defense to addressing Meletus, he would have been acquitted quite comfortably (36aûb). Yet just as Meletus could not be content with accusing Socrates on behalf of the poets, and had to drag in Anytus and Lycon to represent the respective interests of the artisans and rhetoricians, now Socrates will call upon the city itself to throw its dead weight behind them. He will do so by accusing public opinion itself of corruption and impiety. He forges an alliance against him on sacred ground common to both pious right and profane left: a belief in an adversarial reality sustained by thumos: erotic energy inverted by anger and fear. It will no longer be possible for the jurors to vote in favor of Socrates without recognizing that they themselves, and indeed Athens itself, have been guilty of the very vices Socrates was unjustly accused of. Now, like Tiresias in Thebes, Socrates is forced to accuse Oedipus/Athens! There can no longer be any middle ground in this quarrel; the laws dictate that a citizen who does not take sides in times of revolution is guilty of criminal indifference.[17] Like a good soldier, Socrates will not go home as he had done in the case of Leon of Salamis (32c) while others obeyed the evil orders of the Thirty. Like Achilles avenging Patroclus, he takes the offensive against those besmirching the glory of his fatherland: *patrokleos*. Yet this is only possible because he believes that Athens is capable of learning from his example. His adversarial conduct here must be seen as divinely ordained, and based on a hopeful disposition. This is the final tragedy—one that exposes the limitations of the tragic way of life. While Euripides' apocalyptic *Bacchae* exposes the primal fury beneath Dionysian exuberance, and earlier Aeschylus's *Eumenides* and Sophocles' *Oedipus at Colonus* sought but to appease this terrible power; now Socrates will surpass the dying Oedipus and battle against this mother of all fury.

Socrates points out that he could not adequately defend himself against the specific accusations of impiety and corruption without consideration of the implicit basis for their being preferred against him; neither does he think that he should. He does not simply occupy himself with the outcome of his trial, by getting these charges dismissed by any means necessary. Thus while Plato does not provide the speeches of the new accusers, Socrates reconstructs their true foundation: the older unwritten accusations made against him. He goes beneath the positive law to reveal its sacred substratum.

As a good and conscientious citizen he finds it necessary that, instead of concerning themselves solely with his eccentric behavior, his fellow citizens could only judge him properly after they have understood his life and the principles animating it. This process began with the enigmatic message from the oracle that Chaerephon brought to Socrates from Delphi. Though Socrates was not present at the time, his self-understanding began through the strange intercourse of a god of restraint, his intoxicated illiterate prophetess and a notoriously batty enthusiast. Yet this philosophical Odyssey ends in a very different manner. By his striking conduct at his trial, Socrates sets out to make the culmination of this long strange trip of self-discovery as public and explicit as its origins were obscure and distant. Like Orestes, Socrates is ordered by Apollo to punish his mother and brave her furies. We recall that Meletus went to the city, as to his mother—to complain of Socrates' impiety (2c). As Clytemnestra, he seeks to awaken slumbering chthonic powers.[18] Now, as the sacred furies of Athens possess its men-folk, Socrates, like Orestes, calls upon Apollo as his witness. He will claim that that the Oracle of Apollo gave him his orders.

Although Socrates will speak plainly in everyday non-technical language familiar to any Athenian man on the street, his conclusions will fly in the faces of his jurors. Indeed his speech will turn out to be a radical indictment of popular tradition and conventional wisdom. He will not address the jurors *en masse* by appealing to their self-righteous but easily manipulated collective consciousness; rather, his dangerous strategy will be to address them as so many potentially thoughtful individuals. They will only be able to attend adequately to his words by uprooting themselves from the collective mentality in which they are comfortably embedded; as we noted, his homely language addresses and shames their slothful souls! While their minds are used to dealing with ritual, jargon and platitudes, Socrates' deeds have gained authority through his ability to rule his body; his plain words will force Athens to understand him. These words will drive the Athenians out of the security of the cave. Avenging himself on Aristophanes, he will seem to set their houses—or at least their household gods, on fire. This was why the prosecution warned against his seductive way of speech. Yet, this is also because, in a typically quixotic gesture of fairness to his prosecutors and jurors, Socrates goes out of the way to stress the radical implications of his trial with words that both arouse the soul and torment the body. He is very much aware that a man can only leave the cave of his own free volition, not through heedlessly succumbing to the seductive rhetoric of another.

This is why Socrates tells his jurors that to judge him correctly, on the basis of the charges that Meletus, Anytus, and Lycon have preferred, they must first be relieved of the prejudicial slanders that have been told about him and themselves since their childhood. Through the myths of the poets, the lies of the politicians, and the trauma of the war; they have been separated from their souls, the truth about the past, and indeed reality itself. He is assuring them that it is safe to leave their dangerously thumotic underground shelters and return to erotic reality. In other words, Socrates is telling the jurors that it is they who have unwittingly been exposed to corrupt and impious influences since their childhood. These lies presumably pertain not only to him, but also to their own common values and self-understanding as Athenians. These jurors must be purged of this corruption and impiety before they can even properly apprehend the meaning of these terms, leave aside being competent to serve as judges of a case as complex as that they are presently faced with. They cannot judge him correctly from within the perspective of the cave and he knows that they know themselves to be, *qua human*, yet capable of transcending it mentally, albeit not necessarily with the power to rule their wills.

From Socrates' standpoint it is the height of absurdity that patients suffering from an insidious disease depriving them of self-knowledge about their condition should presume to judge their physician. While he would regard this very presumption as further evidence of their malaise, they would be outraged at his hubristic attitude towards the traditions and institutions of his native polity: both Orestes and the prisoner returned to the cave should submit to the righteous authority of the womb that gave them birth. The absence of any middle ground between the positions staked out by Socrates and his accusers makes any compromise impossible. If Socrates is innocent then the Athenians are guilty, and vice versa. But this is also why he must explain his deeper fundamental loyalty to Athens in the *Crito*.

It seems that the confusion surrounding these charges and counter-charges will only be dispelled when Socrates and his judges can provide each other with adequately substantiated accounts of their respective world-views. Although Socrates is in a position to render such a justification of his life, it is quite clear that he is the only one in the courtroom who can do so. As we saw from the *Euthyphro*, the Athenians' pious refusal to probe or question the sacred origins of their traditional values suggests that the very attempt to inquire into the essence of piety is deemed impious and corruptive.[19] We have gone from Euthyphro's clearly unjust prosecution of his father to studying the merits of Pheidippides' claim to educate and examine his mother. While Socrates famously substituted education for retribution, to the Athenians it is death to be alienated from a collective identity that rewards conformity with soulless immortality of the sort promised Abraham. The soul's desire and power to see the forms threatens the cave's sanctity.

Our study of the *Euthyphro* cleared out the thorny thicket of problems surrounding the Greek concept (*hosion*) that we translated as "piety." We now discover that the concept commonly translated as corruption (*diaphtheirein*), also less archetypal in its associations, is provided with a very interesting and suggestive ancillary meaning by Plato. While the literal meaning of this word "destroy, ruin, cripple, weaken, slacken, or dissipate" has to do with physical destruction, Plato also uses the phrase "having changed nothing of his color" (*ouden diaphtheiras tou chromtos*) in a highly suggestive point in his writings. These words are used in the *Phaedo* to describe Socrates' calm demeanor as he receives the fatal cup of Hemlock from his executioner (117b). We are also reminded of Achilles' threat to leave for the rich wasteland of "fertile Phthia."[20] Simply put, Plato uses this pun to suggest that Socrates was not "corrupted" by the fear of death. While the Hemlock would corrupt his body in the literal sense, and Socrates was well aware of this, we are assured that his *character* is unaffected by this grim prospect. Otherwise put, his soul, although originating in the cave, has an integrity that ultimately transcends it.

As Socrates and Plato seem to use the term, corruption is closely connected to the power of the fears of the body to overwhelm a soul's self-possession. Yet corrupt Athenian conventional wisdom views this concept in a diametrically different manner. This self-possession threatens the autochthony of the cave and the *oikos*. While Socrates is steadfast in his moral awareness that virtue is stronger than vice, associated with his belief that the gods won't allow a good man to be harmed by those worse than he (30c), this assurance seems to pertain only to matters concerning the soul. In the case of the body, however, we must concede that the fears of *Hoi Polloi* concerning *its* susceptibility to corruption are far more legitimate; we are dust and must return to our autochthonous origins. Athenian piety is founded on the fears of the self-righteous body. When it is examined from this pusillanimous and purely corporeal perspective, Socratic intellectualism, with its concomitant indifference to the interests of the body, and the possibilities of vicarious existence offered by the cave, certainly appears to be both impious and literally corruptive. The very recent experience of plague, siege and famine would surely have made the Athenians aware of death's power over the soul and idealistic virtue. One generation earlier Thucydides depicted how easily piety itself succumbed to the power of *statis*.[21] This fear can also be used to tighten our religious bonds to the cave or the empty tomb of the body.

If we take Aristophanes as their best representative, Socrates' most intelligent opponents maintain that since human reason cannot rule over a basically irrational reality, soothing myths are the best remedy to the blind but not-unjustified fears of the body regarding the undiscovered country of death. Since the body cannot reason intellectually, humans ruled by bodily exigency (the vast majority of any human community) may only be "educated" by traditions and time-honored stories that conserved social stability and maintained the appearance of permanence in a rapidly changing world. The giant shadows and sacred flames must not die out in the cave.

We must remember that it is never questioned whether the results of these supposed investigations into heavenly and chthonic matters are accurate descriptions of the nature of things; even Aristophanes seems to have very little respect for the truth value of stories about the traditional gods or cosmologies. Traditional piety, a barely disguised code word for social stability, dictated that potentially transcendental values like truth and justice had to be superseded by more fearful concerns or seen by their light. This is why Euthyphro's hyper-literalized piety is so absurd; it is also why Plato ceaselessly deploys new myths that lead back towards an eternal erotic present, the dance floor between the teeming earth and beautiful sky; he seeks to replace older myths that have become too literalized and too reified to transport the soul beyond itself. But sadly Plato's urgent warnings concerning the primacy of spiritual things, matters beyond the range of the body, have been translated by Neo-Platonism into materialistic or naturalistic terms as literal accounts of heavenly matters and things beneath the earth. Later, more skeptical readers assume the invalidity of these literal accounts to mean that Socrates and Plato also held to an ultimately atheistic view. For ourselves, we must not forget the nub of Socrates' interpretation of the Oracle's words: though the divine exists, no man can know god's inner essence. Instead we have immediate awareness of our moral duty, unclouded by calculations involving willful gods.

It is now clear that when Socrates claimed that the Athenians had already been prejudiced against him by his earlier accusers, he was merely drawing attention to a much greater problem. Socrates himself obligingly lists the various accusations that his older enemies brought against him. He was accused of being meddlesome, investigating taboo cosmological matters, making the weaker speech the stronger, and teaching this way of life to others (19c). We must recognize that all of these positions stand in direct opposition to the cynically manipulated and fearful world-view upon which post-war Athenian piety and conventional wisdom was founded. As we saw, post-war Athenians lived off past glories and old resentments; their vicarious existence could be likened to the collective resentment of the Trojan War veterans in Hades. Aristophanes' ideal spectator combined the self-righteousness of the many with the fearful conservatism of the few.

We have already dealt partially with the pious accusation that Socrates was meddlesome in investigating heavenly things and matters beneath the earth. Ironically this seems to be a materialistic understanding of Socrates' this-worldly emphasis on the soul and virtue. Traditional and god-fearing Athenian piety seems to have consisted of what could best be described as "spiritual materialism." In other words, sacred and divine matters were identified in spatial terms as "things under the earth and in the skies" and justified according to the selfish bodily categories of pleasure and pain, instead of being assessed by their moral quality. These gods were just as selfish and 'realistic' as their cynical worshippers; failure to respect or immortalize these qualities would be punished by mimetic social reality. Viewed from a transcendental Socratic perspective, a vantage that emphasized spiritual integrity and unselfish moral autonomy, so cynical and ultimately hedonistic a stance could only be blasphemous. But even the pre-Socratic cosmological philosophers would have been critical of this kind of spiritual materialism for reasons that would have had very little to do with piety or even morality. Any person possessed of a modicum of scientific integrity would have been critical of a world-view that accepted sweeping statements concerning cosmological themes on the basis of authority, ignorance, fear and habit. But this does not mean that Socrates shared the materialistic amorality of Anaxagoras.

Viewed in this manner, the accusation that Socrates was meddlesome could also be taken as an allusion to what seemed to be excessive scrupulosity on his part. Understood according to its more standard usage, the word usually translated "meddlesome" actually turns out to mean something like "taking excessive pains over" when we are "meddlesome" enough to examine the actual Greek. While the traditional translation "meddlesome" better suits the purposes of those who have an ax to grind or hemlock to prepare, it is clear that being excessively scrupulous could hardly be seen as being impious. Such a charge could be leveled with far greater justice at one who cynically or pragmatically accepted whatever debased mimetic convention was currently in force. Meletus, whose very name means "care," is a fine example of one who professed concern about matters that he was quite oblivious to. Meletus couldn't care less whether Socrates was actually atheist, agnostic or heretic. We have already seen substantial evidence that would indicate that Meletus merely wished to advance his personal ambitions. By contrast, seemingly excessive Socratic scrupulosity is justified on scientific and moral grounds. I will suggest that his grounds for being "meddlesome" also underwent a metamorphosis; Socrates' moral integrity ensured that his originally scientific concern with scrupulosity would soon transcend itself.

When it is understood literally, the word *pereigazomai* turns out to mean something like "going around and examining the business of others." While this sense of being a busybody is closer to the translation of "meddlesome" that we have rejected, we cannot reduce this literal meaning to the proportions of a mere cliché. In other words, Socrates seemed to have occupied himself with critically examining the self-righteous "busy-ness" of those who had no time to question the purpose and meaning of their own governing preoccupations. He was forced to be a busybody by the unreflective behavior of those who, consciously or not, chose to avoid self-knowledge and reduced themselves to the slavish level of busy bodies. Their busy-ness turns out to be based on some implicit "professions" that are not actually examined or lived up to. Socrates' world-view is based on his own activity and experience of reality. His account of the philosopher in *Republic V*—as one with non-coercive interest in the unity of a heterogeneous whole—supports this claim.[22]

Socrates need not have actually investigated matters in the heavens and below the earth to draw the accusations made by Aristophanes in the *Clouds*. It was not necessary that he should himself have conducted the ludicrous experiments lampooned by the Comedian. Indeed, one could claim that only familiarity prevented Athenian men on the street from seeing that their own religious rituals were far more absurd than the procedures supposedly carried out at the Socratic "Think-Tank";[23] every nation or cave seems to have its own thumotic markers or totems. For the purposes of purging conventional wisdom and piety, it sufficed that Socrates asked people to explain the meaning of the astonishing claims made about matters of a celestial and subterranean nature by those implicitly or explicitly claiming to be sufficiently versed in these matters. He did not need to actually possess positive scientific knowledge concerning these things to be moved to skepticism by the evidently outlandish and unfounded beliefs of his fellow citizens. His Delphic revelation was sufficient to help him see that all of these claims were false. Yet to many Athenians, he wantonly exposed the old gods to ridicule and offered no substitutes (for human pusillanimity) in their stead. Likewise, although he did not study matters under the earth, Socrates told the Athenians that they lived uneducated and alienated from the fullness of reality in an underground cave bunker constructed out of fears and prejudices.

Turning now to the other unspoken charge that he made the weaker speech stronger, we should first pay attention to an obvious, if unintended, sense in which this is true. Socrates clearly goes out of his way to add substance to the thoroughly nebulous charges preferred against him by Meletus. As we noted at the beginning of this chapter, Plato also follows this practice in trying to make the arguments of the various hostile interlocutors of Socrates more virile and beautiful in his dialogues than they were in real life. Yet this is not merely a way of turning the other cheek to one's adversary. As Glaucon suggested in Book II of the *Republic*, it does not suffice to merely gain a, temporary, rhetorical victory over one's opponent (358b); the inadequacy of the refutation will only suggest that the position championed by the refuter is just as dubious. Like a Hydra, the defeated argument itself will merely grow more mouths if its very essence is not confronted and refuted. While a rhetorician can have no higher expectation, Socrates believes that the fabric of reality is better and less fickle than Machiavelli's *Fortuna*. This cosmos is to moral virtue what the universe is to scientific knowledge.

As for the allegation that Socrates made the weaker speech stronger, the claim that Socrates championed "Unjust Speech" against "Just Speech" is not seen as part of the popular opinion concerning him. Socrates, in other words, recognized that he was not being accused of championing or advocating injustice; rather, he saw that he was situated by the many at the other extreme: nurturing what is currently weak but potentially strong against what is seemingly strong but potentially weak. He is not being unjust; however he was thought to be imprudent and reckless in exposing the conventional wisdom of the status quo. Socrates scandalously does not seem to be bound by these norms or implicit conventions. He will not accept that what commonly passes for justice in the eyes of the many is, consequently, legitimate. The truth of the matter was not that Socrates made the weak speech stronger; rather, it was that he made the strong speech of violent *ananke* appear weaker than it desired to appear. In this spirit Plato shows how tyranny inevitably ends in madness and misery; unjust speech reaps just punishment from within itself.

The weaker speech is not necessary the weaker argument; rhetorical effect does not carry with it a guarantee of dialectical soundness. We see in the *Gorgias* how a very strong speech, able to convince a large audience amidst conditions conducive to emotional persuasion (454e–455a), could well turn out to be flawed and sophistic once it is subjected to logical scrutiny by the individual. The popular rhetoric of a competent demagogue must be understood as strong speech according to this way of thinking. Yet, Socrates is not simply interested in the analysis of speeches. In the *Apology*, he continues his lifelong examination of the conditions of the possibility of this misleading rhetoric. In other words, he is not content to refute the individual Hydra-head; his mission is to assail the body of the Hydra—that vast and angry reservoir of prejudiced public opinion that continually spawns new mouthpieces to pander to its insatiable appetites and titillate its craven fears.

In the Callicles section of the *Gorgias* we see that the quantitative strength of the many, like the demagogic argument, withers away and is exposed as the weaker *logos*, once it is dragged out of the cave and subjected to the light of reason. Although the collective loyalties or "family values" of the cave/*oikos* are necessary for the human animal's survival, especially in childhood, they become falsely misleading imperatives at the truly human level of free political deliberation. The unity of truth must be defended against an angry chorus of lusts, slanders and fears. Socrates real offense is to show that the spiritual soul is stronger than the clamoring desires and the body.

Aristophanes' charge that Socrates investigated matters above the heavens and beneath the earth was refuted by our recognition that Socrates merely pointed out the impossibility of the knowledge that poets professed of these things. Indeed since the *Phaedo* (109a–d) and the cave myth of the *Republic* suggest that he ridiculed the idea that the local cave or *oikos* was identical with the natural domain of human action, investigating beyond the heavens simply corresponds to leaving the false horizons of the cave to study the natural world and other cultures beyond one's own. The claim that Socrates made weak speeches stronger must also be reversed for the truth—that he revealed the weakness of so-called strong speech—to be seen. Incomplete human nature is supplemented by freedom and reason and made capable of political or cultural transcendence; yet it is always tempted to accept thoughtless piety and freedom-destroying myths in exchange for the security of an Egyptian fleshpot. The exodus from the cave is what Aristophanes sees as Original Sin. While the poet panders to the wish to end all thought, and bring the End of History, in a way reminiscent of circle-men finding their other half, Socrates, with seeming impracticality and perversity, holds the contrary position: individual acts of deliberate judgment must replace piously affirmed and furiously defended collective truths based on sacred honor rather than reality.

The rhetorical force of what the poet Aristophanes would cynically call a strong speech would be particularly susceptible to Socratic analysis. Just as Socrates famously denied that Justice consisted of the advantage of the stronger, pointing out to the likes of Callicles and Thrasymachus that the merely physically strong would be ignorant of their best advantage, a rhetorically effective "strong speech" would, quite apart from being false, bring no benefit to its hearers. Its very purported strength consists in the power to move people to wallow in their old falsehoods and act against their soul's best interests. Understanding the truth about these deleterious effects would reveal the weakness of a strong speech and expose its presuppositions.

We should also recognize that Socrates never sought to move people to act against their better, or worse, judgment. Such a strategy would fly in the face of his seemingly "over-scrupulous" conviction that virtue could not be achieved by the rhetorical means of deception or imitation. This meant that he would never make a rhetorically weak speech "strong" by infusing emotive elements that interfere with the integrity of the deliberative process. His conduct in the *Apology* is the only proof needed to bear out the truth of this contention. The strength of his speech consisted precisely in this refusal to accommodate to otherwise compelling heteronomous pressures that detract from his exemplary integrity as human being, citizen and philosopher.

We see here the deeper ironic significance in the claim made by Socrates that he was fighting against shadows. Like shadows from Hades, the older accusations then leveled against Socrates by Aristophanes, and mindlessly reiterated by those of his ilk at the time of the trial, seem to be negative or inverted images of the real issues at stake here. These matters could not have been stated positively without disclosing the very fictions from which the poets and politicians derived their authority in Athens. Perhaps most of the old accusers could not even see the truth of the matter as we have stated it. Most successful liars usually convince themselves that they are being truthful: rather than remembering the immediate experience he is asked to recall, even a truthful person will usually merely remember the last time he told the story. In other words, in as much that they suffered from "Cave Vision," his enemies could not apprehend reality apart from the a priori categories of dogma and prejudice that Socrates was anxious to liberate them from. In this clash between individual integrity and collective solidarity, the many seem to find vicarious glee in observing the tragic fates of those who resisted irrationality. Too old for erotic pursuits, they take pleasure in wasp-like resentment and resigned righteousness.[24]

In order to completely dispose of the old accusers, and vindicate Socrates' robust denial of their allegations, we must now turn to the final old accusation: that Socrates *taught* others to be meddlesome, investigate cosmological entities, and make weak speeches stronger. These accusations have already been substantially weakened by our recognition that Socrates himself did not perform any of these actions. Yet this does not dispose of the question of whether Socrates did not exercise sufficient prudence or "care" in ensuring that the youth who admired him did not arrive at positive and dangerous conclusions by observing and imitating his enigmatic negative practices. This, after all, is the crux of the explicit allegation that Socrates corrupted the youth of Athens. Meletus seems to have thought, along with Aristophanes, whose name literally means "best revealer," that it was best to not reveal the collective chains of political theology that held a polity together. Socrates however doggedly fights the view that the whole was either irrational or under the power of unfriendly gods. This to him would be impious.

While we are compelled to defer consideration of a significant part of this question until later, we can deal with the earlier accusation that Socrates taught his disruptive practices to others. It should first be noted that by distinguishing between the earlier accusers and the present charges presented by Meletus, Socrates seems to be suggesting that his jurors should distinguish between what he was then and what he is now. Meletus's own charges reflect a change in Socrates; they seem to describe conduct less weird and more politically subversive than the picture painted by Aristophanes. From being an investigator of forbidden matters beneath and beyond the earth, he is now merely a believer in strange gods. In other words the once prodigal escaped prisoner has returned to the cave as a smuggler of ignorance and irony. Further, where Socrates was once accused of being a busy-body and teaching the art of making the weaker argument stronger, he is only charged with corrupting the youth; we are not told how this corruption occurs. There may be some basis for concluding that Socrates has become more enigmatic and his ways are less easily discerned. Yet he seems to teach and corrupt by simply being himself and refusing to conform.

The first accusers seem to describe somebody who was far more public in his activities and inquiries; that Socrates would have contributed to the French Encyclopedia, Wikipedia or even Wiki-leaks. This is consistent with the picture Socrates provides of his "cosmological phase" in the *Phaedo*; he describes himself as one who believed that adequate mechanical explanations of the genesis and corruption of all cosmic phenomena could be arrived at through properly scientific means (96a). His disappointment with Anaxagoras had to do with that sophist's mystical invocation of *nous* as a principle of rational *ananke* instead of explaining precisely how it ordered the cosmos to the advantage of all its constituent entities (97c ff). While the pre-Socratic Socrates did not arrive at any final comprehensive account as to just how the cosmos was constructed, he seems to have believed that such an explanation was both possible and desirable. Meletus indicts a man who seems to produce corruption far more mysteriously; it is almost as if Socrates were accused of witchcraft rather than sophistry. The sophists and orators see something demonic in his ability to see through them. They do not know of his gift of the gods, the revelation that humans can know nothing about the gods or the underworld. As we shall argue, he merely knows reality outside the cave along with evidence that the gods are benevolent.

In comparison to what he had become by the time of his trial, the pre-Socratic Socrates could have been naively optimistic in his belief in the unlimited power of science and human reason. This un-ironic approach towards truth would certainly have led Socrates to be quite imprudent in believing that enlightenment was just around the corner. Just as Christians at the time of Christ would have little difficulty in giving away their earthly possessions before the imminent apocalypse, Socrates would have seen little need to practice discretion when he regarded the ultimate truth as information soon to be attained and then easily shared with others.

Although Socrates would not have sought to teach cosmology, since he clearly had not attained the objects of his studies, the pre-Socratic Socrates would have not been opposed to sharing the results of his on-going investigations with others. He would most likely have been genuinely shocked by the unexamined lives of the many, the absurdity of the mythical accounts that easily satisfied their curiosity, and the amazing power that rhetoric had to stifle their critical capacities. It is more than likely that in the course of these free and wide-ranging discussions he first displayed that lasting dissatisfaction with conventional pious explanations that earned him the reputation of being meddlesome and sophistic in his criticisms of both the content and the style of conventional wisdom. It was only later in life, after the message from the Oracle, that he realized that in as much as he could "teach" anything at all, the content of this human wisdom would consist of no more than the impossibility of finding, leave aside teaching, the ultimate truth about things. This would necessitate his famous second sailing or shift to an indirect approach; the look of God as "The Good" is more productive than a scientific analysis of the divine nature.

We could clarify Socrates' position better by contrasting it with that of a celebrated sophist and teacher of rhetoric. Gorgias famously maintained that although there was no such thing as truth, even if there was truth, it could not be apprehensible by the human mind, and even if it could be known, it could not be communicated.[25] Socrates would have rejected the claim that there was no such thing as truth, though he would have agreed with Gorgias's assertion that the human mind could not apprehend ultimate truth. Socrates would also have held that the human mind was capable of knowing all it needed to know; finally, he would have accepted that it was impossible to transfer this human truth through teaching. Unlike Gorgias who would have said that in the absence of controllable or transmissible truth, rhetoric had to create disposable truths, Socrates chose to purge the cave of artificial truth and recollect the way to what man could not control but had to be guided by things beyond the cave. The sophists showed the leaders of a polity how to deploy the vast body of conventional opinion and traditional lore as a "standing reserve" of political power: this resource of formless emotions and perceptual matter could be twisted and manipulated to serve the needs of the passion of the moment.

Even though, as we have taken pains to observe, Socrates does believe in revelation and inspired words, he is deeply skeptical of efforts made by politicians and priests to turn the winged words of literature into gelded theological dogma—indeed since Plato was to coin the term theology itself, he would surely disapprove of this word being abused and used to describe efforts to reduce interactions between the human and the divine into reified doctrines about divine matters after the style and spirit of Euthyphro. Further, while official theology leaves as little room for dissent or play as a Soviet-era referendum, and has little trouble excommunicating those who choose not to follow its *ananke*, Socrates is well aware that revelation is the lovechild of divine essence and mortal contingency. Problems arise when specific and time-bound utterances are read literally and transmuted into absolute divine mandates. Winged words must not be twisted around and bound to each other as chains of convoluted dogma.

Socrates now points out that he is quite different from those sophists who participated actively in this poetic process by which a democracy created truth for its citizenry. While both Aristophanes and his new accusers hoped to exploit the hostility that the Demos felt against "wise-guys" who knew better than them, thus hiding their own, more insidious esoteric manipulations, Socrates suggests that he served as the champion of the Democracy against its corrupters by exposing their lies. Whereas the sophists earned large sums of money by teaching the wealthy young men of a city to detach themselves from their fellow citizens for self-serving reasons, Socrates' poverty is proof of either incompetence as a corrupter or incorruptible virtue.

By stating that the sophists gained both money and gratitude from their students, Socrates is suggesting that he incurred both poverty and ingratitude as a result of his own efforts. This claim is further attested to by wealthy Callias's curt response to Socrates' inquiries concerning the education of his sons (20b). Since Callias knew Socrates quite well and frequently socialized with him, his abruptness on this occasion was not occasioned by snobbery but rather by the unwelcome subject matter of their conversation.

Differently put, the "over-scrupulous" Socrates—who like any good midwife is not afraid of asking indelicate questions about embarrassing matters—has made Callias admit that the means he has chosen to advance the interests of his sons are somewhat shameful. Otherwise he would surely have not been disconcerted by Socrates' inquiries; human nature being what it is, most parents are, if anything, over-anxious to gain honor by attesting to the cost of the expensive education that they give their children. Socrates' assertion that he would have been "pluming and preening himself" had he possessed such knowledge, would surely extend to one like Callias who is in a position to buy his children virtue and wisdom. Callias's implicit shame suggests that an exaggerated emphasis on ends has caused him to employ disgraceful means; it is as though he has apprenticed his sons to a successful drug-dealer. Callias is doubly ashamed because Socrates has made him concede that he, one of the most prominent and illustrious dignitaries of Athens, is incapable of teaching his sons the virtue of "human being and citizen" through his own example. Such impotence is self-evidently shameful.

Yet this kind of behavior, although not the same as that previous impiously hungry speculative zeal which Aristophanes mocked, is also clearly an activity that many could find rude and obnoxious. Trying to explain why he behaves in this manner, Socrates admits that he does indeed possess a certain manner of wisdom (20d). This, however, is a lowly species of human wisdom; a form of piety that he distinguishes from that "greater than human" comprehension which most persons intend when they employ the word "wisdom." Differently put, while Socrates' earlier eccentricities were occasioned by his quest *after* wisdom, his new behavior results from an insight into its sublime nature. Then, wisdom was a noun, a Promethean treasure wrested from heaven in defiance of the gods; now, it is a verb, part of human virtuosity demanded by the gods. Then it led him out of the cave; now it orders him back with a mission from God.

Differently put, if wisdom or virtue were a noun both qualities could be produced and transferred by a god or wise king. This would mean that human nature would not need to remain incomplete and erotic. A human being could become a happy animal, the Last Man or, better, an efficient machine with a theology or program that could be followed exactly and literally without need to judge or discriminate; humans would simply obey their King or Shepherd and virtue would flow like oil. Perhaps this was why the Old Testament God did not want the Israelites to have a King; as he explained to Samuel, this meant that they rejected their God—who will be what He will be—and His prophets.[26] Virtue only emerges when humans in their incompleteness struggle with an enigmatic hidden deity; such a god keeps alive the literary aspect of Theology and prevents piety from becoming either arid scholasticism or crass idolatry. But how do we find this hidden god? Here we turn to Chaerephon's embassy to the Oracle of Apollo at Delphi.

II. The Apollo Mission

Socrates reveals that his present mode of questioning was inspired by the Oracle's answer. This suggests that Chaerephon's news ended the pre-Socratic period of our protagonist's life. All the distinctively Platonic dialogues, with the possible exception of the *Parmenides*, must thus occur after this significant transformation of Socrates' self-understanding. But what could have made Chaerephon go to the Oracle? Socrates' perplexity on hearing the Oracle's response (21b) suggests that he was already quite aware of his condition of radical ignorance, and disillusioned with metaphysics. It seems that Socrates' self-understanding of his intellectual accomplishments was very different from the opinion that his enthusiastic friend held of them. While it would be temptingly convenient for some to conclude that the *Clouds* made Chaerephon seek oracular confirmation, this play was staged in about 422, long after the dramatic date of early Socratic dialogues like *First Alcibiades, Protagoras,* and *Charmides* that are set about ten years earlier.

I have argued elsewhere that it was his erotic attraction to Alcibiades that aroused Socrates from his Cosmological slumbers;[27] this, however, does not negate the significance of Apollo's Oracle. While I stand by my contention that it was probably this erotic experience that made Socrates aware of the paltriness of his cosmological investigations, it was the message from the Oracle that made him see the positive value of this recognition. Perhaps, since Chaerephon still believed in Socrates' wisdom, he fatefully sought oracular confirmation of his conviction.

Although its deepest implications only become evident to him about a third of a century later, let us consider Socrates' first reaction to the glad tidings that Chaerephon, as unlikely an angelic messenger as Euthyphro, has given him. Far from breaking into a *Magnificat* of praise, our barren midwife's son is uncharacteristically lost for words. Never one to repudiate his convictions in the face of contrary opinion, Socrates finds himself numbed, like many of his future interlocutors and victims, by the Oracle's revelation. But how could he be both aware of his ignorance and yet be smart enough to know that the Oracle has falsely understood his wisdom?

Siding with his incredulous judges, against fanatical Chaerephon and the manic Oracle, Socrates now agrees to "teach" them the basis for the charges preferred against him (21b). Since he seems to have been doing this for some time already, we can tell that Socrates is no longer dealing with the older accusers who corrupted his jurors, but finally preparing to address the explicit charges of Meletus. Pondering the Oracle's enigmatic words caused Socrates to embark on his remarkable second career as the champion of self-knowledge and scourge of false opinion.

Socrates' "teaching" will take the form of an autobiographical recounting to the jury of how the Oracle's words developed the full implications of what he already knew. Such a self-referential course of action was very much in keeping with the way the Oracle functioned. Many of the laconic utterances of the Pythia could only be satisfactorily deciphered by the questioner becoming aware of the blind spot that usually eluded human investigation: the polymorphous soul of the inquirer himself. As Heraclitus saw, a man's character or ethos is his *daimon*.[28] The baffled questioner finds his soul probed by an opaque response that yields insight into the origin, rather than the satisfaction, of his desire; self-knowledge is worth more than fortune's prizes.

This moment of self-recognition is also crucial to any adequate appropriation of the Platonic literary corpus and the legacy of Socrates. When Kierkegaard sagely stated that the various Platonic dialogues were but mirrors in which readers did not see Socrates' soul but only their own,[29] he too was recognizing that the manner in which we respond to a Platonic work reveals much to us about who we most essentially are. This capacity to force its readers to interact with the text seems to be what is most divine, or at least oracular, about a Platonic dialogue.

The Delphic Oracle's famous complementary maxims, "know thyself" and "nothing in excess," draw attention to the fact that the vice of excess stems from an vulgarly pragmatic obsession with results that leads the actor to neglecting his integrity. This suggests that ritualized acts of piety, even those executed flawlessly, are sullied by the thoughtlessness or selfishness of the mimetic agent. It is in this context that Socrates' reputed excessive scrupulosity must be seen as turning us from the vice of torturous interrogative excess towards the self-possessed virtue of moderation. There is a direct proportion between the soul's capacity to rule itself and its ability to see a cosmic order held together by beauty rather than power. Excessive pains taken with observing the letter of the law, or obsession with the material conditions of a spiritual action, suggests a disharmony between ends and means and reveals much about the seeker and his quest. The knowledge appropriate to man eventually turns out to concern psychic integrity rather than technical ingenuity or priestly purity. Spiritual materialism, whether in service of human apotheosis or pagan piety, becomes the new target of Socrates' meddlesome interventions.

For now, even though he has humbly recognized the extent of his own ignorance before the highest mysteries Socrates, altogether characteristically, will not accept without challenge or verification the Oracle's pronouncement that no man is wiser than he. Despite Chaerephon's triumphant interpretation of the Oracle's words to mean that Socrates was indeed preeminent in wisdom, Socrates could not take this claim at face value. That would lead to the absurd conclusion that *Chaerephon* was Socrates' superior in wisdom since he had known all along what Socrates, the wisest of all men, had doubted! Alternatively, one could distinguish between the content of wisdom and our meta-knowledge about its availability. Socrates did not allow Chaerephon's simplistic interpretation of the

Oracle's answer to obscure the inherent ambiguity of her words. True to form, he would carefully study this cryptic utterance. At the least, given his present condition of skepticism about the possibility of reliable scientific knowledge about ultimate reality, the Oracle could be referring to his unswerving dedication to the truth, and not falsely praising his possession of transcendent wisdom. This disposition would not change.

To recapitulate, Socrates' distinctive pre-Socratic habit of rationally analyzing everything into its mechanistic elements was shipwrecked by the clash of the *Nous* of Anaxagoras with the *Eros* of Alcibiades. He came to the recognition that he knew nothing and could never know anything about the highest and most divine things. Eventually, his "Copernican Revolution" or what Cicero called "the bringing down of philosophy from the heavens to the cities of men"[30] resulted from Socrates dwelling with the consequences of seeing via Delphi that the ultimate truth could never be at our disposal; we can only become aware of its existence and benevolence. This in turn derived from his juxtaposing the baffling experiences of *Eros* and *Nous* with the enigmatic message from the Oracle. While *Eros* made it very clear to him that there was a higher realm of *Nous* which could not be apprehended through mechanistic methods, the Oracle suggested that if he was the wisest of all men, this exaltation had much to do with this recent double humiliation. The Socrates of the *First Alcibiades* is quite hubristic in his desire to open up a vast empire of wisdom and power to his beloved.[31] Yet something happens to prevent him from consummating this love as a teacher of wisdom. He now knows that while there is a dimension of higher truth, this realm is beyond our capacity to grasp or master. Yet, crucially, this knowledge helps us to see a priori that all claims to understand or control the ways and weaknesses of the gods are false. We should also avoid the anthropomorphism of viewing the divine in terms of irresistible power that overwhelms our deliberative faculty.

Not even batty Chaerephon could understand the Oracle to mean anything more than that Socrates was the wisest of *mortals*. Further, since possession of ultimate wisdom by man implies the corollary ability to subject it to human control, it follows that any truths that could be known, changed or modified by man were not the ultimate governing principles of reality but merely derivative and contingent facts. While the wisest men would presumably be receptive in some limited way to the highest order of reality, they never enjoy sufficient access to the transcendent things-in-themselves entitling them to claim to know these truths. Keeping with Descartes' recognition that man is a compound of infinite imagination and limited wisdom,[32] we see that human wisdom consists in a continual heed-fulness to these verities and a concomitant liberation from all claims to wisdom in excess of human limits. This also is consistent with the *Euthyphro*'s theme that direct interaction between the divine and human is not possible. It follows then that part of our service to the gods has to do with the destruction of any claims either about the usable content of past contact or of knowledge how future interactions can be made to occur. This is perhaps linked to Socrates' claim to be the only living practitioner of the true political art.[33]

However all of these deductions, though contained in the Delphic Oracle's response to Chaerephon's inspired question, will only be drawn very much in the future. At the time he first heard them, Socrates seemed to have viewed the Oracle's words as a daunting personal challenge, the true meaning of which would only emerge after he grappled with living according to the challenge they posed. If he is to take the revelation of the Oracle seriously, he must conclude that he knows neither himself, nor the extent of human wisdom, adequately. Also, since he is convinced that the Oracle is wrong, he must subject this matter to the test—through empiri-cal verification and falsification—thus continuing to maintain the very tireless interrogative posture that seemed to have distinguished him from all other men. In other words, he understood the Oracle to mean that instead of studying *everything*, he must now question *everyone* (including himself) with the same interrogative fervor that he had previously reserved for the natural realm. He evidently had to seek human truth, and this quest had to be pursued in the horizontal realm rather than the vertical. He would discover that ephemeral human wisdom would turn out to be a verb rather than a noun: an activity, not an objective possession or permanent condi-tion. By functioning in this manner, Socrates soon recognized that he him-self would have to function as a kind of witness to the truth that Apollo wished to proclaim through him. Socrates' wisdom would have to consist in being a signifier rather than the one signified. This was what Heidegger meant when he praised Socrates for continually asking the same questions. The beginning of human wisdom (and true end of the Olympian gods) could be signaled by the word from Delphi that the God was well pleased with Socrates' wise ignorance.

Although the evidence overwhelmingly suggests that he did so, up to this point we have not attended to the question of how it was possible that Socrates, that paradigm of intellectual rigor, could have believed in ora-cles. This is perhaps one of the most disconcerting questions that contemporary readers of the Platonic dialogues have to confront. While it is for the most part quite possible to regard Socrates as a defender of enlightened rationality, fearlessly confronting the dark forces of superstition, our hero's claims to be privy to divine revelation remind us of just how alien and distant his world was from ours. The problem is not merely that Socrates was genuinely pious, albeit in a uniquely eccentric manner that only a few of his own contemporaries could understand or emulate. Our difficulty is compounded by the recognition that, just as we only possess the texts, and not the musical scores, of Greek dramas, and marble statues without their gaudy paint, we know very little about the *gestalt* of Greek religious consciousness that Socrates shared with his fellow citizens. Our key must be the unequalled insights provided by their classic literary works into the unchanging limits of human nature.

In the crudest terms, while we tend to regard Socrates as an enlightened contemporary confronting forces of superstition and self-righteous stupidity that have changed very little over the 2400 years separating our times, the parallel must not collapse before experiences that place him on the far side of this temporal divide; as noted earlier, our own age is as familiar with the religious fundamentalism of Euthyphro as it is with those proud descendants of the sophists who would reduce everything to power and the manipulation of matter and language. It is *our* scientific barbarism, enriched by the conceit that our culture is divinely privileged, that threatens to destroy the very possibility of human existence today. To understand Socrates' relationship with Apollo, we cannot ignore the Dionysian underbelly of our Platonic character rendered youthful and beautiful; but nor can we afford to discount his very real devotion to a transcendent divine influence addressed here by the name of Apollo.

When considering the *Euthyphro* we entertained the hypothesis that Socrates was interested in somehow taming and redeeming the chthonic religious forces animating Greek piety. It was clear that he did not question the reality of these powers. The very profession of ignorance so steadfastly maintained by Socrates in the *Apology* would not make sense had he not been aware of forces both above *and beneath* him that he could not adequately comprehend. Indeed Homer's wisdom consists precisely in his insights into the passions and desires animating human nature, not in his very anthropomorphic projections of the gods that were made to understand these powers. We must carefully distinguish between the incorrigible substrate of man's animal nature, the dark chthonic powers that Socrates was morally superior to, and the enlightening but enigmatic "Hyper-

Uranian" influences that Socrates himself was very much aware of being attracted to and actualized by. While the chthonic influences acting on different human beings are localized by time, space and culture, Socratic philosophy seems to assume that all humans, however the accidents of geography and history have dispersed them, hold both the same animal drives as well as the same self-evident Hyper-Uranian archetypes and erotic vectors in common.

The *Euthyphro* showed that Socrates was not an unbeliever regarding the possibility of divine revelation and inspiration. It was as an intellectual who also believed in divine authority that he seems to have been outraged by the way most persons reified the content of revelation, and generally behaved as if they could somehow control the gods themselves through a kind of technique or manipulation. As poetic revelation is not knowledge about divine things, or merely human knowledge of human things, it can only be divine knowledge of human matters. But since genuine poetry is divinely inspired it is synthetic, not analytic in merely putting in verse data that can be humanly amassed, and not under the rational control of its poet-maker; it is thus easily misinterpreted. As Socrates saw, inspired poets were often the worst interpreters of the revelation they delivered (22b). Since poetry is divine knowledge granted to us in a poet's ignorance, its right exegesis requires a gift of the god Hermes, interpretation or hermeneutics, to one too barren to give poetic birth himself. Among other things, this meant that it was ultimately up to the supplicant to, intellectually and/or existentially, interpret the meaning of the oracle he received. This was precisely the approach that Socrates followed in the case of Chaerephon's oracle.

The supposition that Socrates believed in oracles receives additional confirmation from outside the Platonic corpus; Xenophon recounts how Socrates advised him to consult an oracle before embarking on the ill-fated expedition of the Ten Thousand under Cyrus. Socrates even went so far as to rebuke Xenophon for incorrectly phrasing the question that he put to the Pythia; when his friend asked what he should do to come home safely, Socrates said that he should have asked whether or not he should embark on the expedition.[34] This hardly suggests an attitude of affable tolerance on Socrates' part; evidently he did believe that Xenophon could learn something from the Oracle, even Socrates' chastisement is somewhat oracular. The *Euthyphro* supports this position: Socrates viewed his own trial in much the same spirit. The *daimon*'s hint that he not prepare his defense meant that this encounter was worth undergoing; it did not promise that his life would be preserved. That was not the highest priority in Xenophon's case, or his own.

In attempting to understand how Socrates could have trusted in oracles, we must remember that the Pythia was no mere fortune-teller. We learn from the *Eumenides* of Aeschylus that the shrine to Apollo at Delphi was located at a much older site that had previously been held successively by Gaia, Themis and Phoebe: three metamorphoses of a pre-Olympian chthonic principle.[35] Apollo's shrine at Delphi thus represents the imposition of a relatively rational "Apollonian" Olympian order upon primal chthonic forces that were still functioning quite actively at the substratal levels of both the cosmos and the human soul. This also meant that one called upon the assistance of Apollo, through the Oracle, to defeat the influence of malign chthonic forces that could not be alienated from the polis. As we shall soon see, these very powers seem to be supporting the furious hostility that Socrates excited in his victims. Just as the dead could kill the living in Aeschylus's *Libation Bearers*, the collective unconsciousness of a polity or culture definitely wielded great power over those who belonged to it.

Our immediate concern however is with the metaphysical implications of the state of affairs that we have just discussed. In the bluntest terms, the Greeks did not believe in a cosmic order that was created ex nihilo by a timeless omnipotent God. The view they took of reality allowed for the possibility of a far greater degree of contingency and freedom than any monotheist system of theology could consistently uphold. A Greek oracle could not provide definitive forecasts concerning an already predetermined future. Oracular pronouncements, frequently derided today on account of their vagueness and ambiguity, were expressed in terms of symbols; they tended to deal with universal patterns rather than particular events, with meanings not facts. Ultimately, as we shall argue, brute physical facts or happenings derived their meaning from this higher symbolic realm but were not caused by determining (or predetermining) divine agents. The Oracle does not know how we will react to the god's words. As with tragedy, what happens matters far less than why it happens and how we respond. Necessity likewise only defines the limits within which human meaning is conserved. There is no *sub specie aeternitatis* or God's-eye view of the future. As the *Gorgias* asserts, the Cosmos consists of interactions between Earth and Sky, Gods and Mortals (508a). The Delphic Oracle's very location, the so-called Omphalos or Center of the Earth, suggests that the hub of cosmic activity does not reside in some totally transcendent timeless heaven. The on-going drama of good and evil has human meaning.

The purpose of oracular utterances seems to have more to do with drawing the supplicant's attention to spiritual influences that he was not adequately aware of. We observed previously that an Oracle would attach particular importance to self-knowledge; this would be because most persons were often prone to ignore the strange complexities of their own souls. The scientific mindset is typically prone to deny the influence of subjective factors over its supposedly objective and logical grand designs. Without adequate self-knowledge a man could squander even the best and most promising opportunities that fate sent his way.

Rather than providing an infallible perspective on future events, it is better to regard the Oracle as making it possible for the supplicant to gain a fuller appreciation of the present. By providing self-knowledge lacking in the person making the inquiry, the Oracle would do more than provide a simplistic perspective on a highly ambiguous future; instead, by promoting self-awareness, the supplicant could approach the future with a far better awareness of the internal resources that he could draw upon. It was in this sense that Aristotle noted that virtue was more enduring than scientific knowledge.[36] Whatever the future brought, a proper psychic disposition would have the most influence on whether its effects would be beneficial or malign. Destroying the supplicant's "cave-like" view of reality, an impoverished egotistical perspective that could only be sustained by false necessities of fear and superstition, the Oracle would deliver him from illusions limiting self-knowledge, thus opening him up to the fullness of what lay beyond the cave as well as the reality of what was in it. Socrates played a similar midwife's role in Athens.

It is also interesting to note that most of the authenticated inquiries put before the Oracle took the form of questions posing a choice between two alternatives; it was far cheaper to ask the Oracle a "yes or no" question.[37] This suggests that a simple prohibition in the form of "don't do x" would often have sufficed. The famous *daimon* of course functioned in much the same fashion when it forbade Socrates to follow a certain course of action. It seems clear that regardless of how terse the response of the Oracle, the best opportunity for self-knowledge occurs much later, when the supplicant retrospectively endeavored to interpret its meaning in the context of this sliver of divine light shed upon the course of his life and the quality of his soul. Immediately, as in the case of Socrates, the Oracle would seem to function more as catalyst than as answer; we are moved to act rather than being led to know. What makes the *Apology* different from *Oedipus Tyrannus* is the nature of the god revealed; the Oracle does not trap Socrates in his cruel destiny, it is more like Tiresias in helping him to realize his destiny. Far from providing closure in the form of a conclusive answer, an end or beginning of an end, the Oracle rather seems to provide the impetus and confidence to embark on a new second sailing or inner odyssey of self-exploration. Who I am has much to do with how I see myself, order myself, order reality and interact with it. At the level of knowledge, this process could be seen to parallel the famous "second sailing" described in the *Phaedo* where Socrates rejected as inadequate the mechanistic trajectory of Anaxagorean cosmology (99d). This metaphysical counterpart to the psychic revolution described here also reflects Socrates' turn from science to philosophy.

While we have so far emphasized the provocative psychic aspects of the Delphic Oracle's pronouncements, this does not mean that the Oracle serves a merely therapeutic function. The very willingness to put a question before the Oracle, providing of course that the inquiry is properly phrased, indicates that the supplicant is prepared to be attentive to a standpoint that transcends his own idiosyncratic perspective on things. At the very least, this means that the perspective now adopted or sought is universal rather than particular. The Delphic Oracle is certainly not a protector or patron, rather its role seems to be to establish a connection between universal truth and personal enlightenment—to bring into harmony the macro and microcosmic aspects of truth. The implication of this position seems to be that by the attainment of genuine self-knowledge, gained by the stripping away of blasphemous rumors about vicious gods and their selfish plans, the individual will forsake parochial perspectives and petty egoism to adopt a higher standpoint serving and promoting the good of the whole. A crucial distinction between necessity and freedom may be drawn here: while a simplistic view of the future would seek early warning of what is violent, inevitable and necessary, human wisdom and the true political art dictate that we guide the clashing potentialities of the future towards the best of all possible outcomes. The *Gorgias*, one of the most Socratic dialogues, fully develops the meaning of this liberating revelation. Here Socrates solemnly states that cosmic reality is interactive and rational; it consists of harmonious relations between all the parts of the whole. It is not a violent struggle waged between irrational gods and human lies.

The case of Socrates provides a fine example of how challenging the Oracle's words could be if they were heeded attentively. Far from merely confirming, and thus refuting, the opinion of his enthusiastic friend that he was the wisest of men, the simple word of assent pronounced by the Pythia made heroic demands on Socrates that would result eventually in his death and intellectual apotheosis. Even if Chaerephon's query had been answered in the negative, it is quite possible that a similar burden would have been placed upon Socrates: he would then have been directly obliged to go in search of the wisest mortal. However the subtle difference made by the Oracle's affirmative answer turned out to have far-reaching implications with regard to Socrates' altered understanding of what true human wisdom amounted to. As we suggested earlier, the Delphic Oracle left its lasting mark on Socrates in the form of giving divine sanction to the internalized *daimon* that he trusted implicitly. This reliable internal touchstone enabled him remain immune from the nihilistic effects of the moral vertigo that afflicted post-war Athens.

Just as Socrates sought to reconstruct the meaning behind the Oracle's cryptic words, we have attempted to provide an explanation of his post-oracular conduct that explains the link between the Oracle's speech and Socrates' stirring but scarcely less opaque deeds. It is clear that Socrates understood the daunting implications of taking the Oracle's words seriously; likewise, it is necessary that any intellectually honest encounter with the spirit of Socrates should confront the existential implications of the challenge that he poses. Knowledge can no longer be regarded as booty one could bear violently away; it is relational rather than substantial. Yet this relational knowledge is also distinct from sophistic relativism or pragmatism in requiring continual attention to both the transcendent but hidden order of truth sustaining it and the soul reflecting it.

The meaning of Socrates' repudiation of cosmological wisdom (and the very mindset of possession) for human 'philosophic' wisdom (a *way* of striving governed by humble erotic dedication towards a higher order of truth) is that men can only function as adequate defenders of truth by the continual profession and cleansing practice of ignorance. This means that there is sufficient truth in the world for a good life. It would also seem to follow that we ourselves may live such a life and adequately 'know' Socrates by dedicating ourselves to a way of life that follows a similar mixture of erotic and purifying influences. In other words, we cannot imitate Socrates by reproducing the identical material conditions that he lived under. Such an eternal return of the same is impossible, and so mindlessly mimetic an approach only produces a nauseating skepticism. But while Socrates' virtue is hard to emulate, the Oracle's word has relevance for all.

The corrosive values of fear and violence must not eclipse our human power to see the rational beauty of the cosmos. As Crito must see, one cannot be virtuous through another.

After pondering their import for a long time (21b), a process that we have endeavored to follow here, Socrates tells his jurors that he finally decided to investigate the meaning of the Oracle's words. In keeping with his newly found interest in human "horizontal" wisdom, as distinct from the previous cosmological "vertical" direction of his studies, he accordingly sought out a politician who was popularly thought to be wise (21b–c). All appearances suggested to him that he had found somebody wiser than himself, so he could pass on the hot potato of being the wisest of men. The qualification *"entautha"* (here) is important because of its overtones of place. Here, in the public space where his examination of this politician was conducted, in the statesman's very element, his cave, he would surely be expected to display the sort of wisdom that Socrates had vainly sought through means of private study (21c). We should note that despite his irony, Socrates does not confidently expect to discover that this politician is supremely wise. In other words, he does not expect to immediately falsify the words of Apollo's mouthpiece. Rather, his main purpose seems to be to probe the Oracle's strange words and await further developments.

It is also possible that Socrates, once he despaired of seeking wisdom regarding the highest things, was now content to seek illumination at this merely human horizontal level. Though from the standpoint of the gods, he was the wisest of all men in his complex awareness of the impossibility of knowing the highest things, Socrates was yet capable of learning practical matters, beneath the dignity of the gods, from others better schooled at the lower human level. It is thus possible that he could have sought human prudential wisdom that was based purely on human nature while remaining leery of sweeping metaphysical accounts about ultimate reality.

But, even if this wisdom existed, it could surely not be used as an exact science of the sort that so attracted Charmides.[38] As the case of a great leader like Themistocles seems to show, the very exercise of this art seems to corrupt the soul, leading to tragic results. The hero is but an instrument of the gods; when he forgets that he is inspired and exercises power in his own right, hubris destroys him. Because one's *daimon* is hidden from oneself until the time of one's death, those seeking fame in their own time become artisans, rather than heroes, before posterity.[39] Jesus's earlier mentioned words about a prophet not being honored in his own town pertain to both the prophet and his familiars, as much as to Hegel's great man who cannot impress his valet for reasons that have to do with the valet's baseness and the hero's humanity.[40] Also, removing enshrined ignorance is not the same as acting with inspired prudence towards contingent matters.

Thus since such practical knowledge could consistently and respectfully recognize the probable existence of gods, and not interfere with traditional practice, to the extent that it is symbolic rather than literal, it would not make any positive claims about matters beyond its human limitations. While Socrates, functioning as a Hume rather than a Kant, could prove the impossibility of specific claims to false knowledge, he would not be satisfied with his negative wisdom until he had acquired what we could call practical reason: knowledge of how to act virtuously in the political world. This could well have been the knowledge he sought from the unfortunate politician that he accosted at the beginning of his public career. This, after all, was why Socrates chose to commence his "second sailing" by questioning a well-known politician; this man would reasonably be expected to be the kind of man most conversant with the limitations and capacities of all-too-human knowledge. Both parties were soon to be bitterly disappointed by the outcome of this conversation.

Upon closely studying this man (*skopon*—literally looking through) and conversing (literally dialoging) with him, Socrates soon found that he only seemed wise—both to the many as well as to himself (21c). It seems that the politician's transparent ignorance appeared in striking contrast to the opacity of the Oracle when Socrates "looked through" him. Yet, when Socrates tried to make this smug individual see that he was not as wise as he supposed himself to be, he only incurred the furious hatred of both the politician and many of those present at this dialogue (21d). If Socrates had any expectation that this man would be grateful to have his radical ignorance and freedom revealed to him, he was speedily relieved of his false opinion in this regard.

While his account of the event is ruefully ironic, it is possible that Socrates was, at the time, genuinely distressed at the anger and resentment that he excited in the humiliated politician and his henchmen. The naïve character described in the *Phaedo*, an account partially corroborated by Aristophanes' *Clouds*, may have been shocked to realize that most men were far more attached to the *appearance* of wisdom than to the truth itself. It was only later, after many experiences of the kind described in the *Apology*, that Socrates fully realized their significance. As Rousseau teaches us, *amour propre*, concern with one's reputation, is inversely proportionate to self-knowledge.[41] The more self-knowledge one has, and concomitantly the fewer illusions and overweening desires, the more time and energy he has to help others. In the case of Socrates, this busy-ness consists in ridding them of their debilitating illusions. This skill of healthy exegesis can coexist alongside the power of those who, like the poets, are inspired to act well—if not wisely. We thus have poets/makers of truth and exegetes—actors and interpreters—as well as their imitators: artisans and politicians; while artisans believe that their limited powers of imitation makes them wise in all things, politicians—false exponents of the true political art of the *Gorgias*—use their awareness of the poet's un-wisdom to rule the credulous ignorance of others; their ancestor is Anti-nous of the *Odyssey*. While true poets and exegetes are actors, inspired by divine *causes*, artisans and demotic politicians merely concern themselves with the production of desired *effects* on demand. It is likely that inspired exegetes like Themistocles became bad politicians when they imagined that the divine power that they channeled came from within; for such men a short and glorious life as a hero is surely preferable to a long picaresque career as a politician.

Even if Socrates had been partially forewarned by the Oracle to expect that other men would be as ignorant as he about the highest knowledge concerning human things, he may not have expected them to be as passionately "chained" to ignorance as he was devoted to the truth. When he earnestly sought practical wisdom at the horizontal level he met with dull mimetic habit; at the vertical level, where he expected simple piety, he was shocked to discover ugly hubris and arrogant cynicism. In other words, blasphemous religious superstition had usurped the place best occupied by pious ignorance; additionally, it allowed freedom, the condition for virtue to be supplanted by a combination of the smugness of the rich and the self-righteous stupidity of the many. The chthonic Furies offer our seemingly unfinished souls completion. They provide animal instinct and blood knowledge, the righteous certainty of a "mama grizzly," thus making it needless for us to interpret signs, judge prudently and act tentatively. This local theology or common sense cannot be justified rationally; when questioned, its possessor only becomes literally furious. One has to "be there" to "get it"—for local theology to be meaningful.

His first fateful conversation helped Socrates to see that he was wiser than the politician in knowing that he knew nothing about the essence of the good and noble (21d). While Socrates is supposed to have said in this context that he knew he was ignorant, his words support my contention that the subject of his investigation was the "good and noble." i.e., human virtue. Despite this setback, Socrates questioned many other politicians and invariably met with the same ignorance while incurring additional hatred. It took him a while to see that this very activity on his part was identical with the true political art. The "pain and fear" (21e) with which he responds to this hatred suggests that Socrates was both pained by this alienation from the collective certainty of the many and did not yet have the ironic self-possession typical of his actions in Plato's dialogues. Also, his public discovery that a man's popular reputation was usually inversely proportional to his prudence or self-knowledge could scarcely have contributed to Socrates' popularity in democratic Athens. Far from being concerned with what was truly good and noble, the politicians and the many understood these values only in terms of winning and losing. Still piety led him to continue with his investigations, a mission he suggestively compares to the labors of Heracles (22b).

Heracles was required by the Delphic Oracle to perform various tasks; he realized his destiny by freeing the literally pagan Greek countryside of many malign chthonic influences. Socrates exposed sophistic influences in much the same spirit: not because the tasks gave him pleasure but because they were required of him by the Oracle. *Eudaimonia* is not identical with physical pleasure; the latter has more to do with fleeing the burdens of consciousness and conscience. Socrates' many battles for the true human virtues against dangerous intellectual misconceptions are foreshadowed by the heroic deeds of the greatest of all Greek heroes who destroyed monsters and made the world safe for man. Just as Heracles was hated and tormented by Hera, the goddess of jealousy (love of one's own) and the Olympian representative of the supplanted Mother-Goddess, we see that Socrates incurred the insatiate fury of chthonic influences on account of his activities on behalf of Apollo. Likewise while Heracles madly slew his children Socrates was blamed for neglecting his sons by his manner of death. Finally, Socrates also emulates Heracles in setting the stage for his own death and eventual apotheosis.

It is also noteworthy that the Stoics and Cynics later used Heracles as a heroic exemplar of their ruling virtues of simplicity, endurance and philanthropy. Of course the mediating principal for this strange identification of the brutish hero with cerebral philosophy was Socrates, the philosopher-hero. Heracles was also typically depicted as being both stupid and lustful. Socrates seems to use his constant ironic professions of ignorance and erotic incontinence, his constant clubbing of himself with professions of ignorance, to imply a parallel with these unlikely attributes also. Therefore, throughout the *Apology*, great emphasis seems to be placed on Socrates' emulation of Heracles' selflessly heroic deeds, tragic acts that seem to have flown in the face of the shrewdly calculated self-interest that served as the generally accepted measure of prudence from the Themistoclean and Periclean Empire to post-war Athens.

Socrates' unpopular interrogation of the politicians seems to have established that while men like Anytus are self-evidently skilled in the business of shaping public opinion, they are usually as unconcerned as they are unfamiliar with the truth of the matters that they harangued the many about. The politicians thus derive their skill from exploiting the vast body of popular opinion and folklore that was created originally by the poets. The politicians are ignorant because they fail to see themselves as bad and ignorant poets. Still desirous of proving his own inferiority in wisdom, Socrates accordingly turned to those who knew themselves as poets, the writers of tragedies and dithyrambs, to show Apollo, the god of poetry and music, that he was more ignorant than the poets about their own art (22a–b). It is significant that Socrates does not include the Comedians—those like Aristophanes—in the ranks of the poets. One possible explanation for this omission is that a writer of comedies was far more like a demagogue; their works were quite deliberately written to pander to and influence the more vulgar elements of the *demos*.

Yet once again, upon questioning the true inspired poets, Socrates found that they were astonishingly ignorant of the meaning and origins of their own *poiesis* and did what they did "by some kind of nature when they were inspired" (22c). These poets turned out to be incompetent at interpreting their own works. Socrates had to conclude that, like the diviners and oracles, even the best poets were but inspired channels of noble things. As such, they were unable to display even the skill of a corrupt politician in *producing* a desired popular effect. The politician could consciously make bad poetry, in the sense of interpreting events falsely, albeit to his own advantage,[42] while a poet turned out to be more fool than knave, bad actor than crafty artisan, in sincerely misinterpreting his own work and being unable to distinguish between genuinely inspired insights and false rhymes. Apart from failing to see that the content of their revelation pertained to human rather than divine matters, the poets also falsely prided themselves on being the wisest of men (22c), as the creators of their productions, instead of seeing that they were but the instruments of mysterious higher musical powers.

It would seem that while the poets memorably depict the actions of heroes and prophets, who live fully in and see the present, they fail to understand the fullest meaning of these striking actions—that yet demand to be represented now, even if they are only understood later. For instance Homer, in depicting the lives of Achilles and Odysseus, saw them as playthings of the gods. It is only much later that men like Plato saw that the true meaning of these poems pertained to the tragedy and comedy of human life, along with the many passions and powers that were vividly if inaccurately depicted as divinities. The powers of noble action, sublime temporal representation and essential understanding make up a triad of terms that correspond to the transcendental trinity of goodness, beauty and truth. These powers are also divided; they never inhere in the same person at one time.

The poets seemed to be necessarily ignorant of the true nature of their own art. This meant that their works had to be posthumously rescued from the Cave and made to shed light on the human things. The selfless task of artistic expression seemed to necessitate that they were only inspired when they eschewed the conscious arts of manipulation and interpretation that were practiced by demagogic politicians. The case of Simonides comes to mind here: his short glorious lines "Go tell the Spartans…" contrast poorly with his long and sordid career as a paid hack and sycophant to tyrants.[43] Faced with the choice between being a knave or an inspired fool, most poets foolishly ended eventually up choosing knavery. Many poets blindly viewed themselves as inspired creators of literal truth instead of appreciating the intermediary character of their profession and the subtle quality of the revelation that passed through them. Although the implicit dichotomy between conscious manipulation and unconscious creation is quite elegant, suggesting that creativity and control can only be exerted at the expense of each other, its practical implications are quite difficult to defend. Can we be presumptuous enough to say that Euripides and Sophocles, to single out the most eminent tragedians of Socrates' adult life, were ignorant?

Socrates' position seems more tenable when we see that he is chastising the poets for their lack of wisdom, for not realizing that their poetic genius did not make them wise in all matters—especially in those concerning the gods. This claim is more plausible, but Socrates is also maintaining that the tragedians did not even understand their own works. Does he mean that instead of exorcising the passions that corroded the Athenian polity they preferred to make shadows in the cave, thus only seeming to flatter and appease the savage forces disintegrating the souls of their fellow citizens? Isn't it better to view Sophocles and Euripides as interpreters of

Homer? Are they not critics as much as poets? It may be fairer to see Sophocles as being more poet than critic, while Euripides is the opposite. We must also remember that just like Shakespeare, the tragedians wrote for the many and for money; perhaps the deepest significance of these plays only become evident to those like us who fortunately or unfortunately have the Apollonian libretto without the Dionysian music, just like the afore-mentioned classical statues stripped of their gaudy paint. The great power of "blind" bards like Homer (his name just as appropriately means hostage) was not actualized (or ransomed) as wisdom in their own time.

As noted in our discussion of the *Euthyphro*, the poets and dramatists of Classical Athens had much greater prestige and influence then than their fellow practitioners enjoy in our day; they were political theologians not entertainers. While far more fame accrues to a singer than a songwriter (or a President than a speech-writer) today, in Socrates' time a dramatist was a public intellectual who had much greater *kudos* than a masked actor. While the Athenians repeatedly chose Sophocles to occupy the highest offices in the polity, they would have certainly not have elected an actor—one who merely spoke words written by others—to these exalted positions.

Now Socrates clearly accepted that the great epic poets and tragedians were in fact inspired. No one with even a passing familiarity with the works of the great Greek epics and tragedies could say otherwise; the comic poet Aristophanes however, while exceptionally intelligent and witty, neither seems nor claims to be the agent of the gods. If anything, he seems to stand for the Maternal Powers and good old-fashioned common sense. This clarifies our question; the crucial issue for Socrates seems to have to do with the content and applicability of poetic inspiration. We have seen that the politicians, instead of deriving the basis for their actions from prudentially gained knowledge of the baser aspects of human nature like Aristophanes, justified their self-serving actions theologically; they enact-ed the will of the gods—as expressed through the works of the tragic poets—to the general public and shrewdly understated their own influence and input. Meanwhile poets, dependent on political patronage, were seen as infallible messengers of the gods. This allowed their paymasters, cun-ning politicians, to exercise power without responsibility. The images of Homer and Hesiod, the official theologians of the Athenian polity, were translated into politically correct dogmas that denied the possibility of individual identity apart from the tribal substance; Odysseus's discovery of the soul has no place in the tragic underworld. Though the gods of tragedy at their best were more like *daimons*, products of divine intercourse with mortal inspiration, the usual sources of poetic imagination were political or demotic, and the consequences were both blasphemous and misanthropic.

By suggesting that poets were intermittently inspired oracles rather than wise theologians, Socrates is drawing an important distinction between the respective territories of *theos* and *logos*, reason and revelation. Although by his constant recourse to poetic authority, Socrates grants that the tragedians were often inspired in their insights into the *human* condition, he does not have a correspondingly high estimation of their statements concerning the gods. Their cosmological forays were as impotent as the quasi-scientific attempts that he once made to penetrate the divine things-in-themselves. They could not see that their wisdom had to be turned around. Yet since the poets preferred to see themselves as theologians rather than oracles with insight into human things, as divine spokespersons and seers of the future instead of insightful reporters of the chthonic compulsions pervading the present, their pride made them incapable of assessing or interpreting the true value of their own revelations. They surrendered the human domain to politicians wielding the profane powers of sophistry and rhetoric. Socrates would also have expected a poet's life to live up to the rational implications of his poetry and professed beliefs. This was a standard that few men could measure up to, either then or now.

Unlike the far more independent comedians, who prided themselves on their originality and creative liberties, the tragic poets self-consciously derived their productions from a vast body of mythological lore that dated back to Homeric times. The basis for their theology was the poetry of Homer and Hesiod; these poets were regarded as authoritative expositors of the Olympian gods. As such, the poets of Socrates' day could not go beyond these hoary sources to provide simpler accounts of the gods or the cosmos in their own words. According to Socrates, this meant that the poets he interrogated were fundamentally ignorant of the very divine matters that they were said to be infallibly familiar with. Differently put, because they merely provided footnotes to Homer and could not transcend his authority, the tragedians of his day were no different from the rest of humanity in their state of fundamental ignorance concerning ultimate reality. Despite the seemingly transcendent *source* and divine power of poetic revelation, their interpolation of its *content* was profane and anthropological, not sacred and theological.

To understand Socrates' interrogation of the poets we also recall that while he probably never met Aeschylus, who is far closer to the humanistic spirit of the *Odyssey*, Euripides was not too popular in his day.[44] Agathon was probably far more typical of the tragic poetry of the day than Sophocles, who often seems to despise the human ingenuity of Odysseus's strivings against divine curses, aristocratic honor and chthonic fury.[45] Sophocles and Euripides shared deeply pessimistic views about the gods and their disposition towards man. The only difference was that while the one preached pious submission, the other exposed primal irrationality. While their views served as a valuable check on the hubris of Democracy, the toxic effects outlived the good. By emphasizing the misanthropy of the *Iliad* and the special effects of the *Odyssey,* instead of drawing out the slow humanistic progress from the Trojan War to the reformed Kingdom of Ithaca, tragedy after Aeschylus made its audience more resigned and susceptible to rhetorical manipulation. Sophocles, for instance, sees all claims to human rationality as foredoomed by the cruel irrationality of the ultimate principles of reality; gods, chthonic powers or fate, the end result is that all human striving ends badly. While Aeschylus saw progress as issuing slowly though suffering and understanding, Sophocles tells us that suffering gives understanding and Euripides angrily reveals suffering beyond understanding.

Matters were complicated further when poets were elected to high office on the basis of supposed insight into divine matters. Plato's *Ion* displays the absurd state of affairs that ensues when Homer is regarded as the ultimate basis for the prudential art of a general. Even if a proficient strategist could cloak his expertise in suitably Homeric idiom, this approach would be liable to be imitated by others less intelligent, and consequently more likely to believe that the strategic art was infallibly derived from Homer himself. Again we see a disastrous inversion of rhetoric and art— ends and means. While we can learn much about human nature from Homer, he cannot teach us about battle formations. One wishes that literalists of our time could make this distinction. The poet must constantly fight against the temptation to control effects within the cave instead of being open to humbling causes outside the cave quite beyond his ken. The true art of the exegetical second sailing is in making hypotheses adequate to the phenomena and inquiring into the conditions for their possibility. The poet's progeny, like human fortune, is always mixed. Divinely inspired words are often mixed in with all-too-human dross. Even Jesus says that men cannot separate wheat from chaff;[46] perhaps this is why the help of the paraclete is needed.[47] The poet is often incapable of judging between his children because he may love those less inspired works into which he mixed more of his own labor. As Aristotle saw, love has more to do with loving rather than being loved, and giving than receiving.[48]

The true and timeless greatness of Homer was not derived from any implicit claim to provide journalistic accounts of scandalous happenings on Mount Olympus, it came rather from his inspired and unmatched ability to represent the *poros* and *penia,* the concomitant grandeur and misery, of the human condition. The Olympians described by Homer were epiphenomenal shadows of the passions moving the likes of Achilles and Odysseus; though vividly personified by the blind Bard, they were invoked as hypotheses to account for powers wielded by heroes that could not be explained in merely human terms. Likewise Homer and Hesiod themselves were to be viewed in the same uninspired manner that denied the true nature of their genius. Instead of being seen as great creative virtuosi, they were portrayed as Olympian journalists who somehow stormed heaven and gained access to the secrets of the gods. In short, the real problem is not with the great poets, it is with pusillanimous mortals who insist on taking their every word piously and literally—thus denying and obscuring both the erotic genius of poetry and the sublime truth about the human spirit that poets somehow reveal. While it is possible that the two personae are present at different moments in the life of the same poet, divine inspiration and critical acumen are rarely found in the same author at the same time, even with regard to the same work. While we may distinguish true inspiration from its evil twin, furious intoxication, by noting that while the gods are always subtle, they are never malicious or unjust, the *Apology* strongly implies that there are no perfect texts or exegetes. As Lessing saw,[49] human erotic striving must stand in for wisdom.

In his brilliant essay on the *Ion* Allan Bloom suggests that though rhapsodes like Ion could be said to be inspired, this inspiration derived from their audiences rather than the gods.[50] As Ion unwittingly discloses in the eponymous dialogue, although acting as if he is inspired, he pays very close attention to his audience to control the effect that he has on them. "If I make them weep, I shall laugh because I am making money, but if they laugh, I shall weep because of the money I am losing" (535e). It is perfectly reasonable to suppose that successful poets gain inspiration from their audiences. In other words, these poets would function as public oracles in giving expression to the deeply hidden truth immanent in the collective political unconscious of their polity. It is this truth that would be represented through the not inappropriate idiom of those traditional myths and founding archetypes that both held a polis together and preserved its continuity with the past. Of course, this account also suggests that these poets were not divinely inspired, in the sense of having transcendent truths revealed to them by the gods, but merely inspired from below by chthonic powers. One thinks of a sometime genuinely inspired musician faced with a choice between living as a day laborer, continually depending on the daily manna of inspiration, and cynically pandering to his public to gain both power and money from their rage.

While someone like Aristophanes is open and self-conscious in his desire to appeal to, and evoke belly-laughs from, the earthier elements of his public, the tragedians saw themselves as agents of divine revelation. The illusion is even harder to overcome because the epics from whence tragedians derived plots and characters were universally supposed to be of divine origin. It would clearly have been difficult for these worthies to distinguish adequately between the merely mimetic and truly creative aspects of their complex and rather less than self-consciously reflective relationship with their audiences and cultural substrata. These pragmatic links, which resemble those spoken of in the *Ion* and the famous cave image of the *Republic*, only served to bind poets and demos closer to each other in a relationship of mutually sustained ignorance. As movingly as the tragedians depicted men being destroyed by divine deception, they didn't reveal that these very representations themselves deceptively projected human folly and psychic forces on the gods. While Feuerbach claimed that Christianity attributed all that was good about us to god, while reserving evil to humanity,[51] tragedy hopelessly pits human virtue against divine vice.

This seems to be why Socrates finally turned to the artisans (22c). As a sometime stonemason, he may have expected that these persons would have been aware of the difference between what could and could not be known. It is one thing to work with stone, it is quite another to know what stone is in itself. Unlike the greatest poets of the day, who turned out to be little better than popularly inspired channels of collective emotion, the best of the artisans were genuine creators and thus fully aware of the capacity and limitations of their own handiwork. Daedalus could be expected to be more reflective than the mimetic Icarus. This awareness would presumably have made the artisans better able to comport themselves in the state of endemic ignorance that marked the human condition. Sadly, the artisans' true confidence in one area of competence only led them to believe themselves wise in matters far beyond their capacity (22d).

Instead of knowing that they did not know anything that was not as clear and distinct to them as their own handiwork, the artisans were prone to regard the fundamental principles of the cosmos as artifacts and thus, in principle, as knowable as other artifacts. As Archilochus would have put it, they were hedgehogs who thought they were foxes. This materialistic attitude towards reality could well be representative of a democratic tendency to regard all things as malleable and subject to convention and negotiation, or supply and demand. Conversely, as we have seen from the *Euthyphro*, the Socratic profession of piously reflective ignorance suggests that though they must be attended to and cared for by humans, the greatest matters cannot be known or apprehended in the same way by which inanimate objects are crafted and possessed. Socrates' own turn from cosmology/stonemasonry to midwifery, from making images of the divine things to leading souls out of the cave or womb, can also be seen to fall under this heading.

Once he had reflected on the deluded ignorance that he found in politicians, poets and artisans, Socrates saw that the Oracle's words meant that he is far better off than all other men in being aware of the extent of his ignorance. Socrates claims to be made an instrument (or artisan) of the gods "to show that human wisdom is worth little or nothing" (23a); his annoyingly homely analogies must be viewed in this light also, since prudence deals with normal experience. The suggestion is that he is exploding human claims to transcendent wisdom, rather than denying the possibility of a self-consciously human "practical reason" that is self-consciously aware of its own limitations. Indeed, if he were to hold that second order human wisdom were also impossible, he would be denying that mankind could even be aware of its own ignorance. Apart from denying the possibility of sophistry, such a nihilistic position would also serve to deliver humanity up to the very religious charlatans and dogmatic fools that Socrates is manifestly anxious to show up and refute. Additionally, speech itself becomes absurd if the very possibility of shared human understanding is denied. Conversely, once the shock of disenchantment is over, shared awareness of metaphysical ignorance, the freedom to finally speak honestly, often edifies and unifies people as much as mutually exclusive esoteric dogmas tend to alienate, separate and stupefy them.

For all these reasons Socrates believes that the truest and most pious interpretation of the Delphic Oracle amounts to a divine command that he examine and refute the claims of any man, whether Athenian or foreigner, to be wise regarding the highest things. In other words, one could only interpret the human meaning of the poets. A man may be a fine philologist, and master every detail of secondary scholarship on a technical detail of a work of metaphysics, and yet be indifferent to, or incapable of, grasping the truth that even Aristotle never transcended the human condition of ignorance, likewise mastery of the interior lines of a system often obscures its tenuous origins. By stating that he must come to the aid of the gods (23b), Socrates is making a remarkable statement about the limits on divine power that is very consistent with the conclusions we arrived at when studying the *Euthyphro*. The gods seem to need the service of men; while they provide the necessary inspiration, the actual physical deeds that the gods require have to be performed by mortals. Carrying out this divine mandate is why Socrates lacks the leisure either to attend to the tasks of the city "worth speaking of" or the tasks of the family (23b). This suggests to the careful reader that while he is indeed performing a political function, this labor is one that is carried out through words and deeds rather than by pure speech or solitary contemplation.

Emulating Odysseus, Socrates illustrates virtues that the gods them-selves cannot directly embody in the physical world. His thought-provoking deeds throw a spanner in the banal, mindlessly efficient, mimetic mecha-nisms that rule normal life in the cave; these categories cannot account for his behavior. It cannot be denied that there is method to his madness. Socrates is trying to point beyond himself to the gods as he smuggles pious ignorance back to the cave. If he, in his self-professed ignorance, cannot be the source of the higher than mortal wisdom that his actions indicate, then a thoughtful observer should deduce that there clearly are gods, or transcen-dental forces, who inspire these actions of interruption and interpretation. It is only at the very end of his life that he becomes an inspired actor.

Just as blind Homer inferred the existence of the Olympian gods through his observation of heroic human powers, Socrates wishes to imply that conventional standards of goodness are derived from a less than divine origin. As we saw from the *Euthyphro*, Socrates is trying to move from the coercive power of Zeus to an Apollonian model of divine-mortal interac-tion that is less adversarial and more harmonious. In the language of Empedocles, the gods of Socrates rule through love rather than strife. Since such a "synergistic" view of the cosmos depends upon virtue being freely chosen for its own sake, it follows that these "novel" gods of Socrates educate humans through the subtle means of wonder and inspira-tion. His abrasive speech aims to scrub the barnacles off the soul that make it, like the Sea Glaucus of the *Republic*, incapable of seeing itself and undertaking a second sailing.[52]

Returning to our place in the text, we can now see why the refuting art of Socrates, the aspect of him that the wealthiest and most leisured young men love to imitate, cannot be viewed in isolation from the gentle way of life that it is founded upon. The rough tools used by the stonemason's son are but obstetrician's instruments, delicately wielded to advance the self-less ends of a midwife's child. Seeming physical damage and psychic discomfort is inevitable when a soul is brought into the world. A great deal of Socrates' unpopularity is attributable to those who imitated his speech rather than his deeds. It is noteworthy that while he possesses neither wealth nor leisure, his imitators had both of these commodities in abundance. Moreover, while he is trying to overturn the unhealthy practice of mindless imitation, the wealthy young men about town unwittingly illustrated the extent of civic corruption when they thoughtlessly imitate Socrates and turn his pious exegeses into nihilistic politics. Additionally, while his imitators are pleased by the ignorance that they maliciously reveal, Socrates, if we take his sworn words seriously, is still genuinely distressed by both the ignorance that he discovers, and the hatred that he incurs. It makes little difference if they mindlessly imitate his words or react thoughtlessly to his deeds; both behaviors reveal a staggering lack of self-knowledge and indicate how much the city was corrupted by mimesis. Socrates would have been both corrupt and decadent if he had derived any pleasure from this Sisyphean activity.

We are now ready to deal with the substantial issues involved in the explicit charge of corrupting the youth of Athens. Socrates' imitators may more justly be accused of corrupting the youth than he. This is because when they set about mindlessly imitating his dialectic with malicious intent, while remaining willfully ignorant of his purposes, the practices of these false disciples circulated a nihilistic or cynical take on Socrates' devoutly undertaken mission. This practice persists to this very day among those who dogmatically assert that Socrates was a closet atheist who cared only about philosophy. While Socrates himself was swift to assure his interlocutors of his own ignorance about the matters that he sought knowledge of, and often sought their participation in his investigations of the negative potentiality of metaphysical ignorance, his imitators and enemies were content to take this manner of speech for nihilistic wisdom itself. While his pious enemies hated him for his exoteric revelation of what they mistook to be nihilism, his imitators reveled in the false liberty they derived from exposing bankrupt political theology of their fathers. Since his imitators were almost always too rich and powerful to be attacked directly, it was more feasible for those chastened by humiliating encounters with their own ignorance to blame Socrates, the reputed father of their unjust and fatherless nihilistic words.

Socrates suggests that instead of being enraged by him, or his imitators, the self-righteous politicians, poets and artisans should be angry with themselves for their false pretensions to wisdom (23c). He is not merely the scapegoat for his imitators' misdeeds; even these less than admirable young men are not as culpable as those in whom they accurately detected unwarranted claims to wisdom. In other words, the "corruption of the youth" was only piously deplored by the older generation because it led to the unwelcome public revelation of *their* deluded self-complacency and moral impotence. The real cause of corruption had far more to do with their banality than with their offspring's evil; the latter was only an effect of the former. The wealthy and dissolute youth of the polity would not have been so cynically opportunistic in their twisted use of the Socratic method if had it not been for the bad example jointly and severally set by their oligarchic fathers and the *demos*. While the sophists were responsible for introducing the mindset of nihilistic cynicism, and Socrates was blamed for introducing the dialectic that led to its revelation, the Athenians ultimately had only themselves to blame for creating a context within which these abuses could take place. Keeping with his claim that nobody would corrupt those he had to live with, Socrates said that those who sow corruption often don't live around it long enough to reap its bitter harvest;[53] the evil that men do does not merely live after them, it is also only discovered posthumously. Once their folly or hypocrisy is recognized, by moral mutants like Callicles, the transition from implicit selfishness to blatant shamelessness even seems virtuous in the sense of being more honest. This loss of shame goes well with demotic cynicism and a certain form of professional process-driven righteousness that seems to be derived from a priestly concern with form and ritual purity.

Socrates contends that the real reason animating the virulent hatred mobilized against him is that he speaks the truth and holds nothing back in conversation (24a). But he has suggested that since his opponents live and flourish through jealously guarded and venerated falsehoods, they cannot tolerate any challenge to their accustomed way of life. They would not have been as sensitive and resentful to honest inquiry if their lifestyles were better than an ugly assemblage of shadows, lies and myths held together by habits and thoughtlessness. Socrates was not accused of spreading falsehoods about things above and beneath the earth for a very good reason; as he pointed out, he did no such thing. He was hated for introducing a method of inquiry that exposed the falsehood of sacrosanct opinions held concerning these matters by the Athenian polity. In other words he had revealed that the Athenian poets and politicians were guilty of fabricating and disseminating false opinions and unjust interpretations about the highest and lowest matters. As Thucydides and Euripides revealed, the Athenian Empire was held by modes and orders of political realism that could not be spoken of by decent men without shame. Socrates died for exposing the "sins" of those who knew not, and preferred not to know, what they professed.

But quite beyond exposing the specifically Athenian attitudes about empire and power itself, regime-specific topics that although controversial could yet be legitimate political subjects, Socrates does far more than beat and punish the fathers of Athens, men like Pericles and Themistocles; he also outrageously exposes the mysteries or maternal principles that constituted the very basis of the city. While the sky gods of the city are erotic—to the extent that they inform the *telos* of the polity—they are political through and through. Just as the gods of the *Euthyphro* argued and wrangled over the best meaning of justice or beauty, the Athenians could and did debate (albeit often under the guidance of daimonic statesmen like Themistocles or Pericles) over the best strategy for the city to adopt as it pursued glory and riches. Since these debates defined what the many collectively held to be honorable or shameful, Socrates, among other things, pitted dialectic against rhetoric and reduced the certainty of the many to perplexities that shamed and confused the individual citizen. As we suggested earlier, he made the weaker arguments of reason resist the supposedly "stronger" rhetoric used to move the body politic. His irony withstood the brazen rage of the self-righteous demos, forcing those comprising this thumotic mob to think as individuals.

The real issue goes deeper than the synthetic a priori assumptions of the regime; rhetoric always claims to be reasonable even as it acts under the power of desire. Socrates seems to be polluting the very cave/womb itself by publicly trying to bring the pre-political *drives* under the rule of reason. Callicles had earlier accused him of being unmanly and fearful of (re)entering the public space; now, fortified by his gift of the gods, just as Odysseus was told by Hermes the Giant-slayer that the encircler (Circe) would not unman him,[54] Socrates descends to the womb-like depths of the subterranean prison to bring freedom and enlightenment to his swinish fellow-citizens. While his invasion of Hades is bound to arouse the fury of the underworld, only thus can he reveal the black gold of Pluto: the dark store of angry energy used by political theology to bind the city to itself. While many deny the sky gods, none deny the sanctity of life, body and family. This means that the sky gods are disposable masks; true power resides in the sacred, as opposed to the divine, in the chorus of chthonic fury that now cries for the death of Apollo's votary. If the sky gods are a city's insurance agents, the forces of life, body and family are its utility providers.

III. The Schooling of Athens

Once Socrates has exposed the hidden chthonic origins of the older slanders about him, and identified his real accusers, he is free to attack the explicit accusations themselves. Through his questioning of Meletus he will display the bad influence that Socrates' older accusers have had on the younger generation. Thus Meletus, in his evident condition of ignorant opportunism, is the only witness Socrates needs to prove the validity of the claims he previously made about his older accusers. The grumpy old men making up the jury will probably have seen that Meletus, the self-appointed champion of the good old ways, is himself a corrupt youth. Aristophanes would surely have blushed before this grotesque caricature of himself. Meletus is either an accomplished and precocious hypocrite or terribly foolish; he is either morally or intellectually corrupt.

Yet as Socrates exposes Meletus to public ridicule, he does so at great personal cost. The more discerning among the jurors, those most likely to be receptive to the spectacle that he has presented, will also recognize that if Socrates is not to blame, then Athens is profoundly at fault. Socrates, as we observe earlier, has challenged the jury in a way that will not let them take refuge in a shadowy middle ground between Meletus's position and his. They would be like the cowardly men who straddle the *methoria* in the *Euthydemus* (305b–e). If Socrates is innocent, then the jurors must recognize their own individual and collective responsibility for both the corruption of the youth and the strangeness of the gods of virtue worshipped by Socrates. As Socrates pointed out, he would be convicted not by the superior arguments made by Meletus and Anytus but by the power they presupposed and pandered to, "the slander and envy of the many" (28b). All that Socrates can do is expose the hidden source of the corruption of the old, and hope that some of his jurors will belatedly attain some knowledge of the blind forces animating their fury.

Turning now to defend himself against the explicit accusations preferred by Meletus and Anytus, Socrates first exposes the absurdity of the charge that he alone corrupts the young. How could the moral strength of the many be so much weaker than the questions of one ignorant man? Meletus must reluctantly admit that, save Socrates, all of the Athenians make the youth noble and good. He is led to make this exaggerated claim by Socrates' questions, which challenge him to keep widening the number of benevolent influences, *Eumenides* on the youth to include every one of the juror-judges, all those present, all the councilmen, all of the assembly-men, and finally the entire citizenry of Athens. Apart from shedding some light on Meletus's demagogic political ambitions, this interrogation also shows that he at least nominally rejects the suggestion made by Socrates that others could have contributed to corruption by use or misuse of his methods. This leads to the absurd implication that, since only Socrates corrupts the youth, those many Athenians said to have been corrupted by him miraculously continue to be a good influence on others.

Perhaps the only "wriggle room" out of this predicament would be for one more intelligent than Meletus to maintain that all of these bodies of men were *collectively* good influences on the young, even though they were individually susceptible to corruption. This, after all, is the idea behind trial by jury: the belief that the whole is greater than the sum of its parts, an idea that has sadly mutated into our belief that private vices lead to public virtues. Such an argument runs parallel with the view that the poets were inspired by the collective body of the Athenian demos, the General Will of the "democracy of the dead" rather than its dull individual elements. Although we may have reason to disagree with this conclusion, based on what we have seen of Meletus's motives, this is more logically consistent than the untenable corner Socrates has backed him into.

Yet such a position is diametrically opposed to the view of Socrates that while a few may be able to improve, the many only have the power to corrupt (25b). We may conclude, in a less optimistic vein, that the many corrupt precisely through acting as a mob; in such a situation the collective intelligence of the whole is clearly much less than the potential of its constituent parts; chaos is less than order and far inferior to justice. This is the strength of the weaker argument, rationally speaking. True to his mission as midwife, Socrates may be seen to have elicited out of Meletus an admission that the latter was not consciously aware of; far from being edified by the collective unconscious of the demos, he was actually corrupted by its blind self-righteousness. The contrast between the respective preparations made by Socrates and Meletus for the trial is quite instructive. Meletus, although carefully rehearsed for his political debut, has prepared for this event by a lifetime of being immersed in the prejudices and passions of the demos. He will seek to animate the sacred fury that Athena, perhaps disingenuously, hoped to turn towards the external enemies of Athens in the *Eumenides*.[55] Meanwhile Socrates, although he has not prepared a speech on the express instructions of his *daimon*, will also explicitly state that he has prepared for this culminating event of his life.[56] Just as Meletus will serve as an inspired spokesperson for the blind fury of the many, Socrates will claim to be possessed by the *daimon* that has guided the course of his life. He is not a loosely cobbled together collection of fears and cravings. He is not a zombie.

Returning to the case of Meletus, it also follows that because it is absurd to intentionally corrupt those one lives alongside (25d), the many involuntarily corrupt each other through their ignorance and fear. One is reminded of how the plague spread. By the time the many belatedly recognize that corruption has taken place, their minds will have become incapable of knowing how it could have come about. Here Socrates drops his accustomed profession of ignorance to indignantly reject the implication that he does not know that is bad to do evil (25d–e).

While Socrates may not be able to define certain winged words like justice and evil, he is certainly aware of the principle that it is wrong to do or disseminate evil and would not do this consciously and willingly. In other words, the *Euthyphro*'s distinction stands; while the origin of the command "evil should not be done" is mysterious, the rule is as universally known on earth as it is on Olympus. Any disagreement is about what evil is in a given situation. Unlike philosophy, which affirms principles while being critical of their practice, *thumos* which seeks to do good to friends and impose evil on strangers, denies the basic command to avoid evil underlying the forms of justice and piety that it insists on seeing punctiliously carried out. Mindless imitation corrupts this power to see the whole and judge the ultimate particulars appropriately. Political theology of the kind espoused by Meletus is all about politics in the basest sense: it believes in neither the divine nor the logos. While Socrates knows that definitive knowledge of the essence of qualities can't be gained, kept or given, false opinion masquerading as certain knowledge of good and evil becomes the means by which our formal awareness is corrupted and seduced. An Idea or look may only be seen by the individual soul. It cannot be represented as a physical sign that is visible to the mob. The many are usually ruled by rationally groundless revelations made by orators and poets, and reified by artisans. The brazen voice of demagogic common sense, rhetorically induced, selfishly motivated and furiously upheld, usually out-shouts the privately conducted, public-spirited, deliberation of the sort that Socrates encouraged. In a demotic age the gods have fallen from the sky and become chthonic furies of their former selves. As such, they are easily deployed by demagogues.

Distinguishing between the soul's moral knowledge of the divine and sacred thumotic piety is essential to an appreciation of what Socrates is defending in the *Apology*. The vain desire to present the appearance of being wise in matters beyond human understanding all too frequently causes clubs or gangs of power-hungry men to band against each other and ignore the self-evident moral precepts that should unify them. Since *thumos* has no object beyond itself, moral corruption results from the hubristic desire on the part of those in power and their sycophants to avoid admitting to being finite and not qualitatively distinct from the rest of humanity; they insist that all power—and their own especially—is sanctioned by the gods. This means that every "is" within the pale of identity is *ex officio* invested with the aura of an "ought." In contrast, best and most memorably embodied by Socrates, moral virtue involves more than personal integrity in speech and deed; once given freedom by the bursting of its *amour propre,* it also feels the compassionate desire to protect others from the contagious effects of injustice and impiety—Socrates' selfless education of Euthyphro comes to mind. While Eros sees the other in the light of the good, *thumos* is akin to nationalism in that it only knows itself by the lurid glow of adversarial categories. As we saw, Meletus was not ashamed when shown not to have given any thought to the charges he made against Socrates (24d). All pious outrage certainly does not come from God. Socratic piety is best defined as refusing to let God's name be used to justify or sanctify *thumos*.

Meletus cannot see the full implications of his confusion of opportunism with piety; this is why, in his willing susceptibility to the contagious power of collective corruption, he performs an act that visits much damage on the Athenian polity. The belief that Socrates, the thinker, is stupid and selfish enough to corrupt his fellow citizens is a projection of Meletus's own vices upon his antagonist. Although, Socrates denies that evil is performed for its own sake, Meletus's "care-less" conduct is a striking example of how corruption perpetrates itself. Just because evil is rarely deliberate, it does not follow that acts of incontinent wickedness cannot be posthumously whitewashed and collectively justified once men are morally blackmailed into defending them. Theology becomes casuistry: reasoning backwards to make otherwise scandalous deeds sacred.

All this suggests that a slothful preference for a condition of vain ignorance is the truest reason why communities generally prefer the public spectacle of retributive punishment to the private admonition and instruction that Socrates chose to administer. Because the people are generally ignorant of the causes of corruption, and since they tend to formulate their political theology in terms that are more chauvinistic than rational, we end up in a situation where even asking the question "what is piety?" is deemed impious. While it certainly is true that "rare spectacles" of the kind described by Machiavelli can deter unruly human passions and instill sacred awe through fear, we must also see that because conditioning of this kind does not address the intellect, such an approach does little to encourage true virtue to be sought for its own sake.

Even if we go against the evidence and suppose him to be animated by piety, a crude voluntarist like Meletus does not understand or care why Socrates acts the way he does; he merely wishes to change the older man's behavior by threatening him with death. This kind of "shadow-conditioning" is typical of the mindset that the philosopher meets in the subterranean polity. Just as the literal minded Homeric theologian perceived the soul as a mere shadow of the body, the poets likewise made it seem that the individual conscience is but a function of powerful unconscious and collective influences; even Aristotle seemed to subscribe to a more consciously constructivist version of this approach; he first places deliberation within the capacity of every citizen's soul but then prefers to rely on the mimetic power of the *spoudaios*.

The famous cave analogy of the *Republic* suggests that Socrates championed precisely the opposite point of view; he believed in the ability of the soul to rule itself and its body virtuously through its power of transcendence. If man did not really have a soul, then he was but a slavish shade capable of neither thought nor autonomous morality. Seth Benardete's insight that the shades in Hades live in a state of eternal frustration is most relevant here;[57] blinded by self-pity, the gods of this living Hades only expect to be honored by vulgar mimetic rituals and thoughtless flattery. The best mortals curry favor with these gods by leading inferior members of their species in acts of abasement. In exchange for this, they would expect to be regarded as divinely appointed rulers and guardians.

The youth are corrupted when they learn to see warped accounts of the past as sacred destiny; their inherited passions would likewise be accepted as the will of the gods. Such an incestuous loop could never be transcended without the very intellectual awareness that had been repudiated out of the combination of a mistaken piety and the conviction that most mortals could not stand to know the truth of Silenus—that it was best not to be born in the sense of leaving the cycles of ritual, reproduction and resentment that made up a cave.[58] Individual transcendence of any kind is ruled out; the guardians merely participate actively in the regnant political theology and preside over the eternal return of the same. As we have seen, this sad state of affairs was caused by some Dionysian poets' mistaken opinion as to the source of their art; believing themselves to be divinely inspired, they identified chthonic influences, the selfish behavior of tyrants and/or the collective passions of the demos as authoritative voices of Olympian gods. The resulting theology was mis-anthropocentric and morally corrosive. Self-evidently unethical practices could be piously emulated once the gods were identified as their origin and the demos in question were seen as their exceptional favorites; this was why mimetic poetry of this sort was denounced in the *Republic*. The *thumos*-filled gods of life, body, and the cave are very different from the erotic gods of the soul that cannot be known, represented or flattered. The morality that trickles down from the thumotic gods is an ugly witches' brew of fury, fear and fraternity.

We may now see why Socrates was accused of bringing in or worshipping gods other than those believed in by the Athenian polity. Expressed in the bluntest terms, it would seem that the transcendent divine virtues he serves through his mission have nothing to do with the blindly self-referential furies that possess the city. While the original indictment—according to Diogenes Laertes—reads "introducing,"[59] and Xenophon's account has "carrying in,"[60] Socrates boldly but piously amends this to "*believing in* novel *daimons*"[61] when he makes his defense speech. It follows that the corruption of the city is blamed for the seeming novelty of the gods Socrates serves and assists. The traditional forms of veneration earn his contempt precisely because they do not inspire transcendence but cater to selfish and incestuous impulses militating against political moderation and human actualization. Thinking posthumously, Socrates must teach the fainthearted that virtue is sufficient to withstand even the strongest thumotic pressure.

We have already paid attention to Meletus's imprudence in simultaneously maintaining that Socrates is both an atheist and one who introduces strange gods into the city. Meletus's only recourse here would be to claim that Socrates was a ironic hypocrite who did not practice what he preached, but this would (a) be inconsistent with everyone's experience of Socrates' eccentric religious conduct, (b) in conflict with the thoughtless orthopraxy that passed for piety in Athens, and (c) also draw undue attention to how Athenian political and religious institutions were run. The issue is one of henotheism: Meletus's charges tacitly acknowledges these daimonic voices from the gods of high places, and rejects them in favor of Athens's own furies, fire and cave. Likewise post-exilic Jewish religion, which denounced the (sky) gods of the high places and insisted that sacrifices could only be offered in *the* Temple, underwent a similar ethical transformation once the chthonic Temple was destroyed in 70 C.E.[62]

Socrates had earlier simplified the indictment against him by provoking Meletus into combining his two charges. Meletus must accept that he corrupts the youth by teaching them to forsake the gods of the city in favor of the novel *daimonia* introduced by Socrates. This means that the charge of political subversion is subsumed under the broader accusation of impiety. Like Euthyphro, Meletus claims that justice, which to him is the angry self-righteousness of the many, is derived from piety. But this is also consistent with Socrates' stated position here: his politically significant actions stemmed directly from his divinely commanded mission. By proceeding in this manner he is also compelling the Athenians to pay attention to several seemingly innocent but probing questions about the ground of revelation, a subject that would normally be off limits on the grounds of its impiety. I shall suggest that these queries do far more than damage the credibility of Meletus; they also indicate the possibility of reconstructing a Socratic view of a cosmos that will emphasize the role of the anti-voluntaristic virtues that he embodied. Such a view of reality must radically discount the possibility and value of dogmatic knowledge, the origin of a sacramental order, and look to the transcendental powers inherent in human eros and practical reason. In other words, the basis for such a way of life would be the Oracle's implied claim that Socratic ignorance about the gods was a necessary and salutary feature of the human condition. This holy ignorance requires virtue to be practiced for its own sake, rather than out of a desire for selfish or tribal advantage in either this world or the next. Philosophy is yoked to moral virtue by this view of the human condition; both may only flourish when it is seen that positive power-yielding revelations about divine powers and desires are both impossible and undesirable. Only then will divine insight about human things be available alongside simple probity.

As suggested earlier, in attempting to understand Socrates' position concerning the poets, the genuine value of revelation derives from its ability to shed light on human rather than divine or sacred things. While we previously concentrated on a popular poet's ability to give voice and seemingly divine sanction to perverse chthonic influences, Socrates' own *daimon* was not unlike other great poets in calling attention to the heroic potentialities immanent in human nature. Put differently, just as genuine prophecy simply sees what is essential in the present clearly and does not lay claim to infallible knowledge of the future, true revelation speaks of a difficult beauty that is always possible; it is gained through erotic power over oneself, the power to justly rule one's desires, not by taking the thumotic line of hawking recipes of how to flatter gods and exploit men. The inspiration given by these ideas frees us from the dead weight of the past and our fear of change and the unknown. By reminding man of his best capacities, which are internal, not mimetic or sycophantic, it re-collects and re-integrates the human spirit in the present, thereby empowering man to face future uncertainties with a better sense of his powers, virtues and limits.

The Oracle's revelation, as interpreted by Socrates, also goes beyond what can be empirically known in denying the very possibility of human wisdom about the gods. This Delphic intuition into the inaccessibility and undesirability of cosmological power thus functions as a *daimon* in delimiting the roles of gods and men and freeing the latter to find true happiness by dedicating themselves simply to the practice of virtue. As the *Euthyphro* hints, only in this way can we serve the gods and do what cannot be commanded: participate in a cosmic order based on the idea of self-transcendence and common amity. Virtue must be freed from the yoke of piety and the burden of sacred resentment. We can only see the present clearly when we are not blinded by darkness at noon, when we do not allow hopes and fears to distort our moral sight. The basis for these distorting fears is fearful belief in a jealous deity who cares only for our submission.

Once we recognize that the content of revelation is self-knowledge, that true moral knowledge is about ruling the self or microcosm according to the pattern set forth in the cosmos, rather than dependence on revelations of divine foibles, it is possible to see what Socrates found to be so valuable about ignorance. When one is aware of the radical extent to which the human condition is separated from certain covenantal binding sacred rituals a very different paradigm of the self emerges. No longer seeing ourselves as sullenly opportunistic slaves seeking only to flatter power, or angry day laborers who would gain violent hegemony for a few gaudy nights, we recognize the extent to which human life is both interdependent and fraught with contingency. Our dark chthonic roots, volatile inter-subjective relations and mysterious access to the realm of ideas and inspiration all suggest that egocentric thumotic behavior is absurd and foolish.

After we are relieved of the great burden of these illusions, it is possible to negotiate a relationship with the cosmos that is based upon a truer view of the self and the world it dwells in. Socrates' temperate "conscientiousness" appears in striking contrast to the claims of the wise-guy sophists that happiness and excellence are all about accumulating power by tricking men or the knowledge of how to befriend and influence gods that was claimed by the professionally pious. From the standpoint of the unenlightened (and un-lightened) ego, the value of gaining wisdom about the foibles and lusts of the capricious gods was exceedingly practical. This lore was supposed to help one accumulate wealth and pleasures in this life and outsmart death in the next. However, on seeing the highly dubious provenance of this information, and recognizing the equal absurdity of a supposedly spiritual substance that compulsively pursues pleasure and flees pain, it well behooves the soul to live in a different manner and seek another kind of wisdom.

When Meletus heatedly accused him of being an atheist, we saw Socrates point out that the linked accusation—that he introduced (and believed in) strange *daimons*—caused these charge to contradict each other (26e). Socrates' position was that one could not consistently believe in *daimons*, supposedly bastard children of gods, without also acknowledging the existence of their parent gods (27d–e). Socrates' *daimons* are not sufficient conditions for their own existence; they point beyond themselves towards transcendent origins. It seems that Socrates' belief in gods' existence is empirically founded upon his personal experience of *daimons*. Almost like one who claimed to have been abducted by aliens, Socrates is convinced that no merely human source could adequately account for what has been revealed to him. In making this personal confession, he is quite unlike those more orthodox believers who concede that *daimons* could exist because they believed in gods said to have spawned many offspring. This belief in the gods themselves is based upon poetic and parental authority and coercive cultural practices. Yet, ultimately, the authoritative poetic accounts of the Olympian gods are themselves not empirical but inspired. This means that some superhuman power acted upon them to inspire accounts of the various Olympians and their lives. But, since neither Homer nor Hesiod claimed direct acquaintance with an Olympian deity but were explicitly reliant on their muses, does their inspiration prove the existence *and establish the essence* of any divine beings more substantial than Socrates' *daimons*?

When Socrates states that *daimons* were the *illegitimate* children of the union of a god with a mortal (27d), he could be coyly identifying himself as one such mortal. On pondering the implications of Chaerephon's message from the Delphic Oracle, we see that Saul is also among the prophets: Socrates seems to have joined the ranks of those involuntarily impregnated by an unknown divine force. By patiently teasing out the implications of the god's enigmatic words, and staying within the limits given by his *daimon*, he has carried this unusual spiritual pregnancy to term. More daringly, we identify this impregnating power as Apollo, though even this assertion does not convey any other information about the essence of this "far-shooting" god, only the nature of his relation to mortals. It is noteworthy that this *daimon* was conceived by not following orthodox rites of piety: as Homer often memorably illustrates, divine promiscuity frequently runs foul of the sacred jealousy of Hera. Zeus the lover sows but does not reap; Heracles is but the most famous case of a divine grace that violates the claims of the sacred. Just as there was said to be no salvation outside the Church, Hera, and Meletus who flies to her as to his mother, declare that is no salvation outside the sacred order: there are no anonymous Christians or *daimons*.

The role of his notorious *daimon*, the offspring union with the god, is not revelatory or theosophical but personal and ethical. Instead of filling him up with juicy bits of Olympian gossip or other privileged information concerning transcendent matters, Socrates is only provided with negative self-knowledge by this *daimon*. It is as if he has been given bones and gristle to chew on by Prometheus[63] instead of the choice cuts of flesh that a typically self-consumptive thumotic tyrant seeks. Otherwise put, far from giving man inside information about *their* desires, the *sophrosyne* granted by the gods takes ultimately the form of a challenging imperative that we understand why this humble pie is the best of all possible portions from the god's table. It impels Socrates to abandon his familial and scientific interests to spend the rest of his life deconstructing the very possibility of mankind knowing anything about the gods beyond the virtue expected of us. These are the Herculean labors slaying false mythic monsters that also attracted the displeasure of Hera: the goddess of the sacred and jealously familial. Hera's religion thrives on the guilt generated by human envy of divine power. It feeds on strife and resentment.

I am suggesting that Socrates' celebrated *daimon*, this limiting force that guides by negation, sets him on a path or destiny parallel with his continual remembrance of, and reflection on, the Oracle's message. This *daimon* never required positive actions but only intervened to stop Socrates from acting in certain instances. This suggests that its primary focus was to remind him of what he could not know and thus could not serve as the theoretical basis for his actions. The word "*daimon*" derives from the Greek word meaning "division" or "allotment." It could both refer to knowledge of what was not permitted by the gods and also allow for distinctions to be made between what was and was not humanly possible and appropriate. The paradoxical awareness that he was the wisest of all men, since he knew nothing, made Socrates "daimonically" reveal the folly of seeking to escape or transcend the human state to those who would otherwise seek this false knowledge or else despair of their capacity to be virtuous. He would do so first in specific cases, and short dialogues, before revealing the principle, as he interpreted it, at his trial. While this denial of theosophy meant that piety without justice was not possible, this ignorance itself gives emancipation from the endless labor of trying to appease many mad masters. Just as the Sermon on the Mount assured the desperately poor and exploited peasants of Galilee that they were not, despite their taboo-ridden religion, hated by God and punished for their sins whenever something bad happened, Socrates complements the faith of the Athenian democracy that any normal person was capable of excellence[64] with his Delphi-aided discovery that no one has special know-how or unfair advantage in the erotic ascent towards the sunny uplands beyond the cave of the *Republic*. If this technical wisdom was available, then rule by a benevolent despot becomes logical. Its lack requires a mixed regime reflecting divine eros and powers for virtue and vice present in all of us.

Socrates' curious belief in gods on account of their illegitimate offspring means that divinely inspired human beings are the basis for his piety. Rather than showing charity towards men because of his belief in God, Socrates believes in God because he sees the divine spark in human nature. The human capacity for *daimon*-inspired virtue suggests to Socrates that there is a purpose and meaning to the human condition that goes beyond what a purely materialistic cosmology would suggest. While most accounts of the divine were framed in the terms of what Aristotle was later to call "efficient causality," Socrates' daimonic experiences led him to think otherwise. This occasioned his opposition to what we called "spiritual materialism"—the tendency to view the gods as infinitely extended embodiments of our vices, powers and appetites. Here it is also relevant to consider a form of misanthropic theology that uses rhetorical assertions of divine omnipotence and omniscience, language better suited to Caesar than Christ, to squeeze out human virtue and turn temperance and autonomy into prideful pagan vices. By contrast Socrates' daimonic model puts human flesh on a divine armature.

The subsequently developed Platonic theory of the archetypes, especially insofar as it concerned those humanistic qualities (such as justice, love, friendship, temperance and courage) that he was almost exclusively interested in, finds its legitimate origin in Socrates' celebration of the limits that were imposed by the gods upon human behavior. Instead of trying to know Apollo as an anthropomorphic being, endowed with caprices, lusts and other personal quirks, Socratic ignorance suggested that this god would have wished us to concentrate on the humanistic virtues that the divine power traditionally referred to as Apollo inspired in man. As is suggested by the *Euthyphro*, we best please the gods by being the best we can be, not by blasphemously trying to curry favor with them—thereby suggesting that the gods had all the vices and lusts of mortals. In other words, we should try to emulate and study the lives of those heroes who embodied the best of all human potentiality and displayed the limits imposed by the gods on mortal prowess. While all we have said regarding self-knowledge recalls the celebrated Delphic command "know thyself," we cannot forget that the other, equally renowned, oracular maxim "nothing in excess" could be applied both to human conduct and to the manner in which man should conceive of the gods.

Such a position is also completely consistent with Socrates' passionately held position that the ultimate values governing human life could not be those cravenly derived from the fear of death and danger (28d). Socrates invokes the *beau ideal* of Greek manhood, Achilles, as a witness on his behalf. According to Socrates, "the son of Thetis" regulated his life by standards of honor and justice. He rejected the possibility of a long and safe life upon seeing that it would come at the cost of dishonor and cowardice. Likewise Socrates refused to save his life by going into exile because he felt that this would be abandoning the ground that the gods had required him to defend. Denial of these limits is evil; as Solzhenitsyn reminds us, it is equivalent to the loss of self-knowledge.[65] In other words, the position that Socrates had to hold was defined in both spatial and moral terms; through his *daimon*, the gods had established a certain perimeter that he had to live within. This allotment, again literally his *daimon*, was his fate and self-knowledge; anything beyond it stood for the moral and metaphysical excess forbidden by the Delphic Oracle.

But, more paradoxically, Socrates says that he had to man his outpost (28d) and defend a cosmic order that he could not himself know, beyond feeling its stamp in his soul and its erotic reflection in others. He thus had to occupy a middle ground between those believing in revealed truth that could easily be known and preserved by mimetic means, and those sophisticates who claimed either that there was no truth or that it was created by the will of the most powerful. As noted earlier, Socrates offends both right and left by holding that while there is a transcendent cosmic order, it could not and should not be possessed as an object of knowledge or reduced to thumotic proportions. Emulating Prometheus and anticipating Lessing, his *daimon* reassigns the respective lots of gods and men; the truth belongs to the gods, man's destiny is to strive for virtue.

Socrates described his position as a just speech (28b), and stated that any "anthropos" or un-gentleman-like human being who would accuse him of being shameless in running the risk of dying, was speaking "ignobly" in urging him to value life over virtue. Implicit in this is the view that only such a position, clinging to life at any cost, truly represents the so-called 'unjust speech' that Aristophanes and his other old enemies accused him of fostering. It follows that when he was accused of making the weaker argument the stronger, Socrates was saying that the fear of death, widely seen as the strongest argument of all, should not serve by default as the highest principle governing a human life. Rather than being jealous of their unique essence and striving to actualize it, the ignoble pusillanimously deny their potential and prefer to be ruled by spite, envy and regrets. We are reminded of the Parable of the Talents; life cannot be preserved by not being lived.[66] Burying one's talents underground is the Biblical equivalent to refusing eros or grace and imprisoning oneself in a cave in implicit preference of the security that slavery seems to provide.

Because his self-knowledge enabled him to recognize that a human being was more than a bundle of fears and desires, Socrates refused to regard pain and pleasure as the governing principles of his life. His attentive study of Homer seems to have taught him to emulate the virtues of great men instead of piously supposing them to be utterly unlike him and specially favored by the gods. His steadfast conduct during and after the bloody battles of Potidaea, Amphipolis, and Delium (28e) also testified to his loyalty to his comrades and fellow citizens. These bonds of solidarity also ensured that he would take his stand in devastated post-war Athens and not abandon his beloved city at the time of her greatest peril.

The fact that on each of these battles the commander who stationed Socrates at his post perished in the fighting is also significant.[67] There is ample testimony to show that Socrates' inner self-mastery helped him to preserve his composure and serve as an example and rallying point when his less self-possessed comrades tended to despair. The aged Socrates conducts himself during his last retreat in such a way that the best ideals of Athens were preserved through him; though he died in battle, his memory inspires us to follow his example as a self-possessed citizen and human being in a time of total cultural chaos. If the gods who placed him in the Athenian courthouse (28d) were soon to be swept away by a rising tide of cynicism and pessimism, Socrates, acting in the spirit of the *Euthyphro* and following what we could playfully call a magic deeper than time itself, ensured that they would be replaced by worthy successors. Likewise, disheartened and bewildered persons of good will in our time, the age of the Death of God, could surely profit immensely from following the *daimon*-like example of Socrates.

Socrates tells us that his condition of inspired ignorance helped him to outsmart the conventional wisdom of his day, the belief that death was the greatest of all evils that could befall a man (29a). This unfounded dogma was linked to the fearful "wisdom of the body" the materialistic idea that accumulating pleasure and avoiding pain was the meaning of a human life; even the honor/shame values of the thumotic *aner* represented a minimal advance over these still subterranean categories. These heteronomous influences only served to divert a man from the only knowledge that was immediately self-evident to his soul–the absolute obligation to do what was good and to avoid evil (29b).

Good and evil seem to be concepts that could be understood in two very different ways. The first approach takes its bearings from the body and reduces these moral categories to the sensual proportions of pleasure and pain. Seeing good and evil in this manner alienates the soul from itself and pits it in an adversarial relationship with the rest of reality. In other words it is counter-productive to view heaven in hedonistic terms; if its joy in paradise can only be consummated by the envy and unhappiness of those deprived of the company of seventy-two black-eyed virgins, that soul is badly damaged. The other way, taken by Socrates, sees good and evil according to how a soul is related by eros and logos to itself, the polis and the cosmos.

Regardless of what it knows about the cosmic order, and discounting the stimuli constantly provided by occasions for pleasure and pain, the virtuous soul seems to be sustained in its moral autonomy by an awareness of what is wrong. As Socrates puts it, while he does not know about the things in Hades, he is aware that it is bad and shameful for a man to act unjustly and disobey his betters (29b). He could just as well be saying that because of this moral awareness, he does not live as if he were already in Hades. We know from the *Odyssey* that the shades in Hades do not recollect who they were; in our context, this means that they lack self-knowledge. As previously noted, the word Hades means something like "no idea"; this means that one who lives as if he were in Hades is too distracted by the bonds of pleasure and pain, and the powers of honor and shame, to see or actualize his unique potential. Such an account describes one who enacts the infinite labors of the damned in Tartarus,[68] imprisoned by his own resentments in a place of eternal frustration: his own shrunken and opaque soul. Others, who spend their lives hating and fearing, are effectively chained to the very evils they chose to be negatively defined by; being freed would entail the loss of identity. The negative examples provided by these shades should give us the energy to break out of the bonds holding us in this domain of regret and wasted potential, leaving the dead to bury the dead.

As Socrates sees it, he is at a point where he must choose between fleeing from two different kinds of evils: things he knows to be bad and things that he does not know anything about (29b). Most humans also prefer abuse to being ignored. This is in keeping with a thumotic outlook that transforms the old dictum to love friends and hate enemies[69] to a mindset that loves what is familiar and hates what is strange,[70] regardless of the moral content of these acts. When Socrates says that he will not depart from his divinely sanctioned way of life, even if he must face death as a consequence, he is not afraid of changing a familiar way of life. He means rather that he would die spiritually by departing from the role that the *daimon* has revealed to be his essence. He is destined like Odysseus to be constantly erotic, to seek and strive beyond himself, not to be mired by habit in the familiar. If anything, this is not dissimilar to the choice Achilles faced. Were he to leave for "fertile Phthia" he would choose life, but only at the cost of the everlasting fame that his glory-thirsting spirit yearned for. While he would live longer, he would "waste away" and not be Achilles. The name of Achilles would not possess that archetypal quality that it has now.

Socrates has presented his case to the jurors in such a way that they have to condemn either his way of life or their own for corruption. As Callicles saw, the choice to view reality through Socrates' eyes meant living in a world turned upside down.[71] Either they are already living in Hades or Socrates should be sent there. Socrates is fully in agreement with his accusers. As Anytus put it originally, either Socrates should not have been brought to trial or he should be sentenced to death (29c). According to Anytus, now that matters had progressed this far, Socrates' acquittal would make him an irresistible role model for the youth of the city—thus leading to their complete corruption. Anytus's argument is aimed at those in the jury not convinced of Socrates' guilt. He suggests that they were in a situation where they had no choice but to vote for his death. Even if Socrates was not guilty of corrupting the youth before his trial, if spared he would now be so much of a *cause celebre* that the feared corruption would certainly ensue: his way of life would be implicitly ranked over that of the city fathers and disrupt civic order. It would thus seem that Anytus has been corrupted (or blackmailed) by Meletus to the point where he will, as we will see, go on to corrupt the jurors.

By this argument, Anytus seems to have being pushing for the undecided jurors to view condemnation of Socrates as something akin to ostracism: an exclusionary procedure that would violate the individual's rights but turn out to be greatly beneficial to the community. More provocatively, Anytus is also appealing to Socrates to conduct himself like a man who had been ostracized, a challenge that would later be taken up in the *Crito*. Anytus is saying that if Socrates were sincere in not wishing to corrupt the youth, he would see that they would be corrupted by his acquittal. Thus, either Socrates sought to corrupt the youth by his previous conduct, or he does so now by refusing to plead guilty. Either way, he was (or would be) a corrupting influence and had to be eliminated. We're reminded of the dialectical sophistries of *Darkness at Noon*: but any appeal to "bad faith" denies the soul's capacity to rise above institutional truth and sacred lies.

Viewed from this perspective, the aggressive strategy adopted by Socrates seems to only make things easier for those jurors inclined to agree with Anytus. Socrates' explicit allusion to Anytus's sophistic argument revealed the extent to which he refused to pander to those elements of the jury that were receptive to it. It seems as if he is gratuitously shaming these wasps; they are too old to feel the sting of eros and so must content themselves by living as part of a self-righteous swarm of furies. As his speech continues Socrates even sets out to echo Anytus's cynical rejection of any middle ground, implicitly positing that the banal and mimetic morality practiced by the majority of Athenians was ultimately not virtuous but morally corrosive. As we shall see from the *Crito*, Socrates would even be critical of those among his friends who would "talk the talk" but not "walk the walk." Obeying Solon's aforementioned law regarding neutrality in times of regime change, Socrates agreed with Anytus that apathetic neutrality was culpable as far as his trial was concerned. Many present-day readers naturally predisposed to side with Socrates would surely be disturbed by so polemical an exclusion of even the very possibility of an existentially uncommitted middle position here.

Socrates here provides the jury with an example of the manner in which he has hitherto spoken and will continue to use. He will ask his fellow Athenians if they were not ashamed of themselves for caring so much for wealth, reputation and honor while disregarding the values of prudence, truth and spiritual excellence (29d–e). He finds this to be especially disgraceful because Athens is the greatest and best reputed of all cities for wisdom and strength. By speaking these extravagant words of praise to a city still struggling to recover from the humiliating conclusion of the Peloponnesian War, Socrates underlines the fact that he is reproaching the Athenians as a loyal citizen, and not talking as a disembodied philosopher who dwells in the clouds. Even more remarkably, he believes himself to be commanded by Apollo to pursue his mission in Athens; he is a new Orestes, come back for a rematch with the Furies who have taken possession of the Acropolis. Socrates goes on to tell the jurors that he is especially energetic in his pursuit, questioning and chastisement of them, his fellow citizens, since they are closer to him in kin (30a). The truth of this claim is surely established beyond any doubt by the manner in which he continually hectors and exhorts his jury.

In many ways Athens does not seem to have recovered from the "help friends and harm enemies" mentality of the Peloponnesian War. Indeed the tremendous bitterness accumulated over twenty-seven years of incredible expenditure of life and treasure, culminating in siege, starvation and civil war after a humiliating surrender, seems to have created a reservoir of embittered fury that could only be compared to the murderous forces unleashed by Hitler after the Great War and its bitter aftermath. The bellicose honor culture spawned in this context would militate strongly against any admission of guilt or culpability, tending rather to furiously denounce any calling into question of its fundamentally chauvinistic values: deeply

rooted in human nature, fostered by the judgeless jury system, and shamelessly pandered to by Athens's democratic politicians. Yet Socrates is most
irreverent in his fearless exposure and condemnation of these predatory
and materialistic ways of using the past. His contempt for Athenian
"exceptionalism," in contrast to the exemplary virtue that the School of
Hellas should have practiced, is as deliberate as it is dangerous. While the
Athenians feared death in the sense of no longer being the most feared of
the Greek polities, Socrates saw that his city would only survive by making a qualitative jump beyond the tragic ethos. Odysseus, his new paradigm, made a similar leap by becoming more than a crafty pirate and sacker of cities. Instead he became the first man capable of ruling himself and
keeping his promises, to himself and others. By practicing and attaining
self-mastery/temperance, he was the first to refute Helen's hoary old
excuse: "a God made me do it." This model of the human soul would be
the origin of democracy; Odysseus will grant citizenship to his swineherd
and cowherd: former slaves who were yet capable of keeping their word
and ruling themselves.[72] This ethical emphasis also prepared the way for
the birth of Christianity out of the sacrificial confines of Second Temple
Judaism.

Socrates' way of philosophy is clearly political in its very essence. As
he excoriates the materialistic lifestyle that lives along the pleasure-pain
axis, Socrates also rejects the possibility of a sentence that would permit
him to pursue a private contemplative life–something akin to the way
Aristophanes accused him of living in the *Clouds,* or that pursued by
Aristotle when he refused to let Athens sin twice against philosophy.
Seemingly, the virtues that he urges on his conversational partners (prudence, truth and the excellence of the soul) could only be adequately realized in a fraternal setting. While this may have something to do with the
special nature of *his* own mission, the absence of objectively available wisdom necessitates that virtue has to do with thoughtful deeds that bridge the
gap between pure private thought and mindless collective works.

The unique nature of his own mission is further emphasized when
Socrates tells the outraged jury "until the present, no greater good has
come to the city than my service to the god" (30a). This seems to be equivalent to the "true political art" that he alone claims to practice in the
Gorgias. We should distinguish here between Socrates himself, and the
divine task that is being conducted through him. This, presumably, is the
job of going around to persuade people that (a) excellence of soul matters
more than bodies or money and (b) all good things in life–both private and

public–come from virtue. By selflessly performing these tasks, Socrates serves as a public *daimon*, separating good from evil, and soul from body while reminding the Athenians of their spiritual obligations. His point was that philosophy, or at least virtue, lay within the power of all.

But is it yet reasonable for Socrates to tell the Athenians his service to the god is the greatest good they have received? This claim is certainly more tenable in our time than it was in his day, or even in Plato's. By making such an extreme statement to his fellow citizens, this public pest places his mission above the lives of such preeminent Athenians as Solon and Themistocles, individuals who re-founded Athens and saved the city from certain destruction, and mythic figures like Theseus. Since he is a man of seventy addressing living Athenians, perhaps we could take him to mean that he is saying that no one in his lifetime has rendered a comparable service. There is no doubt at all that Socrates considers himself to be better than the poets, but what of the statesmen? Themistocles, we recall, was ostracized just before Socrates was born and the records of men like Pericles and Cimon certainly contain notable blemishes. While Cimon was ostracized for his pro-Spartan sentiments by a group of democrats led by Pericles, the proud imperial policy of the latter was certainly one of the major causes of the Peloponnesian War. Were it not for Socrates, perhaps the short glorious life of Athens would not be remembered any more than the career of Achilles, which, like the *Iliad*, ultimately may have been immortalized by the less glamorous *Odyssey* and the exploits, in speech and deed, of its picaresque hero.

The ultimate basis for this amazing claim seems to be Socrates' examination of those men reputed to be wisest in his time. If we follow his belief that prudence, truth, and the good of the soul matter more than wealth, reputation and honor, the commodities that the politicians and poets have gorged the Athenians on according to the *Gorgias*,[73] then Socrates' words make sense; they are fully consistent with his teachings. Moreover, bearing in mind his position that virtue is the source of "all good things for human beings, both public and private" (30b), Socrates is but the only person who reminds the Athenians of this all-important truth and practices "the true political art" instead of either flattering the *demos* shamelessly or cowing them through superstition and fear. When claiming that his mission is "the greatest good up to now" (30a), Socrates certainly does not rule out the possibility that someone else could render an even greater service in the future. Perhaps this man would be more successful than Socrates in showing the Athenians, and the school of Hellas, their true potential. One such man would be Plato, an exegete inspired by the actions of Socrates.

Socrates now warns the "men of Athens"—his jurors—that he does not fear their anger. It was this very fear that led to the corruption of both the politicians and their leaders; this primal rage was the source of the false wisdom of the politicians, the poets and the artisans. Socrates can resist this angry monster because he is confident that, even if it kills him, "it is not permitted for a better man to be harmed by one worse than he" (30c). He warns the angry jury, employing an expression used by teachers many times since, that, in seeking to do him evil, they will hurt themselves far more than they will harm him. This is a fundamental precept of Socratic teaching: the paradoxical idea that it is worse to do evil than to be victimized by it. It is also the very origin of the classical idea of a soul: a substance that is both capable of knowing itself and justly ruling its body cannot be harmed by the evil of others as long as it is virtuous and true to itself.

Socrates has found that false wisdom causes men to act unjustly–towards themselves and others. This type of folly, moral ignorance, is closely related to the false theosophical wisdom that he gladly renounced all pretensions towards. As noted earlier, this delusory wisdom obscures the simple self-evidence of ethical knowledge; corrupted and deluded men believe that esoteric rituals and sacraments exempt them from the moral imperative to live with virtue and integrity. Ignorance due to corrupt thumotic mores occludes the erotic self-motion of the soul to its *Telos*.

Yet it is easy to see why this teaching concerning the effects of evil should be so difficult to accept as a maxim regulating actual human behavior. Even those who accept Socrates' other fundamental precept that moral ignorance is the cause of evil would find it difficult to entertain the very naïve conclusion that seems to follow from these two principles: the view that it is ignorant to believe that evil can do harm. We must see that Socrates does not say this. Indeed, he has just told us that he "perceived with grief and fear that he was becoming hated" (21e) and that his mission has generated "enmity harsh and heavy to endure" (23a). Yet like Zarathustra, or Odysseus, he is an inverted Achilles: invulnerable only in the heel.[74] Among other things he is pained by his clear-eyed recognition that the performance of evil harms the doer far more than the victim. We see from the *Gorgias* that moral ignorance can lead to the willful performance of evil acts that will grievously damage the soul of the actor and even affect his ability to know himself or see the extent of the psychic damage he has done to himself, injury that exponentially exceeds the material damage that he can inflict on an enemy. While Socrates sees the effects of evil better than others on account of his moral virtue and/or ignorance of the sacred, he does not glory in the suffering of his enemies because he is aware of the damage that a corrupt soul can visit on others.

While investigation of this position would take us too far from our present topic, and has been discussed by me in another book, we must also pay attention to a closely related Socratic idea that moral ignorance leads to false conclusions concerning the identity of our foes. This basic precept of Socratic-Platonic morality, best articulated in dialogues like the *Republic*, suggests that the Athenians do not even recognize who their real enemies are.[75] The obvious inference here is that the *demos*, wallowing in a state of moral ignorance and false wisdom, is its own worst enemy. Penned like sheep within the dark confines of their poetically constructed cave, the citizenry manifestly lack self-knowledge. While we've already noted the tendency to identify the familiar and unfamiliar with friends and enemies, it is also noteworthy that in this pathetic condition, the Athenians could not see the tremendous spiritual wounds that they inflicted on themselves, whilst battling shadows and chasing projections. Accordingly they would denounce, as a corruptive influence and blasphemous enemy, anyone opposed to the practices of catering to the superstitions of their blinded souls or pandering to each whim of their diseased body politic. The Acropolis thus lost the erotic high ground and became a fury-ridden necropolis.

This is why Socrates is convinced that he must appeal to the jury to prevent them from bringing great evil on themselves; by conveniently making him a scapegoat for their evils, they will only worsen the very conditions of corruption and pollution that plague the city. Socrates calls himself a "gift of the gods" (30e), a prophet, sent by Apollo to awaken the Athenians from their spiritual torpor. By choosing to scapegoat him, the Athenians were both acknowledging that there was a problem and stubbornly refusing to deal with the real issues involved. The original "gift of the gods" was granted by Hermes to Odysseus when the latter was setting forth to rescue those of his crew whom Circe–the encircler–had turned to swine or circle-men[76] in the sense of falsely limiting animal natures. It made it possible for him to retain his wits and even survive an expedition into the underground cave of Hades. The same could not be said of his crew. The Trojan War and its aftermath led them to make constant attempts to escape the human condition and regress to a false pre-human state, despite their king's best attempts to drag them back to reality. Zeus killed his last comrades for sinning against the Sun; this suggests another parallel with the cave and *Republic*. Likewise Xenophon reports that Socrates claimed to be the only Athenian to survive the Peloponnesian War and Fall of Athens without losing his integrity.[77] The rest of his generation, like Odysseus's crew, were destroyed by their harrowing ordeal. Yet, just as Odysseus came home to found a new political order for Telemachus and his friends that he himself, like Moses, could not participate in, Socrates gives Plato and his peers insights into virtue and reality that, surviving his execution, will found Western Civilization.

Returning to our text, we note that while there was common agreement that something was rotten within the Athenian polity, a conclusion underscored by the terrible conclusion of the Peloponnesian War and the tyrannical rule of the Thirty, there was great disagreement over what this was and how it could be resolved. Part of the difficulty had to do with the fact that the left and the right, the democrats and the oligarchs, offered very different accounts of the natural condition or healthy regime that had been disrupted by recent events. While the sophisticated intellectuals, commercial interests, and urban poor regarded the era of imperial democracy as the high-water mark of Athenian glory, the more conservative and agrarian elements denounced the demagogic values of urban democracy and looked farther back, with Aristophanes, to the pious traditions of earlier times. Since the two ideals were mutually exclusive, neither faction could impose its nostalgic vision of a virtuous regime on Athens without outraging their adversaries.

These factions had clashed many times during the waning years of the Peloponnesian War. Since the disastrous end of the Sicilian expedition, the oligarchs made violent efforts to radically reform the Athenian democracy. Treasonous acts were commonplace and shameless betrayals of the best interests of the polity occurred frequently as the various factions and opportunists jockeyed for position. The resulting jagged social divisions had very much to do with the catastrophic defeat of the Athenians in 404 and the terrible civil strife that succeeded it. In order to restore the shattered social fabric of Athens, the politicians and populace needed an explanation for the events of the last generation that would enable them to face the future together, and not re-enact the follies of the past. Yet both the democratic and oligarchic factions were both unwilling to accept responsibility for their own errors and well aware that it would be suicidal to directly take the other side on. Indeed, since it fears to reveal its own sacred fury to the light of day or reason, *Thumos* relies on blaming the other for its identity. Thus by default, the impoverished citizenry allowed a volatile combination of demagogic and superstitious practices to rule the daily running of the city. As circuses were cheaper and more profitable than bread, and since man does not live by bread alone, the regime subsisted on a steady–if unhealthy–diet of scapegoats and scandals. Each side needed the other to blame for its own inability to reestablish normalcy and prosperity. As is often the case, the most unscrupulous took the lead in a steadily deteriorating situation where opportunism and apathy marked the conduct of the majority and few sought the common good. Lacking the soul's potential for integrity and resilience, collective bodies, like a demotic mob or oligarchic cabal, are ill-suited for learning. Like Weimar Germany, the restored democracy teemed with old grudges and volatile energies. Here too, demagogues like the democratic politicians of the *Republic* pandered to this beast's every desire.[78]

Such was the prevalent state of affairs in Athens in 399 when Meletus decided to make his reputation in politics by prosecuting Socrates. We have already dealt with his character sufficiently in our prior examination of the *Euthyphro*. It merely remains to be observed that Meletus's accusations that Socrates spread corruption and blasphemy are designed to appeal to both left and right. While the democrats would find Socrates to be a subversive influence, in questioning the idea that inexpert individuals could win the right to preside over affairs of state by virtue of their personal popularity, the oligarchs would profess to be appalled by his blasphemous criticism of traditional religious practice. In other words, Socrates would be presented as an elitist to the left and as a sophist to the right.

In order to maximize his appeal to a large democratic jury, a body composed mostly of ornery older men who lived off their meager juror's stipend, the enterprising Meletus would appeal to the implicit prejudices of the old while explicitly presenting himself as a pious democrat. He would seek to exploit both his own obscurity and Socrates' notoriety. Both sides would believe him to be well disposed towards their interests; the democrats preferring overt evidence to this effect, and the subtler oligarchs choosing to read between the lines. Meletus's indictment would cobble together the most unattractive aspects of Socrates' past reputation as a speculative thinker and interpret them in the light of his present day behavior as an ironic interrogator of those who presumed to be wise or holy. Socrates would accordingly be presented as a nihilistic sophist who found malicious pleasure in spreading moral corruption and religious disbelief through Athens. Meletus had hoped to unite, for half a day, both the oligarchic and democratic factions in their common suspicion and hatred of Socrates, a conveniently enigmatic figure in whom each group could see the traits they most hated in their political adversaries but could not openly attack. This also illustrates how the denizens of the cave battled over shadows.

While Socrates recognizes all too well what Meletus is doing, his strategy of provoking the jury while urging them not to do what is unjust seemed to all to be self-defeating. After all would it not be simpler and more effective for Socrates to defend himself in a manner that would allow his jury to seem magnanimous in its clemency? Doesn't Socrates' hubris play a major role in pushing this sordid scheme of Meletus to a tragic conclusion? However, since Socrates placed the best interests of the Athenians before those his body, he saw well that even if he were to elude the death sentence by accommodating the jury, the larger issues would remain unresolved. The prevailing state of corruption in Athens was such that its true causes had to be identified and attacked without further delay. This was why we have suggested that the previously prudent Socrates saw Meletus's charges, and Euthyphro's interruption, as divine indications that he could no longer hold himself apart from public affairs. Like Achilles he had to reenter the cave wearing, or even flaunting, *his* gift of the gods: the armor of ignorance that made his soul invulnerable. The Athenians had to be awoken from their dogmatic and craven slumbers and explicitly instructed, by both speech and deed, concerning the causes of their malaise.

Socrates compares the polity to a "great and well-born horse" (30e) that has fallen into bad habits of sluggish behavior, presumably the moral laziness caused by its imperial prosperity, "because of its great size" or vast numbers and the democratic way of pandering to its desires and appetites. While the querulous Athenians find his conduct socially disruptive and would rather persist in their corrupt condition of moral apathy, Socrates is obliged by the gods to disrupt this false complacency, even at the cost of his own life. As we saw, although a good many Athenians knew that something was wrong with their polity, they were unwilling to address the real issues involved; this would involve far more social disruption and soul-searching than their shattered post-war nerves could tolerate: they preferred hysterical catharsis. It was far more convenient for the politicians, since their activity seems to consist of maintaining dogmatic slumber through bad poetry, to indefinitely postpone the day of reckoning by using Socrates as a convenient scapegoat.

The subterranean cave regime, most famously described in the *Republic*, shows what happens when endlessly recurring reified images of irrational gods and hubristic heroes are used to seduce the natural desire of the soul for enlightenment. Instead of providing inspiring examples of heroic virtue that slip the surly bonds of earth, the poets tended either to deny the benevolence of the gods or to reject the possibility of transcendence; Euripides and Aristophanes are excellent examples of these reductive attitudes. Likewise, fearing to address the highest possibilities of *Eros*, vain poets and cynical politicians preferred to let this power run backwards and atrophy into blindly self-righteous *Thumos*: anger that mistook pride for justice and viewed ambition as eros.

Even those Athenians who felt that Socrates was correct in his assessment of the prevalent corruption found it convenient to believe that he was irresponsible to precipitously expose the illusions sustaining traditional piety when the common people were unprepared for the onerous burdens of enlightenment. Given their condition, it was considered better for all parties concerned for the dissolute populace to be controlled against their own worst impulses by a democracy stage-managed for the most part by reliable demagogues and cathartic superstition: bread and circuses. In other words, the decadent leaders used the worsening corruption of the many, which was inevitable, given their lack of education, as an excuse to indefinitely defer the introduction of any measures to address this problem. Like many conservatives, they failed to see that justice indefinitely deferred was justice denied. The best Athenians were neither erotic nor introspective; they were self-deprived of both divine grace and mortal self-knowledge.

Those in the know would have been included in a tacit "gentleman's agreement" that they valued their lives and loved their families far more than they believed in the possibility of enlightening the many in the immediate future. This was the code of the cave: life meant more than virtue and family values trumped the common good. Socrates' increasingly overt repudiation of prudent irony exposed the corruption of these gentlemen and excited their furious anger. By not being governed in his actions by selfish criteria, Socrates signifies that one could not subscribe to the virtue by speech alone while being ruled in deed by contrary values of pleasure and pain. Socrates did not believe that the fallen democratic soul could be justified by faith alone!

In his capacity as the gadfly, a robustly winged insect sent by the gods to arouse the thick-skinned horse from its sullen slumbers, and teach it not to fear shadows, Socrates is manifestly negligent of his own welfare and personal interests. By pointing this out to his jurors, he tries to make them see that he is sustained in this unrewarding task by forces that transcend the unhealthy superstition and cynicism pervading the cave. Now, for the first time in the *Apology*, he will speak explicitly about his *daimon*. It is worth repeating here that rather than reasoning in the opposite direction with most other humans and claiming to know the will of god through positive laws, rewards and sanctions, Socrates believes in the divine because of the human capacity to be receptive to intermediary daimonic influence. This leads from the affirmation of human integrity to trust in shared virtues of friendship and liberality, truly political commonwealth, instead of alternating between resentful dependence on angry gods manipulated by order-obsessed oligarchic opportunism and the Dionysian decadence of a demagogic democracy.

Trying to explain to his jurors why he never pursued a public career as a politician, Socrates says that his *daimon* prevented him from doing so. Socrates claims that the corrupt nature of the political process would have led to the loss of his life with little to show for it. This daimonic sign functions like the turning around of the mind in the *Phaedo*; it only turned him away from things but never forward (31d). Again, as we suggested earlier, this means that the *daimon* functioned like an internalized Delphic Oracle in continually reminding him of the impossibility of generating good results through the violent "efficient causality" of politics. Instead of commanding large numbers of people through power and rhetoric, thus relying on the bodily compulsions or direct steering of pleasure and pain, Socrates set out to influence humans with pretensions to wisdom in a subtler way. By individual encounters, he helped his interlocutors to see themselves and assess the implications of their words and deeds according to the spiritual categories of virtue and vice. In effect, Socrates seems to function as a temporary externalized *daimon* for Athens, striving all the time to instill awareness of daimonic forces acting directly on the soul to draw its attention towards virtue and away from vice. These influences, operating through which we could best call "formal causality" work in a way diametrically opposed to the unconscious and/or coercive processes usually governing human behavior. They bring the soul into contact with transcendental sources of power and inspiration that help it to counteract the pessimism and necessity governing the everyday way of the world. Socrates tries to make his interlocutors experience the power of the individual soul undivided against itself to see the ideas. They had to be known not as false images conveyed to the collective body inside the cave, to a collective–hoarse and coarse horse-ness, but as operating on the individuating horses in the soul.

We could view Socrates' *daimon* as the power that allowed him to understand the Delphic Oracle's words in a healthy sense that did not fill him with excessive pride or overwhelm his self-knowledge. It would even be possible to claim that Socrates realized that it was his *daimon*, with its continual reminders of what he could not or should not do, that made him the wisest of men. It is worth noting that his *daimon* never seems to have forbidden him to undertake his pre-Socratic scientific inquiries; rather than deterring thoughtful speculation, its role was seemingly to prohibit rationally unfounded actions as well as to promote continual reflection. In other words, tireless seeking after truth was not forbidden by the *daimon*, only the complacent belief that one actually possessed divine knowledge, rather than reified shadows, was forbidden. The *daimon* thus seemed to interrupt the necessity of habitual processes of "efficient causality" that would have forced Socrates pay homage to the values of pleasure and pain ruling the cave and the body. Its influence also prevented him from entering into thumotic associations with others that would have required that he unquestioningly accommodate himself to their hubristic behavior. His *daimon* is thus like true poetry, which in Auden's Delphic words, "makes nothing happen."[79]

Socrates wants the jury to see that he orients his way of life, and not merely his manner of speech, according to the criteria of virtue and vice–exacting standards that many pay honor to but few obey in practice. He cites as evidence of the efficacy of these values two recent occasions when he defied the powers that be to do what was right, albeit not expedient. On the first such occasion, when presiding over the council, he faced the sacred fury of the demos when they unlawfully tried to cashier a board of victorious generals (32b–c). Later, during the rule of the Thirty, he defied the oligarchs' attempts to implicate him in their misdeeds when he was ordered to arrest Leon of Salamis–a just man (32c–d). On both occasions the persons Socrates tried to protect eventually perished. Like Odysseus, Socrates was only able to call on himself; the son of one of those he failed to convince, Meletus, later accuses him of corruption and impiety.[80] This is why he must cultivate the muses.[81]

These sad illustrations demonstrate the relative impotence of "formal causality" in a public context dominated by thoughtless passions and cynical self-interest. Socrates was lucky to get away with his own life on both occasions. They also suggest that Socrates does not expect to be successful in winning over the jury on this occasion either. He could only hope to prevail in hindsight and secure a moral victory, after the forces of "efficient causality" had secured their pound of flesh. As we seek to recreate the trial of Socrates, it is vital that we should recognize the extent to which even the meaning of this costly moral victory has been obscured by professional moralizing. As suggested before, most of those who piously preach the virtues of Socrates in a classroom would reflexively participate in the academic cashiering of one emulating his practice on their turf. It is this, all-too-easily-broken, connection between ideal and deed that Socrates is vitally interested in preserving and exemplifying—even at the cost of severance from his body.

It seems that Socrates is required by his daimonic destiny to follow a difficult middle course between Scylla and Charybdis here. While he must remove himself from the contagion of a political world governed by corrupt efficient causality, it is equally important that he should not live in solipsistic isolation from the public discourse as a beautiful soul, cowering behind a little wall and only finding satisfaction in saying "I told you so." He must be continually return to the cave to function as a living example of the possibility of living according to standards different from those blindly observed within it. Additionally, if he is truly to show the importance of living a life ruled by virtue, he cannot make his way attractive for the wrong reasons. In other words virtue cannot by definition be chosen for the sake of selfish advantage, whether in this world or the next. This steadfast refusal to offer rhetorical incentive or mimetic knowledge made Socrates a very difficult customer to deal with, as friend or teacher.

Socrates contended that while he was nobody's teacher, in the sense of imparting doctrines, he had never refused to let anyone listen to his words or observe his deeds (33a) and this is precisely how the Platonic dialogue form presents him to us. He suggests that the only pleasure one would receive from keeping his company would be from witnessing the discomfiture of those whose false claims to wisdom were exposed by him (33c). In effect, they would find it "not unpleasant" (32c) to witness the humiliation of notables, while Socrates would garner the blame. Yet, Socrates says that even this derivative pleasure has not caused corruption. This could either mean that those who enjoyed witnessing this activity were either already corrupted or that they profited morally from seeing the illusory nature of the claims to knowledge made by the reputed "best and brightest" of Athens. In other words, part of this enjoyment could very well be cathartic; they would learn that the unjust and ignorant were not happy.[82] The respective ways of living according to virtue and pleasure would clash and Socrates' seemingly "weaker speech" would turn out to be stronger, in the sense of being sustained by the *logos* and not self-destructing, than the windy rhetoric of his overconfident interlocutors. It is self-evident that the enjoyment gained from reading a Platonic dialogue is not sensually derived. The soul is made stronger by the logos of rational speech but it could be seen as weakened in the sense of being cut off from the thumotic reservoir of blind righteousness by being taken out of a collective cave mentality. To the extent that it lacks any innate potential for temperance and integrity, this gross demotic body is qualitatively weaker than the temperate human soul. True virtue inheres in the soul: both family values and nationalism are far too mimetic, they pertain to our animal substrate. The other risk, of cheap moral righteousness unaccompanied by deeds, is what we've tried to guard against by reminding the readers of the *Apology* that they too are accused by Socrates.

For his own part, we must recall Socrates' claims to have been pained and saddened at the profound and widespread moral ignorance (or corruption) revealed by his inquiries, and at the hatred that they excited (21e). After all as we saw, the rich young men who listened in on these conversations were not blamed for the discomfiture suffered by the interrogated one. The peculiar nature of questioning undertaken by Socrates was performed at the god's bequest and not entered into of his own free volition. Had he not been sustained by his *daimon*, Socrates could have suffered from the "burn-out" or melancholia common to those who (like dentists or psychiatrists) practice a disagreeable but necessary task of removing diseased parts of the psyche or body.

In Kantian terms, we can say that Socrates' autonomous virtue had to be its own reward; he could not be sustained by heteronomous pleasure from the sufferings of others without losing all claims to personal integrity. By stripping away all the heteronomous advantages, as Glaucon suggested in Book II of the *Republic*, Socrates is trying to show that he does participate in something that transcends the sensual and egotistic categories that govern the cave, enjoying a higher erotic pleasure of giving that cannot be understood by the effectively two-dimensional or flat-soul categories of the cave and its Cyclopean builders; the Socratic gadfly, like Aristophanes' dung-beetle, has a third dimension of motion: transcendental flight. However, because he must appeal only to their higher impulses, and is speaking far more for their sake than his own, everything depends on the desire of the jurors to believe in categories that go against the blind opportunism most of them have followed for most of their lives. For his own part, and for the sake of his jurors, Socrates has refused to fool some of the demos for even some of the time.

It is for this reason also that Socrates refuses to emulate the customary practice of weeping before the jury and bringing in his children and family to make emotional appeals on his behalf. If he is to be acquitted, it should only be for reasons that have to do with justice; otherwise, by pandering to the vanity of his jurors, Socrates' practice would discredit the very ideals that he has defended in speech. Socrates recognizes that this very refusal to follow convention would offend those too afraid to go against mimetic necessity; by acting in this manner he would implicitly claim to be superior to those not courageous enough to set a better precedent. He defends this behavior as stemming not merely from a dedication to virtue but also from his concern for honor: his own, his fellow Athenians' and indeed that of the city itself. Certain values have a significance that quite transcends the narrowly construed bounds of personal convenience and tribal pride.

Instead of joining the chorus of old men stubbornly chanting that their sovereign polis could do no wrong, Socrates will remind his fellow citizens (after the manner we discussed when considering the *Euthyphro*) of the human capacity to learn from mistakes of the past and redeem the reputation of Athens. Chauvinistic apologists who acted out of a misplaced sense of loyalty to the dead letter of the law would do their polity very little good over the long run. By refusing to rectify the obviously unjust practices of their forefathers, they would only corrupt the youth and alienate the gods who would surely resent their names being used in vain and represented in so blasphemous a manner: as predators or pirates who reap where they do not sow. These views have nothing to do with the Hyper-Uranian or transcendent gods Socrates believed in.

While a mistake is the result of ignorance, it could spawn evil when men deliberately set out to enslave the potential of the future out of a pusillanimously professed loyalty to the dead past in plain sight of the truth. In effect, we only end up blackmailing the past if we demand a mimetic basis for a life of thoughtless piety; by blindly viewing hoary deeds of a morally dubious quality as sacred, we cower under the armpits of knaves instead of standing on the shoulders of giants. Socrates is maintaining that justice cannot be apprehended through blindly following precedent. Sheep-like reliance on custom diverts men from the responsibility of striving towards thoughtful recognition and embodied practice of self-evident obligations governing virtue and piety. The fear of social death is quite as powerful as the fear of literal death. The honor/shame axis to this extent is not much of an advance over the categories of pleasure and pain. Socrates' heroic life continually braved the fear of social death, by ostracide as it were.

Socrates' need to continually restate the importance of living by the ethical criteria of virtue and vice reveals the extent to which the moral climate of Athens was ruled by pleasure and pain. To him the question dividing the right and left, whether these bodily categories should serve superstition or hedonism, was quite irrelevant. Socrates refused to arrive at any accommodation with the jury that would compromise the ideal of justice; he only seeks what is best for the whole: the Common Good, not what is most convenient for all parties involved. Instead of agreeing to a settlement based on a mutual hypocrisy and a shared belief in bodily comfort, he preferred to ensure that the jury explicitly understood the selfish and materialistic values that dominated Athens; it was largely to this revelatory end that he directed his defense.

Socrates also had to show that it was possible to live and die in obedience to the criteria of virtue and vice, sadly compromised words that others only used to advance their bodily compulsions and thumotic thirsts. This is why he is willing to trust in the good and allow the fate of his body to be determined by the lofty ideals ruling his soul. Socrates claims to believe in divine things and he goes on to declare that none of his opponents has genuine belief (35d). Only an impious man will use religion for selfish advantage, believe that gods can be bribed, or hold that the interests of gods and men are naturally opposed to each other. As deployed by self-serving hypocrites like Meletus and Anytus, words like justice and piety were just distorted shadows of the divine verities. In the care and protection of Socrates' opponents, these sublime concepts were blithely deployed to win friends and influence gods by persons utterly oblivious to what they truly were about. Though the *Republic* suggests that the ideas were like artifacts carried behind the prisoners to make shadows in the cave, we could also say that the true ideas were imprisoned and falsely represented by images used by poets and politicians to seduce the innate human desire for transcendence. Here, where piety denies virtue and betrays justice, everything is spelled backwards until the soul is turned around. It is provocative but not inaccurate to say that Socrates tries to ransom and liberate these ideals from their chthonic exile by his heroic conduct on this occasion. As we saw in our study of the *Euthyphro*, he has Daedalus's power to put these images in motion,

boldly calling them out of their graven slumber in whitewashed sepul-
chers.

The furies represent the wasted spiritual potential of dead souls, living
on–like parasitic zombies–in the bodies of their descendants. The waste is
inevitable since the souls in question are not self-ruled but are impelled by
ancient resentments, blind loyalties and sacred psychic forces. If this cur-
dled resentment is not to poison the next generation it must be directed out-
wards, not by external wars as Athena advised in the *Eumenides*, itself a
variation on how her bloody Odysseus is told to go abroad at the end of the
Odyssey,[83] but forced right out of the civic soul. Since they can never
reveal the true source of their power, the tribal furies need to continually
feed on blame. But the primal hatred that pits factions against each other
in a dance of death can only go so far without employing a centripetal
scapegoat to save these self-righteous chthonic forces from attaining self-
knowledge by destroying each other. This is why they need a common
scapegoat, a perfect insider and outsider, both king and beggar like
Odysseus, on whom they can focus their common rage.[84] Socrates, who
acts as King Archon in the *Euthyphro*, was supposed to play this role in the
Apology. Instead he is inspired by Apollo to combine reason with revelation, brave this furious chorus or energy, and demand that both soul and
polity realize their true erotic potential. By exposing these blind hectoring
forces to reason's light he, like Achilles, atones for the death of his father's
glory, *patro-kleos*; he slays Hector, the hectoring furies of Athens in this
case, and avenges Patroclus. Once this is done Socrates does not fear the
living forces of the Underworld; he can go to his death in an exemplary
way. As we will see in the *Crito*, news of his death will come to him from
the sea, in its gentlest form.[85]

IV. The Gifts of the Gadfly

When the jury finds Socrates guilty by a surprisingly slim majority, a result
that he attributes to the presence of Anytus and the shadowy Lycon as
cosponsors of the indictment (36a), the sentencing stage of the trial com-
mences. Meletus proposes the death penalty and it is up to Socrates to suggest an alternative to the jury. We suggested quite a bit earlier that Meletus
was trying to take Socrates on in a game of "chicken" and he acts very
much in this spirit. Despite all Socrates has said, the younger man believes
that he, like all men, is ruled by the fear of death. By asking for the death
sentence Meletus dares Socrates to come up with a counter-proposal of

exile; considering the slim majority that voted "guilty" this alternative would had a strong likelihood of gaining the assent of the jury. Further, by having Socrates offer to go into exile, Meletus will have forced the older man to swallow his earlier boast that he would not desert the post he had been ordered to defend by the gods.

By making Socrates effectively reveal himself as a hypocrite, Meletus would gain kudos from both left and right. While upholding the supremacy of public opinion and political theology, he would also complete the work of Aristophanes and show the Athenians that the philosopher's actions were ultimately governed by the very self-interest he had publicly scorned and ridiculed that very day. However impressive the ideals he defended were, Socrates would have to concede that human beings were governed by bodily exigencies; they all had to grovel before the irrational but compelling power of public opinion and traditional piety. This shared awareness of personal hypocrisy also bound citizens together; it restrained the more reckless among them from idealistic excesses that only spread disorder and angered the powers-that-be, both divine and human.

If Meletus were to see that it was possible for a man to not be dominated by the fear of death and other bodily necessities, his entire case would collapse and the theoretical basis of Athenian radical democracy would perish with it. Once divested of all the rhetoric surrounding it, the foundation of the rule of the many is the supposedly self-evident belief that all citizens were equal. This principle is derived from the truism that all men must bow down before the irresistible power exerted by desire and fear in both the city and the soul. By exposing the power of *ananke* Thucydides' account of the Peloponnesian War dethroned the old heroic ethic and gave both the few and the many new evidence for their respective positions. While the few could claim that the War showed the need for order, however arbitrarily created, the many would see little difference between the best and the least of men with regard to how they coped with the fear of death. If it were shown that some were superior to these seemingly invincible powers, a great divide opens between those who are irreducible to death-fearing bodies and those who are not.

The oligarchic difference between the *aner* and the *anthropos*, the gentleman and the generic man, was based largely on birth and material endowments. It would pale before the new distinction that Socrates would have us draw, placing the temperate human being on one side and both the mimetic gentleman and natural slave on the other; this new order of rank would be based on the criteria of virtue and spiritual autonomy. While

Socrates would be the first to insist that all humans have the requisite *capacity* for temperance, this position visits contempt on all, whether rich or poor, who are ruled by the fear of death. Traditional and reverent ways of appeasing the insatiable powers of fear and desire are hardly consistent with the Socratic attitude of superiority that the soul assumes towards the body and the powers of desire. Such a man would look like Tiresias in Hades: the only person possessed of wits in a *demos* of gibbering shades.

It is because he cannot even begin to grasp these possibilities that Meletus is committed to the belief that Socrates, like the eponymous character of the *Clouds*, will back down from his uncompromising position and choose some way of escaping death. He cannot believe that Socrates is not like other men. Were he better aware of what his professed enemy was all about, an insight that even many friends of Socrates were not capable of, Meletus would surely have chosen not to propose the death penalty. By denying Socrates the possibility of a swift death and probable martyrdom, Meletus would have visited a far worse fate on his adversary. If he had demanded that Socrates go into exile, Meletus would have been far more successful in destroying the mystique and reputation of his aging adversary while enhancing his own prestige with Socrates' powerful enemies and gaining a reputation for magnanimity with the philosopher's wealthy friends. Socrates had feared having to become Euthyphro's student; it would be even worse to acknowledge Meletus as his benefactor. Once uprooted from Athens, and no longer able to lead his accustomed way of life, Socrates' earthly tenure would almost certainly have concluded under less than dignified circumstances. Outside of Attica, he would have been like one of those shades in Hades, a comic shadow of his former self, consumed by regrets. Only through an appropriately heroic conclusion to his life would Socrates have been able to leave a lasting impression on the Athenians.

This was probably one of the reasons why Socrates chose to goad Meletus into asking the seemingly harsher penalty of death. Socrates' own counter-proposal can best be understood as deriving from this same line of thought. Here again, Socrates is both ironic and scrupulously honest in proposing the penalty most appropriate to the crime he was convicted of. From the standpoint of the future of philosophy in Athens, there was only one penalty worse than exile and so Socrates proposes it, knowing full well that Meletus and the jurors would not understand the implications of what he suggests. Gorgias famously recommended that one should fight laughter with seriousness and seriousness with laughter.[86] Since Socrates has clearly turned the tables on Meletus and transformed the comic scene of his humiliation into the grand tragedy of Athens, it is up to his accuser to reverse the genre again and exploit the comic potentiality of Socrates' situation. But instead of doing this directly, by proposing exile Meletus tries to be too clever and, believing that his enemy has no alternative, left it up to him to beg the court for mercy. Socrates, who had employed "rope-a-dope" tactics throughout his career as Apollo's gadfly, is prompt to use the opening. Socrates has just quoted Achilles' dismissal of Thetis' warning that his death would follow that of Hector (28c) Now, like Achilles slaying Hector/himself through a weakness in his own former armor,[87] and thus seemingly sealing his own fate, Socrates attacks his only hope of bodily survival and saves his soul from the possibility of comic dishonor.

When Socrates proposes that his punishment should be appropriate to his worth (38a), this also suggests that his poverty made it impossible for the Athenians to levy financial penalties on him. In a way this very poverty, both monetary and intellectual, has enabled him to be freely critical of the activities of those who valued honors and property over the common good and the soul; in this sense it is the equivalent of Achilles' new armor (as opposed to Socrates' original armor of ignorance which made him invulnerable to his old accusers). While he has overcome war and poverty with every appearance of self-sufficiency, he may not be able to fight the insidious influences of material comfort and social security with similar aplomb–especially since he now has young children to take care of. In other words, while it was easy for Socrates to be critical of what he did not have, the morally corrosive challenges faced by one possessing power, wealth, and privilege were of an entirely different nature.

The suggestion is that were he in possession of the honors and security that others spent all their lives striving after, it would be much harder to keep the admiration of those who had previously looked up to him for his independence and virtue. Once virtue could be seen as leading to privileges, it would be harder to defend as its own reward. Now he would be seen as one who, all along, subsisted by dishonorably and suspiciously sponging off his rich friends, thus suggesting that Aristophanes had not been far off the mark, instead of leading the truly self-sufficient life that he urged on others in very difficult economic times. A religious devotee, who seeks to perform acts of charity for the sake of heavenly rewards, cannot be held virtuous when his actions are tangibly rewarded on earth. Likewise, the exemplary presence that Socrates maintained in Athens depended very much on its not being materially rewarded. Thus Socrates saw that he should never act as if he were assured that pleasures and honors would necessarily accrue from his striving to live a life of virtue. Though worthy of his hire, the day laborer can never expect permanent employment. He only knows his power to live simply and seize the day; he is invulnerable in both heel and soul by not having given hostages to fortune.

This would seem to be the subtler reason underlying Socrates' outrageous recommendation that the Athenians would punish him most effectively by treating him as a public benefactor and granting him free meals at the *Prytaneum* (37a). Socrates as always is offering his opponent the best possible hold; somebody more intelligent than Meletus or Anytus would recognize that their enemy's prestige would wither away in a situation that would inevitably attract much public ridicule and resentment. By comparing him to public benefactors, generals and the kin of its greatest heroes, the Athenians would reduce Socrates to a caricature or shadow of itself. More importantly, Socrates himself would be hard-pressed to maintain his accustomed lifestyle as an ironic social critic in a situation where the effects of old age and unaccustomed prosperity would be likely to corrupt his body through insidiously comic means.

In other words, when Aristophanes symbolically burnt down Socrates' house in the *Clouds*,[88] he drove him out the security of his *oikos* and into the public space to plague the poets and politicians; it is as though Hector forced Achilles to come out of his tent by burning the wall protecting his ships. Now that his cover was blown, he only became more dangerous to the wise. This wholly unintended effect had to be reversed by uprooting the philosopher from his natural habitat in the *agora*, and then kicking him upstairs into the Civic Pantheon. It is hard to maintain the appearance of personal integrity when one is effectively reified by being elevated to a position of undeserved privilege. A man of reason cannot ignore the political priority of appearance over reality; justice must not only be done, it must appear to be done. This is all but impossible for a public figure but very difficult even for a private citizen.

Although Socrates' ironic recommendation clearly has little to do with what the Athenians were likely to do, it sets forth his realistic appraisal of the fate of his divinely appointed mission. Socrates knew full well that he could not afford to lose his ironic distance from the processes of efficient causality that characterized the daily activity of Athenian politics. As he recalled, the two occasions when he was vested with political power also endangered his mission. By killing him, the Athenians would inadvertently lodge him permanently in the Prytaneum in a manner that would render him invulnerable to the corrosive effects of comedy. After his death he would no longer be susceptible to even the appearance of being corruptible by desire and fear; Socrates would be always be celebrated as one who chose virtue over vice all the days of his life. Perhaps this was why Solon said that one should call no man happy when he was alive.[89] By audaciously daring Meletus to throw him into the briar patch Socrates made quite sure that he would not be exposed to the only powers that could corrode his daimonic legacy. Like Brer Rabbit, who was born and bred in the briar patch, Socrates has spent all of his life preparing for death and will not be deterred from following the course of his destiny.

It is only after Socrates tells the Athenians what they ought to have done that he formally offers to pay a fine. He agrees to do this because he does not attach any value to money; he does not deem himself worthy of anything bad. He will merely render unto Caesar the things that are Caesar's without making any acknowledgment of the legitimacy of the rule of money. In other words, making a real sacrifice of something that he truly valued would imply that he was at fault (38a–b). Socrates does not believe in divine retribution and sacrifice because he does not feel that the true interests of gods and men are at variance with each other; he does not subscribe to the adversarial theology that is set forth in the *Euthyphro*. Accordingly, after first proposing a nominal amount of one mina, all that he could afford, he very publicly allows Plato, Crito and several of his other friends to guarantee the more substantial amount of thirty minae (38b).

It is very possible that if he had not made his earlier intentionally outrageous suggestion this counter-offer would have been quite acceptable to the jury. However it would not suit Socrates' purposes for the two proposals to be made separately. If Socrates had only asked to be given his meals at the Prytaneum he would have forced the jurors to kill him, thus placing his fear of exile and prospects for posthumous glory above his divine obligation to educate the Athenians without compromising his honor. Yet if Socrates had simply proposed the penalty of thirty minae, the Athenians would have seen this result as a moral defeat for him. As it is, by agreeing to accept the fine, they would tacitly allow Socrates to continue viewing himself as worthy of being placed amongst the great heroes and benefactors of Athens. Indeed the substantial fine, about nine years wages for a craftsman,[90] would cover the cost of providing Socrates with free meals at the Prytaneum for the rest of his life. Though paying his fine, his friends would instead seem be to covering the cost of turning him into a public institution, as the man unafraid of death, without Socrates getting anything from it. This would seem to preserve both his honor and his life.

At the very least, by linking the fine to his ironic (and non-irenic) preference to be honored at the Prytaneum, Socrates makes it clear that paying the money, which would not come out of his own pocket, frees him to continue his accustomed lifestyle with the implicit blessing of the court. This is underlined by his explicit refusal to go into exile or pursue a silent unexamined life of internal exile or house arrest in exchange for his liberty. Socrates' celebrated statement that an unexamined life is not worth living for a human being (38a) further emphasizes the crucial qualitative distinction between the genuine human and the generic humanoid animal that we have observed earlier. He will not live out the rest of his life as an *anthropos*; this would disgrace his previous life and bring discredit to the god who ordered him to undertake this mission. To paraphrase Mill, Socrates would be dissatisfied with having to live as a pig. We should also note the implicit suggestion that the examined life could not be led outside the city.

Socrates refuses to do anything to discredit the idea that making speeches and conducting examinations about virtue and the other things that he discusses is "a very great good for a human being" (38a). *Logos* is placed above and against both silent anger and prejudiced speech. He recognizes that the supreme difficulty of convincing other men that this idea is worth dying for, not just in theory but in practice, will almost inevitably lead to his being sentenced to die. Instead of trying to convince his jurors to spare him so that he could continue to teach them verbally that virtue is more important than death, Socrates will teach by rare example, by using his willingness to die as the ultimate proof of his belief that virtue and rational speech are not merely possible but also sustained by and consistent with the structure of the cosmos itself. By contrast, the outlook of his opponents presupposes belief in chaos, unjust gods and an incorrigibly flawed soul. Yet there is something about speech itself that will not allow them to make these shameful admissions.

By clarifying the issues facing them so well, he has at least ensured that the jurors will not come to a decision for the wrong reasons, or least for lack of information. He has made their actions deliberate and to this extent has made the few fewer and better and the many, more and worse. They will sentence him to die not out of irrational anger, as a horse would swat a tiresome gadfly, but only after understanding the full gravity of the issues involved. According to the way Socrates has distinguished between their lifestyles and his, if the jurors permit him to live they would implicitly concede that their own unexamined lives, along with those lived by their ancestors, were worthless. They could also no longer participate vicariously in the deeds of the greatest Athenians if they accepted, however tacitly, Socrates' hubristic challenge to their unexamined ways of dogmatic slumber. They realize that he's challenging them to be true men.

This is why the number of jurors who condemn him to die is larger than the earlier majority that found him guilty. Had Socrates not spoken a word in his own defense it is quite probable that he would not have been found guilty at all. Indeed Anytus's view, that Socrates either should not have been brought to trial at all or that he had to be executed (29c), suggest that Anytus and Lycon only added their names to the indictment when Socrates (perhaps through Euthyphro's serendipitous intervention) did not allow the original charge preferred by Meletus to be quashed. This contagious righteousness seems to have been something that grew through apathy. Many jurors would not have understood the primal fury that possessed them, but this ignorance would hardly have inhibited them from voting for Socrates' execution.

The contemptuous composure with which Socrates addresses the large number of jurors who voted for his death suggests that he believed their conduct to be largely motivated by fear. Were they to vote for Socrates' release, they would almost certainly understand themselves to be simultaneously endorsing his position of pious agnosticism concerning the gods and gentle contempt for established Athenian religious practice. Many other jurors, while privately agreeing with Socrates' criticism of popular religion, would have yet been scandalized by his publicly expressed belief that true knowledge of the gods was not available. In other words, while they would have conceded that he did not blaspheme, they would have found him guilty of corrupting the youth by leaving them with nothing to take the place of their discredited religious rituals. Others, who believed that the gods were jealous and capricious, would have been infuriated by Socrates' public mockery of their beliefs. A third faction that included many of the most intelligent jurors, those who would have realized that nothing he said was either blasphemous or corrupting, would have voted for execution because Socrates' very existence was a continual reminder that they themselves were hypocrites.

We must also bear in mind that Anytus had gained some public notoriety for jury tampering. In the fall of 410, about ten years before the trial of Socrates, an Athenian fleet of thirty ships commanded by Anytus had failed to relieve the Spartan naval barricade on the vital strategic fort of Pylos. As a result, the Spartans took Pylos, Athens's most precious bargaining chip, later that winter. Tried for treason, Anytus would probably have been convicted had he not "corrupted" the jurors. While we are not told how precisely this transaction was arranged, Aristotle's *Constitution of the Athenians* describes this event as the first time a public figure exerted undue influence over an Athenian jury.[91] The precise word used by Aristotle, "*Dekazein*," suggests bribery of a group of jurors but greater precision concerning these murky events is not possible. Nevertheless, it is not irrelevant to note that the jury largely comprised of impoverished pensioners that convicted Socrates and sentenced him to death was possibly a good deal more susceptible to material incentive than their victim. The thirty minae that Plato, Crito and the others were willing to spend on Socrates' behalf would have been amply sufficient to pay off thirty jurors and reverse the result of the trial. We might speculate that Plato does not refer explicitly or otherwise to Anytus's prior record because he is more interested in his readers' responses to Socrates. In other words, it would be easy to blame Anytus for the unjust verdict but this would allow the casual reader to avoid acknowledging that the personal challenge and accusation posed by Socrates' stinging words might well have led him to vote along with the majority of the jurors.

Once the jury has decided that he should die, Socrates makes some informal remarks to them before he is taken away to prison. He chides those who voted for his execution that for the sake of a little time, they brought upon themselves and the city the ignominious reputation of having unjustly killed a wise man (38c). These jurors have ensured that Socrates will always be remembered as a wise man though neither he nor they believe this to be the case. Paradoxically, it will also be much easier for the Athenians themselves to celebrate Socrates' wisdom after he is gone. Diogenes Laertes tells us that the Athenians soon repented and banishing the other accusers, put Meletus to death.[92] He says also that they erected a bronze statue of Socrates in the hall of processions, the very place where the embroidered robe of Athena was carried.[93]

Of course a bronze Socrates will grace the "School of Athens" far better than the brazen living gadfly ever could. Now that he is gone, Socrates' ironic words no longer had to be taken personally and praised hypocritically. Thus the great foe of dogma becomes a reified and no-longer-threatening symbol of truth. While we shall reflect further on the implications of this state of affairs later, we cannot refrain from recognizing that for the majority of people the only good truth is dead certainty. Living truth is too illusive, and makes too many outrageous demands on man; it cannot be grafted on to the community values and traditions that govern life in any cave.

Returning to Socrates' last words to the whole jury, we must now pon der the significance of his paradoxical statement that it is easier to evade death than it is to avoid wickedness (39a). This is because wickedness runs faster than death. Since it is impossible for any mortal to avoid death in the end, Socrates must mean that we can only become wicked before we are captured by death; after we die, our physical disintegration ensures that we cannot become subject to moral corruption. This suggests that the body is both the principle of individuation and the precondition for progress in virtue or vice. While death is inevitable, immunity from wickedness or moral corruption, while not impossible to avoid, can never be guaranteed as long as we are alive. This could well be because death can protect us from the constant threat of moral degeneration. But this does not mean that virtue consists only in avoiding vice. Socrates' attack on the idea that we can possess wisdom or virtue, which turn out to be objects of action rather than knowledge, verbs rather than nouns, means that our lives must be devoted to cultivating our souls; the longer we live without practicing virtue, the more likely we are to become morally corrupted through imitating others and obsessively avoiding death. As we have seen, collective banality sooner or later becomes evil. Conversely, though actively avoiding evil by virtue can make us more vulnerable to death, it protects us against the insidious processes of moral corruption. It follows that life should never be seen as an end in itself. We die as humans when we devote our lives to fleeing death. Fleeing vice instead of fighting it only makes one a hypocrite, a short step away from wickedness. It is as if injustice scents fear; it only pursues those who flee death. Nor does avidly battling external evil make us good; it is a self-indulgent way of neglecting to order one's soul in a context that makes us more susceptible to the contagion of evil. The idea that one has unlimited license from the gods to fight evil with evil is a diabolical temptation, a plenary indulgence from Hell

Given the scenario Socrates has set up, it seems that while death starts from behind us, injustice runs towards us. This suggests that one's destined course is to confront injustice and lead a short glorious life. But life in the cave has us facing the wrong direction: fighting with illusory shadows we do not see their evil source. Thus we live "fearing our own shadows" and denying our soul as we fight beside wickedness to avoid death. We can

become involved with those who make shadows and thus become predators rather than potential victims. This strategy brings with it a host of
other evils. While few seek evil for its own sake, many perform morally
corrosive bad deeds to save face and avert death; the worse the state of a
man's conscience, the more likely he is to seek self-forgetfulness in life
while trying desperately to defer the posthumous judgment awaiting him.
By contrast, Socrates' *metanoia* leads him to go back and take on injustice
instead of believing he can outrun mortality. The old Hoplite will not disgrace himself and jeopardize his fellow citizens by jettisoning his impregnable shield, his soul, and thinking only of his own body. Breaking the
shield wall puts every other Hoplite's life at risk. The cave is not a shield
wall. It is an underworld built by poets to sustain an illusion of vicarious
virtue for warriors without shields. It shields limp spearmen with mighty
battle cries from reality.

This wisdom of tragedy echoes the famous choice of Achilles, who
opted for honor and rejected the comic alternative of a life stained with dishonor and ridicule. As Socrates quoted him earlier, Achilles said, "May I
die immediately after punishing the doer of injustice so I do not linger
here, laughed at beside the ships and live as a burden on the land" (28d).
While Achilles is so consumed with grief and rage that he cares little for
the effect his actions will have on others, Socrates' behavior is ruled by his
interiorized sense of shame, his conscience, and his desire to defeat
Aristophanes' power of comic ridicule. The only significant addition
Socrates makes to this paraphrase of a somewhat longer passage is the
word "*katagelasto*" which means "made to look ridiculous." In other
words, Socrates would be a fit subject for men like Thersites or
Aristophanes if he chose to live shamelessly and at any cost. It is irrelevant
whether this shamelessness would be expressed by his way of living or fear
of dying.

Socrates seems to be saying that a life spent running away from pain,
pursuing pleasure and generally following the dictates of the body would
soon gain a deserved reputation for wickedness. He clearly means to
include both hedonism and spiritual materialism under this category. Both
of these seemingly disparate positions obey the dictates of the body; hedonism does so explicitly while spiritual materialism impiously understands
divine and otherworldly things according to this-worldly hedonist values of
pleasure and pain. Both paths lead to spiritual corruption; the question of
whether the starting point is moral sloth disguised as piety or explicit self-
indulgence becomes ultimately irrelevant. Differently put, while some

Athenians implicitly embraced wickedness through their hedonism, others made fleeing death their highest priority and so succumbed to wickedness. Neither faction embraced wickedness for itself, but neglect of the obligation to live virtuously led inexorably, albeit insidiously, to vice. This commonality is best proved by their deeds. Precisely because they hated each other, the demotic and oligarchic elements coalesced to kill the one man in the cave or underworld who recognized like Tiresias that both factions were ruled *au fond* by the same selfish values of their enemies. Yet, as Socrates points out prophetically, the angry Athenians only accelerated their own moral degeneration by killing him. Taking the batteries out of a smoke detector does not ensure that one's house is made fireproof! Because of his commitment to the Logos–a rational proportion between the soul, the body and the cosmos–Socrates' position is that the soul can and must take command of the body. This governance is another instance of the true political art: it requires far more than mindless habit and thoughtless volition. It is only when the soul lives apart from the desires of the body that it becomes exposed to forms of corruption that inevitably harm both soul and body.

Socrates now openly tells the jurors that he knew how to secure his acquittal but refused to pander to them (38d). The shamelessly sentimental practices that were expected at this stage of his trial would have been unworthy of him and truly deserving of punishment. In his awareness of the moral law, Socrates does not dare to say or do anything that would unjustly secure his release. This very self-possession as he approaches his death, and openly takes complete command of his body, leads Socrates to see things that are normally concealed from man by the fears and desires of the body (38c). Just as Patroclus and Hector predicted the imminent deaths of their slayers, Socrates tells the jury that they have unwittingly exposed themselves to fiercer forces of justice.

The Athenians hoped that by silencing Socrates they would deter others from questioning them. But Socrates warns them that their behavior towards him will only provoke many younger and angrier young men (39d), voices that he could no longer restrain, as Odysseus could no longer protect his bag of winds from his crew through his sweet sleep,[94] from being critical of the Athenians in a far more explicit manner. Just as murder only feeds the wrath of the Furies, the jurors cannot escape responsibility for their shortcomings by lashing out at him or identifying corrupt vices as sacred ancestral practices. As he told Meletus, Socrates believes in rehabilitation by education, not in self-righteous retribution. This is consistent with his claim that the Athenians could only ward off future criticism by equipping themselves to be as good as possible (39d).

A strategy of striving collectively towards excellence, relying on eros rather than thumos, rather than employing a repressive policy of mimetic restraint, would seem to be how Socrates would protect the young from moral corruption. By emphasizing the importance of the Athenians "equipping themselves" to be as good as possible, rather than by angrily proclaiming that they are best, Socrates is emphasizing the value of individual forethought and deliberation in the pursuit of excellence. This position is consistent with his implicit suggestion that instead of proclaiming their superiority on falsely autochthonous grounds, the Athenians would have done better to judge themselves by universal transcendental standards. By restraining their citizens in the cave in mimetic bonds of fear and sanctified custom, the Athenians did themselves great harm.

By reproaching the majority of jurors for their lack of nobility in deliberation, Socrates draws their attention to the debilitating effects of moral sloth. As we have seen, he has tried in as conscientious a manner as possible to educate the jurors as to the larger implications of his trial. This approach involved exposing skeletons and raising issues that would have prejudiced many jurors against him. Now that he has "equipped" the incorrigible jurors with all they can learn from him, Socrates is released from the unpleasant responsibility of having to address them any further. He can do no more for them. Foreshadowing his relief at soon being before divine judges in the next world, he is now free to speak to those jurors who conducted themselves in a manner befitting their responsibility as upholders of the laws and address them as judges (40a). In other words, now that he has dealt fairly with the *anthropoi*, he can speak to the *andres*.

We have noted earlier that this crucial distinction between those who are potentially human and those who have actualized this capacity threatened the democratic assumption that all men, and their desires, were equal: either in their impotence before divine power or before death. By publicly sharing confidences with these men, in the presence of their inferiors, Socrates stresses that the difference between the types is not an esoteric doctrine that has to do with possession or absence of privileged information. Rather, it has to do with the manner in which this material is apprehended and held in the soul. It is only with these people that he can speak through myths, poetic language that *hoi polloi* would misjudge by applying the flat-footed standards of literal truth and falsity. While underscoring that all that Socrates has previously said is literally true, indeed this is why

Plato uncharacteristically volunteers that he was present as a witness and guarantor of Socrates' reliability, the distinction also suggests that Socrates is now about to say things that can be misinterpreted.

In other words, while Plato chose to share Socrates' *Apology* with all who could understand ordinary language, we are urged to remember that Socrates' final words, as well as those spoken in the *Phaedo*, can only be adequately understood by those existentially committed to emulating him. The true judges proved their worth by voting against their chthonic inclinations and prejudices; similarly, worthy readers of the *Apology* can distinguish in a like manner between the literal "cash-value" of the dubious metaphysical claims Socrates seems to make here and their metaphorically signified meaning. Neither the confirmed cynic who denies the erotic generosity of philosophy, nor the credulous picture thinker who seeks a secret stairway to heaven, can follow him any further. It is also noteworthy that we are not dealing with a perfect text here. Such a work presupposes a god-like author and a godless world. By contrast, an inspired Platonic work is as feminine as the human soul. Always vulnerable and always fertile, it seems to reflect the subtle dialectical separation between the powers of rational exegesis and poetic revelation.

While the skeptical reader will see Socrates' reference to his *daimon* here as a clear sign to the initiated atheist that this voice was a convenient fabrication, others with different spiritual natures would regard it as an admission that the *daimon* permitted Socrates to hold nothing back on this momentous occasion. Socrates was permitted to dispense with his characteristic mask of irony that prevented him from seeing himself fully. This is why we said earlier that Socrates completely understands the story of his life only now as he addresses the Athenian jury. This could be compared to Odysseus's moving self-disclosure as he tells his story to the Phaeacian court; on this occasion the hero wept as a woman (or soul) being dragged away from the body of her dead husband.[95] Like Odysseus, who on this occasion forsook the customary opacity that had previously led him to call himself *outis* or nobody,[96] a statement not inconsistent with Socrates' claim to know nothing and not to be ruled by his body, Socrates is inspired to discover himself; his mind/soul is now fully present in the cave before its body.

Returning to the *daimon*, careful readers would also recognize that while Socrates has learned to heed this uncanny sign, he does not draw any other unwarranted metaphysical conclusions as to its nature or essence. He knows that he does not know anything about what it is in itself, only that it is and that it has moral authority over him. Accordingly, this ambiguous reference to the *daimon* underscores the way we should read the remainder of the *Apology*; while Socrates has been permitted to practice poetry, we should recall that he is not setting out to provide us with knowledge that he himself manifestly and proudly lacks. He is merely talking about his hopes and feelings to men who have shown some appreciation of what he is about. These simple words contrast strikingly to the melodramatic surface doctrines of the *Phaedo*.

Socrates knows what it is to live as a human being. He does not know what death is; he is wonderfully free of illusions concerning this condition. Indeed, it is this not being weighed down by illusions and false dogmas that frees him to practice virtue. Also, as we have seen, he is far more distressed by the state of "living death" endured by those human beings dwelling in the cave. They fear death because they have never really lived or known themselves. Having been absent from themselves all of their lives, "absentees" in Sartre's memorable phrase,[97] it is no small wonder that the prospect of being unchained from their virtual realities fills the many with great fear and guilt. Although we have suggested that Socrates only really understood the full significance of his life as he presented himself to the Athenian courtroom, he never lost sight of his self-knowledge. It is this clearheaded self-awareness that helps him to clarify the problems presented by his swiftly approaching death for the friends and jurors who still remain with him. Now as he soars above us, like Daedalus on waxen wings, our task is to avoid emulating Icarus in confusing these written texts for tools yielding us virtual virtue and cheap grace.

As Socrates sees it, his death would lead to either an intrinsically peaceful state or to something interesting–the migration of the soul to another place. He compares the first possibility to a sound sleep where the sleeper has no dreams at all; while this comment subtly prepares us for Socrates' dream in the *Crito*, we are also reminded of Xenophon's Ten Thousand hoping to go home like Odysseus: sound asleep on their backs.[98] In other words, one's consciousness is no longer buffeted around by the many fears, delusions, and passions that assail incarnate existence; maybe this life itself has been but a dream. However, this is clearly not the same as non-being, *qua* annihilation. If there is nothing awaiting us after death, because there is nothing of us that survives, we have nothing to fear but fear in this life. So, perhaps Socrates is saying that if our consciousness survives death, it would either survive in a wholly contemplative state as part of *Nous* itself, or be incorporated into another life-context.

So although the possibility of a perfectly contemplative dream-state theoretically includes the possibility of non-being, Socrates is naturally more interested in trying to describe a post-individual condition of transcendence to the extent that it concerns an abiding self. This seems to correspond to the famous trance-like states that were described by Alcibiades and Apollodorus in the *Symposium*. Socrates' account of this "dreamless sleep" hardly excludes the possibility of waking up, as Odysseus did, and finding himself in his true home at last. Otherwise it is quite meaningless to speak retrospectively of this pleasantly refreshing experience as one where all time seems to be no more than a night (40e); this was what Xenophon's mercenaries had in mind.

Whether or not one does wake up into another life or state of consciousness, Socrates is interested in what he could expect to encounter in that next life. Given the importance that he attaches to his daimonic experiences in this life, we cannot expect to be surprised to find that he portrays an afterlife in intellectual and moral terms–criteria having very little to do with the physical categories of pleasure and pain. Socrates has every expectation of continuing to live the "examined life," although Odysseus described Hades as a place where the resentful souls had no recollection of who they truly were. Yet even he must see that Tiresias, the great prophet, was the only one in Hades "whose mind remained unshaken even in death" though the rest of the dead were "empty flitting shades."[99] Socrates seems to view his own life and afterlife in this way.

Now, since Socrates obviously has no ground or warrant for understanding Hades in this highly heterodox fashion, it would seem that we could only hope to uncover the real import of his words by examining them metaphorically and speculatively ourselves. Rather than viewing his tale as participating in that genre of supernatural journalism he so disapproved of, we should try to discern in his words certain crucial themes that he wishes to urge on his friends as lasting memorials of himself and his mission to Athens. It is the form of these speculations that is of far greater consequence than the specific images or illustrations that he employs to make his point.

There is no doubt at all that Socrates wishes to interrogate the dead. Whether he does so as Odysseus or as Tiresias, as one still living or only mentally alive, does not seem to matter very much to him; indeed, one could say that it was this very thoughtful activity that preserved his self-possession. We recall his famous declaration in the *Phaedo* that even if the poison had to be administered to him many times he would not stop

talking (63e), this echoing his refusal in the *Apology* to continue philoso-
phizing as long as he takes breath (29d). I venture to suggest that it is here
too that we may identify one crucial way in which Socrates has indeed
passed into immortality. Wherever two or more are gathered in a conversation that seeks the truth about goodness, truth, or beauty, it could be said
that the *daimon* of Socrates also graces this occasion.

Just as Socrates urged his friends to think of him as happily engaged
in conversations with great souls of yore, Plato and many other Socratics
wrote dialogues that imagined their master confronting many of the peren-
nial themes and questions of human existence. Indeed, even though none
of the Platonic dialogues at least explicitly places Socrates in Hades, the
practical effect of these works is to subject the greatest works in the Greek
literary tradition to Socratic scrutiny. One cannot emphasize too much that
the results of these encounters are not essentially deconstructive–far from
it. Indeed, one could very well argue that, like the shades in Hades, great
ideas and works of literature are only "recalled to life" when they are rescued from a reified state and supplemented or "made supple" or "young
and beautiful" by being made to dance by Socratic interrogation. Even if
Socrates never actually conducted such a dialogue, or could have, the fact
that he ought to have is accorded primacy over factual accident. We only
need look at the *Euthyphro* or Aristophanes' *Frogs* to know that Plato was
certainly aware of this idea. It is only in this way that the Greek literary tradition will be kept forever young and beautiful. Socrates, though not a poet
himself, will serve as the guardian muse and unmoved mover of this pantheon. His actions will inspire poetry and exegesis. By this harrowing of
Hades and slaying of false archetypes, like Odysseus defeating the suitors,
he will go on to redeem the experiences and regrets of the heroes of
tragedy and change the way these works are read. In this context, the fact
that Socrates does not evince a desire to question historical figures like
Solon or Lycurgus is quite significant. He seems to be suggesting that the
most fundamental questions of philosophy pertain to the mythic origins of
Greek culture and religion; he is not interested in questioning men who
would ultimately turn out to be as ignorant as the politicians and poets of
his own day and age.

Any careful reader of Homer will also be struck by the fact that there
are no Trojans in Hades.[100] Plato probably built on this in appointing separate judges for Greeks and Asians in his mythic setting up of a procedure
for final judgment in the *Gorgias*.[101] Since Socrates was so critical of those
laying claim to knowledge or a logos of matters above heaven or below

earth, this image suggests that Hades could be the collective cultural heritage of the School of Hellas. We infer that by fighting the good fight against injustice the archetypal figure of Socrates is safely enshrined in a posthumous Prytaneum. Here even Achilles will not be able to outrun Socrates' interrogations and Alcibiades will marvel at the old hoplite skillful management of the horses of his soul.

While the Platonic dialogues do not present these discussions, and generally confine themselves to reporting imagined conversations between Socrates and interlocutors who are either bright young men or sophists, they aim at producing attentive readers and interrogations of the most fundamental ideas and myths. By imagining Socrates functioning in a role similar to that played by Dante in the *Divine Comedy,* we may begin to understand the sense in which he most hoped to be immortal. He could quite possibly have valued this fate more than a private blissful state of personal immortality. Through his remarkable life and heroic death, he would enter into the company of universal archetypes, figures embodying the highest potentialities and aspirations of the human condition. Though this ideal was most explicitly articulated in the *Symposium*, our readings of the *Euthyphro* and the *Apology* suggest that this was no mere Platonic conceit grafted on to Socrates' austere professions of ignorance. As we have seen, Socratic interrogation is an essential precondition to the preservation of the humanistic wisdom and theosophical ignorance that the gods demand of man. Thus, Platonic transcendental ascent seems to be little more than a playful inquiry into the conditions necessary to produce and sustain one such as Socrates.

It is in this way that we can understand Socrates' assurances to his judges that nothing bad can happen to a good man whether living or dead and that the gods do not neglect him in his troubles (41d). Understood empirically, according to the standards of pain and pleasure that govern the cave and the body, these two promises seem to be outrageous, and even contradictory, in their refusal to accept the reality of things. Taken as referring to the realm of Platonic Ideas, however, a region governed by virtue and moral obligation rather than by the contrary powers of efficiency and violence, his conviction is much more intelligible. Ideas in themselves are indestructible; they cannot be destroyed or defeated by war, plagues, mobs, natural disasters or superstition–however terrible their effects might be in physical terms. Just as friendship finds pleasure in giving rather than receiving, and so confounds the normal economic laws of need and greed, a soul that participates in this domain may have sound reasons for believing itself to be not entirely reducible to matter and material necessities.

In the case of virtuous individuals, those who dwell simultaneously in the realms of facts and ideas "treading the earth and contemplating the sun," Socrates means that such persons cannot be "corrupted" by external phenomena and coercion as long they come under the authority of, and participate in, a higher order of reality. While he frankly witnesses that a good man will be "troubled" by physical and social phenomena, Socrates' point is that travails or injustices need not *necessarily* violate the integrity and character of a virtuous person. While he cannot provide objective proof of this statement, since such an assurance could only be put in the inappropriately materialistic idiom of efficient causality, he confines himself to simply saying that the gods will not neglect a good man. Put differently, Socrates has been inspired to make sweet use out of adversity often enough to see that his faith in the goodness of otherwise unknowable divine powers is not absurd or unfounded. His "gift of the gods," like that made to Odysseus by Hermes, only confers heroic virility, not immortality; as Odysseus's subsequent interactions with Circe and her niece Calypso revealed, the two qualities may even be opposed. Still, the most important insight given here concerns the benevolence of the gods. Odysseus strikingly remarks after meeting Hermes that the gods have the power to do all things.[102] Since Socrates may not be of the same opinion, asking the Euthyphro question: whether the gods aid him because he is virtuous or vice versa–is helpful. Zeus's lament at the beginning of the *Odyssey* that mortals curse the gods for sufferings beyond their allotment, when their excesses are to blame,[103] is closer to the truth. In Odysseus's case, his generous wish to rescue his men from Circe's pen exceeded baser tendencies to succumb to fear or repose in swinish animality. The fact that these very men later remind him not to forget his home suggests that these tendencies, which had earlier led him to recklessly explore the Cyclops's cave, are never fully extinguished in anyone. Like a hero, a day laborer only gets sufficient grace for the day. As long as he is alive he is never essentially superhuman or wise.

This is consistent with one of the main themes of the *Euthyphro* and *Apology*: the stance that privileged knowledge about the gods is unavailable to us because it would give an unfair advantage. This was also why Aristotle rejects the idea that the gods confer happiness arbitrarily; he finds it sufficient to do so on the grounds that this would be unfair/ugly.[104] As the *Euthyphro* posits, the gods don't create virtues–they merely recognize them. This, coupled with the basic teaching of the *Republic* that evil people cannot be happy, leads us eventually to Aristotle's aforementioned stronger claim that the virtuous achieve a true happiness that is more secure than even the truths of mathematics.

This belief in a natural affinity between virtue and grace, although far from proving a virtuous man's invulnerability to the powers of hatred and ignorance, is why Socrates can now claim that even his present troubles have not left him bereft of hope in divine assistance. While we shall continue to discuss in the next chapter the reasons for his being unafraid of death, it is clear that Socrates takes leave of his supporters in the *Apology* with every appearance of serenity. Despite the efficiently laid plans of his enemies, events have worked out so that he will neither be exiled and forced to live apart from his friends nor have to deal with increasing age and have to depend on others in a manner unworthy of him. He has sufficient resources to ensure that the very manner of his death will provide him with a rare opportunity to join the company of the best beloved heroes of his city. While Socrates' enemies have tried to do him harm, he finds in their ultimate impotence further proof of the gods' subtle benevolence. They have turned the intended evil of his foes into good; like old Laertes he now knows that there are gods in Olympus.[105]

Socrates' final request to his fellow citizens has to do with his three sons: two of them are far too young to be guided by their aged father into manhood even if he survived this ordeal. He is not willing to dishonor his name (or theirs) by pleading to live for their sake; he asks the Athenians to deal with his sons as he treated them. He will not put concern for their pleasure or pain before his personal and civic responsibility to live and die as a virtuous human being and citizen. In effect he desires that his sons be treated as the children of one who had died bravely in battle. Socrates wants his sons to be reproached and punished if they are "reputed to be something while being nothing" (41e). In other words, his children cannot claim credit for being "the sons of Socrates" if they do not "care for the things they should" and thus turn out to be "worth nothing" while supposing themselves to be worthy inheritors of his wisdom. The most that Socrates can do for his biological offspring is to provide them with a memory that could be honored, the best his friends can do is to ensure that this living memory is not reified by being turned into a sentimental caricature or a false image of perfection. In reality his legacy is nothing more or less than the effects of a life spent combining metaphysical poverty and ethical wealth. Only someone who emulates Socrates in this manner will be able to make a "strong argument" to be his "love-child."

It is worth noting that Socrates may have had his two younger children for the sake of the city. According to Diogenes Laertius, both Satyrus and Hieronymus of Rhodes say that when the Athenians were short of men and wishing to increase the population passed a decree allowing a citizen married to one woman to have children by another, Socrates did so.[106] This insight also explains Socrates' alleged "irresponsibility" in placing the lives of his children in jeopardy through his intransigence; far from being a charge on the city, they were a gift to it. While we shall soon delve deeper into his unconventional view on the family, it cannot be tacitly assumed that Socrates shares our belief that the sacred love that parents owe children trumps all other moral obligations. We must hold that the rules of virtue and morality are not trumped by the chthonic family values that he has defeated here.

"It is time to go, I must die and you must live. Which of us goes to a better condition is unclear, unless perhaps to the god" (42a). Socrates' last public words reiterate his paramount care for the city. While his uncertainty whether he, in dying, will be happier than his living compatriots could be interpreted cynically, as expressing concern about his own fate, his words may also suggest that he is not too sanguine about their prospects. While his friends are concerned about what awaits him, he is at least as worried about them and their ability to stay on the path of virtue. Socrates is confident that his habits of virtuous striving will lead the gods to help him withstand anything that fortune could send his way, in this life or the next. His experience with his *daimon*, the Oracle and the circumstances of his trial provide sufficient proof of their benevolence towards him. Regardless of what may await him in the next world, his reputation in Athens is secure. He fears more for the living; humans driven by pain and pleasure are far more likely to come off badly as they fight against vices endemic to the soul and city.

Even if Socrates is rewarded amply for his virtue, and remains typically conscious and curious about what goes on in this world, he could hardly be unconcerned if his fellow citizens and friends live in a way that brought vice, corruption and unhappiness upon them. In short, in his erotic concern for his friends and polity, Socrates seems to concur with Aristotle's claim in the *Nicomachean Ethics* that the happiness of the dead is tied in with the lives of those they love on earth.[107] By stressing that even the god, presumably Apollo, may not know which fate was better (42a),[108] Socrates is once more drawing attention to the radical contingency of human matters. In other words while the gods will surely care for a virtuous soul, even divine beings cannot predict which fortunes mortal men would earn for themselves. As our take on Socrates' striking proof of the gods (derived from his personal experience) suggests, these gods cannot intervene positively in the world without the help of the erotic striving of mortals. Socrates himself only decides to die when it is clear that his hero-ic memory will be of better service than the last dregs of life.

If virtue and vice are indeed the ultimate principles governing the cos-mos, then even the gods cannot make human beings better or worse, as eas-ily they could if pain and pleasure were the meaning of life. This is because virtue and vice cannot be transferred through power or mass produced by thoughtless imitation; they can only arise in the human soul as a result of deliberate behavior. Since fate is written by character, our future will depend largely on the choices we make that shape the quality of our souls. Like the Oracle, who could only obliquely indicate the implications of our choices, the gods themselves cannot foretell the future because they do not craft it. This is a deeply guarded secret concerning the gods, one that most conventionally pious human beings neither care to know nor desire to believe in. We recall Homer's suggestion in the *Iliad* that even Zeus must bow before the overwhelming weight of Nemesis that demands the life of his son.[109] While we have identified Hera's jealousy as the counter-bal-ance to Zeus's hubris, our reading of the *Euthyphro* reveals that the real limiting factors are human freedom and virtue. First illustrated by Achilles, human nature possesses an unexpected power to rise out of a cave teeming with resentment and become the origin of a better way of life. This is how we know that there are good gods in Heaven; this erotic capacity for the ordering of the soul becomes the basis for the virtuous city and it sustains our commitment to participate in the beauty of the cosmos.

Crito: or What Must be Done

"You tremble carcass? You'd tremble more
if you knew where I'm taking you!" Turenne.[1]

The final section of this book discusses Plato's inspired speculations about Socrates' stubborn insistence on dying as a citizen of Athens. While Socrates seeks to leave behind an example of moral resilience and civic virtue, Plato's text also highlights the human powers of speech, judgment and law, capacities that lift us out of generic existence in nature and give meaning and happiness to individual life. These powers interact dialectically with their origin: the crude, albeit seminal, ideas of freedom and democracy discovered by Athenian democracy. While it is crucial to study the historical setting of Socrates' stand, the timeless and imperatival meaning of his choice cannot be ignored. The *Crito* can help us to revitalize the Western political tradition.

In the *Crito* Socrates defends himself against charges of cowardice, irresponsibility and irrationality, accusations made by his oldest comrade. He will use the idiom of tragedy to fight the comic chorus of wife, friends, and family arrayed against him. By standing firm, Socrates shows the Athenians that he is unlike Alcibiades and Critias, his notorious former companions, who preferred treasonous exile to confronting their foes in Athens.[2] But he also goes beyond the demagogic anger of Meletus and Anytus in revealing the true meaning of political virtue to the men of Athens. After having demonstrated the power of the virtuous individual to withstand the furies and the false gods, Socrates tries to persuade his fellow citizens that their pusillanimity must betray the great potential of their polity. In so doing, he is also inspired to re-interpret the destiny of Athens and realize the fullest meaning of the idea of law. While Plato's logos of Socrates' death reveals how teacher and pupil "cultivated the muses," the truest meaning of Socrates' refusal to flee has to do with an act of founding, political and religious, the full potential of which has yet to be fully realized. Among other things, this study of Socrates' heroic death poses the question of what a tradition is and how we interact with its essence and origins; instead of demanding that we choose between being chained to a sanctified process or "liberated" from all contact with origins, the *Crito* suggests how a true culture is conserved and realized. Using as its touchstone the heroic integrity that Socrates displayed in the face of death, the *Crito* reveals the meaning of his deed and indicates how this example could become the basis of a temperate polity.

But it is equally important that we note the difficulty of the task facing Socrates. Crito's stunning inability to understand his motives, despite their long association, raises very disturbing questions about the chthonic roots of human nature and the resistance that society, family and body offer to the soul's enlightenment through philosophy. The *Crito* is of much relevance to a time like ours; our own ability to believe in personal virtue is overwhelmed by cynical individuals and sacred institutions, exploiting our doubts and insecurities. This failure in turn undermines our trust in the polity and reality itself, thus ultimately setting up a tragic opposition between human and divine: one ends up either denying man in the name of god or vice versa. Socrates embodies the philosopher's task of mediating between a polity's changing laws and the cosmos's sustaining order. It is insufficient to affirm the primacy of pure essence over crass existence, and emulate Achilles/Athens in preferring a short glorious life to a long craven tenure on earth.[3] Even the desire for undying glory has to trust in resilient virtue and an accommodating reality.

The really heroic task allotted to the philosopher has to do with "returning to the cave" and revealing how others could escape the bondage of the body and public opinion in a way that preserves and develops their joint cultural inheritance for future generations. This "applied" activity of the philosophic "bodhisattva" must be shown to be better than the splendid nihilism of a theoretically Enlightened one, who ascends gloriously into Nirvana while condescendingly telling the rest of us that we cannot follow him to where he goes. Otherwise put, the philosopher must be able to approach both truth and spiritedness in separation from each other; he must show himself to be both a true friend of the many *and* a faithful witness to wisdom, before the two are reconciled. As an honest friend of body and body politic on the one hand and truth on the other, the lover of wisdom must learn to practice the wisdom of love. This is why the *Crito* can be read in two ways: exoterically, as a sincere defense of individual virtue and the rule of law; but also esoterically, suggesting how Socrates' basic insights concerning virtue and the gods could serve as the foundation for a logo-political order that will foster virtue and inspire human flourishing.

This is why we must not regard the *Crito* as illustrating a fundamental abyss separating wise Socrates from all other men; such a caricature would negate the true meaning of the Socratic mission. While the *Apology* read apart from the *Crito* appears to stress the total independence of the soul from the polity, the *Crito* conversely seems to emphasize the soul's complete dependence on the city; read together the two dialogues reveal the vital connection between the virtue of the soul and its erotic access to both the time-bound wisdom of the city and the eternal beauty of the cosmos. Plato seems to suggest that the philosopher is best defined as a friend of this wisdom and beauty; he never claims to have overcome his human limits by esoteric knowledge or divine favor. Even the philosophic soul preserves its awareness of the wisdom sustaining it by the continual erotic activity of shuttling and mediating between the dark memories of the cave and the blinding transcendent order; this link to wisdom is only conserved by its continual existential embodiment as erotic virtue. The real meaning of the *Crito* arises precisely out of our recognition that the interaction between Socrates and Crito sheds light on certain "existential" issues and theological-political perplexities that the erotic soul will surely encounter as it seeks its way out of and then back into the cave. Though this embodied knowledge is earned by a process involving no small measure of suffering, understanding the subtle issues involved should surely lead to more than forgiveness. This very activity should also help to make the questing soul aware of the possibility and beauty of a political life that steers an artful course between sentimentality and narcissistic nihilism. The *Crito* reveals how a polis is both the condition for human excellence and in its shadow aspect— as cave—the place where this potential is born, and often killed.

I propose to bring the same interpretative tools and approach, methods that were used earlier in this work to read the *Euthyphro*, to bear on the *Crito*. My working hypothesis is that Plato, after having presented the explicit position of Socrates in all of its literal purity in the *Apology*, speculates as to the implicit "arguments of his actions" in both the *Euthyphro*, which suggestively examined the implications of Socrates' enigmatic behavior as it concerned the gods he serves (and presumably goes to) and in the *Crito,* which seems to summarize his unspoken attitudes and hopes concerning those he left behind—both individually and severally. While the *Euthyphro* examines the religious implications of Socrates' life, the *Crito* studies his unrealized democratic political legacy; just as the *Euthyphro* defends the "goodness" of the strange gods he is accused of exposing the young to, the *Crito* suggests how the corruption of their fathers could be redeemed. While the *Euthyphro* explains how the polity is corrupted by a bad connection between the divine and human, and the *Apology* reveals some of the sacred powers impeding the prospect of transcendence, the *Crito* subtly indicates what a Socratic political solution to these moral and political problems would look like. It suggests how the problem of sacred inspiration posed in the *Euthyphro* may be resolved, by a community of interpreters: a city that is both tied to its tradition and yet freed by this very tradition of lively conversation with the past from having to relearn the tragic lessons of history from scratch. The *Crito* thus points its readers towards a fuller response to the *Euthyphro*'s questions about how humans serve and interact with the gods. By his use of two unusual literary devices: (a) a dream conversation between the body and soul of Socrates and (b) an equally improbable dialogue between Socrates and the Laws of Athens. Plato seems to imply that we are again in the realm of erotic speculation, albeit firmly anchored to the *Apology.* By this means he suggests how the last best hopes of both Socrates and Athens could be realized.

I will claim that Plato bridges the divide between transcendent wisdom and base common sense by awakening the Athenian polis to a better appreciation of the soul's powers and the gods' limitations. This in turn leads to a more enlightened understanding of the city, informed by the true political art. I will conclude by sketching a model of reality suggested by the deeds and words of Socrates. While my interpretations of Plato's suggestive speculations are more explicit and thus vulnerable to criticism, my reply can only be an invitation to enter the daimonic space opened up between the cave and the gods by the deeds of Socrates and the words of Plato.

1. The Last Temptation of Socrates

Any study of this dialogue must surely begin with its title and go on to explore what is revealed about its eponymous interlocutor. Criton means discernment or judging (for instance, the words "criterion" and "criticism" are derived from the same root)[4] and Crito is thus the last judge, the last representative of Athenian public opinion to come before Socrates and tell him "what is to be done." Crito, it may be said, offers a "practical critique" of the impractically "pure reason" that Socrates seems to represent. Yet, just as Meletus failed to care and Euthyphro's eponymous literalism was utterly inadequate to the task of understanding the divine, Crito proves to lack the very quality that his name denotes. It is surely not without significance that Socrates pointedly refrained from conceding the title of "judge" to his jurors and later, just as suggestively, only used the formal "*dikastai*" to address the minority who voted for his acquittal and were opposed to the death sentence. We now see that he has cause to wonder whether these persons, surely of the same mind and mettle as Crito, were also ultimately lacking the judgment that Socrates rashly praised them for possessing in the final part of the *Apology*. Many of these men may have been well disposed towards him, and reluctant to be associated with the malicious machinations of the prosecutors, but it was much harder for Socrates to help them to see the positive values that upheld him throughout his career. His death, and way of dying, had to be his ultimate means of guiding their unruly souls towards the beauty and justice that ruled his life.

Crito and those like him must see that it does not suffice to do the right thing for the wrong reasons; very different judgments and actions could just as easily be instilled through a mimetic process originating in sacred practices or sophistical rhetoric. Emulating Socrates' caginess, we see that the standard structure of a Platonic work best illustrates this process; his interlocutors may come to reject attractive but false opinions verbally, but as the typically inconclusive end of a dialogue indicates, Plato is most concerned with the spiritual integrity of his readers' capacity for judgment. He is vitally interested in their souls, which by nature and nurture are heterogeneous. These cares become all the more urgent now that Socrates will no longer be present to steer their discussions in the right direction; different human types must be addressed differently. Also, the illusion of permanent secured knowledge is more dangerous than humble ignorance. Even after Socrates (or Plato) has "cultivated" the muses, the "harvest" is not easily reified or readily reduced to rhyming ritual. He does not want to leave behind a body of doctrine.

In Leo Strauss's idiom, those who think they have permanently left the cave through learning some form of Gnostic wisdom or esoteric atheism have only constructed a "cave beneath a cave."[5] They must first be brought down (or up) to the level of common human ignorance, and led to accept our permanent relationship to body and society, before higher goals are pursued. The truth of the matter, well supported by Platonic dialogues like the *Meno,* is that the raw underachiever (the slave) is easier to awaken than his sophisticated but intemperate master. While the latter believes he is wise, it is far more likely that he has only been "vaccinated" against the possibility of erotic madness. While Meno accuses Socrates of numbing him,[6] it is also possible that he has already been rendered immune to wonder by the false art of Gorgias. The soul may be corrupted by premature exposure to the jargon of metaphysics or "language game" of philosophy without any complementary practice or gymnastic to make the lesson set in the learner's soul.

As the *Meno* reveals, there is no royal road to wisdom—not even for the hereditary friend of the Great King of Persia (78d); philosophy and the capacity for judgment must be aroused or awoken within the soul, which must continually choose between alternatives and wrestle with the choices and antimonies that both life and the dialogues teem with. These powers of judgment, the basis for fully human existence, lie within the capacity of every man but are never present to the many; this is the anti-democratic but egalitarian aspect of so-called Socratic elitism. Yet this potential can only be realized after the soul is separated from its chthonic roots or demotic identity and made to see its own ignorance; in other words, there is no Euthyphro-like direct shot at wisdom. In order to shoot down illusions and false knowledge, that democratic weapon, the bow, must continually be bent within every soul of every citizen; virtue cannot be vicariously gained for the many by their heroes. This very recognition uses the faculty of judgment to transcend what is passive and parochial in oneself. Yet, conversely, these critical powers are never really under the soul's rule; they always depend on erotic activity, and cannot be possessed and dispensed as wisdom. Those holding themselves as the highest beings in the cosmos only dig caves for their tyrannical souls. They would be happier as day laborers, dependent on heaven for their daily grace but freed of the enslaving bonds of vanity and vice.

Put crudely, the revelation sustaining Socrates' enigmatic speech and eccentric conduct seems to be is that "philosophy" is a spirit rather than a possession or body of knowledge; the temperance of a philosopher is not something that can be inherited, preserved or reproduced by means of a science or religious process. This awareness could be elicited from Socrates' careful analysis of the words of the Delphic Oracle to Chaerephon concerning him; it is what he seems most anxious to leave behind for us. On account of the relation it bears to the great tragedy that preceded it, the *Crito* may seem to correspond to the *Antigone*; this is because it is to the *Apology* what the *Antigone* is to *Oedipus Tyrannus* or *The Seven against Thebes*. My intentionally imperfect analogy suggests that the first part of the *Crito* depicts an explicit clash between two seemingly incompatible codes or sets of values that has been precipitated by reflection on causes of the tragic *agon* that preceded it. We have already suggested that the subtitle of this dialogue "what must be done" is also of great significance; as we shall see, the crucial question of the *Crito* deals with deeds rather than words. There is now no reason to be preoccupied with the dangers that go with speculation into hidden things; the tragedy has already occurred and the real concern is with how these great events are to be interpreted and incorporated into a long disrupted and recently traumatized collective psyche. The *Crito* goes beyond the propriety of "what should be said" to suggest an ultimate consistency between words and deeds, despite their seeming incommensurability. Since these daunting issues turn out to be embodied and epitomized in the paradoxical relationship between Socrates and Crito at this late point in their lives, it is time to immerse ourselves in the text before us.

We are eavesdropping, hanging upside down like bats, on a conversation between two old men. They are talking in the dark, in an underground prison cell. One of them is a chained prisoner. The other man is unchained; he is trying to free the first man, against his will. We may involuntarily echo the words of Glaucon—the shining one- that shed light on this singular scene: "It is a strange image, and strange prisoners that are being described" (516a). Of course these words were spoken when Socrates described the famous cave of the *Republic*: "an image of human nature in its education and need of education" (514a). Also, but less evidently, this image provides an esoteric perspective on the just city that has just been described to the young men at Cephalus's house down at the Piraeus. This suggests that there are two different ways of viewing the spectacle presented before our eyes and minds. The problem is that the prisoner, whoever he is, cannot be forced to become free. Yet, even if he refuses to free himself, he may still be persuaded to be less of a hindrance to others with greater potential/desire. The cave must not be slandered or polluted. Further, since we cannot live outside the body, or flourish beyond the polity, we must ensure that the freed prisoner does not hold the cave to be as evil as his chains. While there are two truths, they need not conflict; philosophy and politics are not opposed to each other. The one sketches out a fuller account of the whole while the other tends this possibility.

As with any dialogue, the self-revelation of the interlocutor(s) that occurs through their interaction with Socrates is the key to deciphering the secrets of the text. Accordingly, we must examine the character of Crito. He is an older man of some substance, a fellow demesman who is said by Diogenes Laertius to have been "very affectionate in his disposition towards Socrates and to have taken such care of him that none of his wants were left unsupplied."[7] While Socrates' needs were very simple, and the services provided by Crito were almost certainly held in greater esteem by Xanthippe, Crito is the opposite of a casual acquaintance of Socrates; as a "demesman" he may be said to belong to the same "genus"—even though this may lead him to be less attentive to certain specific differences than he should be. On this occasion Crito clearly believes that the qualities that differentiate Socrates from other men matter less than their generic similarities. He thinks he knows Socrates better than the philosopher knows himself.

Crito may be said to have arrived to stand before his sleeping friend, speaking on behalf of Socrates' body, to urge him to fly prison before his impending execution; as Leo Strauss points out, the *Crito* does not contain any references to the soul,[8] perhaps because Socrates is more concerned with the body politic than the already secured integrity of his soul, but this question can safely be deferred for the moment. Crito's identification with the articulate but soulless body is also signified by his ability to enter Socrates' prison cell at a time when no one else was admitted.[9] This is also consistent with Socrates' other conversation with the equally non-physical laws of Athens. Both conversations occur in the "liminal" area between philosophy and politics. Alternately, and more cynically, this could be a sign that Crito has official sanction for his mission from those responsible for upholding the laws in Athens. As a messenger from the invisible forces behind the shadowy laws, he is to Socrates what the wealthy and well-connected Joseph of Arimathea was to Jesus.[10] The problem in both instances seems to be that an amicable relationship, governed by efficient causality, physical contiguity, and care for the material needs of the daimonic friend, could not preserve what both Crito and Joseph found attractive and yet strove to reconcile with their this-worldly wealth and position. While they could try to be solicitous friends of the charismatic figure's body, true friendship could only come through a personal relationship with the elusive transcendent powers that both Socrates and Jesus could do no more than represent. The possession of sufficient material means to be entrusted with the funeral arrangements of an enigmatic prophet says very little of one's capacity to appreciate the spiritual dimensions of his life; the two powers of listening and anointing/embalming may very well be mutually exclusive. The very willingness to be concerned with the proper disposal of the corpse suggests that it is found to be more tangible than the same man's unwritten "corpus" or body of work. Perhaps only the spiritually dead, like barren Antigone, can bury the dead.

Crito accounts for his mysterious nocturnal presence on "death row" by claiming that the guard, who has been the recipient of some favors from him in the past, is accustomed to him (43a). In keeping with the equation of Crito with the body of Socrates, this may signify that because of the material services that he has rendered Socrates' body in the past, the philosopher would be most likely to "let his guard down" before Crito. It is common sense that leads us to expect that it would be before his material benefactor that Socrates will admit, at the end of the day, to being beset by the same carnal concerns, insecurities and fears that afflict all other mortal men. Because Socrates has tacitly admitted his bodily needs by allowing Crito to help him, his oldest comrade is better qualified to discuss Socrates' plight than anybody else. Conversely, as noted before, this dialogue silently asks its sensitive readers if the quality of Crito's "judgment and discernment" is at all superior to the high-minded civic concern that Meletus, whose name means "care." showed during Socrates' trial. Is Crito but the guardian of an empty tomb?

This short dialogue takes place very early in the morning, just before daybreak. As noted, Crito and Socrates cannot see each other, only their shadows; each man only hears, and speaks to, the other's disembodied voice: it is as though their lifelong chain, bond or association has already been broken; they address each other as if they were on ships passing in the night. This is why Socrates and Crito are placed by Plato in a setting similar to that of the prisoners in the famous cave analogy of the *Republic;*[11] here too, only one of them is unchained—though this man's identity may be less than readily apparent. Crito admits that he has sat beside the shapeless form of the sleeping Socrates for some time (43a). When asked by Socrates why he did not wake him up, the well-meaning Crito tells his friend that he wished him to pass the time as pleasantly as possible (43b). Perhaps Socrates realizes, with a pang of guilt, that he has treated Crito in the same way? Crito, who had passed a sleepless night, marveled at how placidly this condemned man slept. Yet, like a reluctant gadfly, Crito is obliged to awaken Socrates to the reality of his familial duties. This is consistent with our claim that Crito represents the corporeal aspect of

Socrates. The *Crito* may thus be viewed as a dream conversation between the body and soul of Socrates. Although he is master of his desires, Socrates isn't disembodied. His dreams may voice anxieties governed, and thus not revealed, by his speech and deeds. They may correspond to lived realities of his cave-dwelling contemporaries, men to whom the ideas are but dreams or fancies.

Crito claims that one reason for his not waking Socrates up sooner, quite apart from his unwillingness to bring him from a condition of blissful sleep to one of bleak awakened awareness, had to do with his own amazement at Socrates' ability to sleep so peacefully given his unhappy circumstances (43b). Crito's preference for entertainment or distraction over existing in a disenchanted reality is what truly makes him belong to the cave after all. This wonderment compounds an admiration that Crito had long held for Socrates' happy temperament; Crito is astonished that his old friend can bear his present predicament so easily and mildly (43b). The question we are asked by Plato here, of course, is whether Socrates' temperate bearing of triumph and disaster is due to his nature or self-cultivation. While Crito suggests that it is the former, Socrates gently expresses counter-wonderment at his (Crito's) being amazed that someone of his age should be vexed at meeting his end. Crito, who is of the same physical age, now rejects Socrates' ironic suggestion that the latter's equanimity before the gates of Hades is natural, pointing out that others of Socrates' age do not behave with similar composure under adverse circumstances (43c). While Socrates grants this point without comment, and the likelihood that Socrates' happy temperament is normal or natural has been minimized; the critical question now becomes whether his exceptional, and seemingly counter-natural, self-composure is a divinely granted gift, or if it is more in the nature of a personal achievement—albeit one realized by making use of natural grace that is available to all men. Conversely, we must likewise be amazed that Crito, who has known Socrates throughout all of the latter's exceptional life, could regard Socrates' "daimonic" nature so "uncritically" and be seemingly more impressed by his capacity to sleep than his ability to live well. Surely Crito must have seen the process of continual striving that turned the sometime comically absent minded cosmological investigator, so gleefully lampooned by Aristophanes, into Socrates—the amazingly self-possessed philosopher? Is it not even more marvelous that Crito's torpid temperament, coupled with long familiarity, has made him immune to the sting of the gadfly and the numbing touch of the stingray? It may well be the case that Crito's ability to sleep through Socrates' continual harpings of the themes of virtue and moral integrity is, although less evident, the greatest cause for wonderment of all, and the true subject of this appropriately named dialogue. Is Socrates guilty about not having awakened Crito? What must be done to rouse the psychic powers that lie bound and dormant deep within Crito's soul? Can he still be freed from his chains, even if he will never leave the cave itself?

Returning to our immediate context and Crito's jealous admiration of Socrates' powers of sleep, we must see that whatever favor the gods have shown Socrates, these qualities could easily be squandered by one lacking the personal integrity to use these gifts justly. While Socrates is proud of what the gods have granted him, other men would surely be embarrassed or angered by this kind of largesse. As we recall, his original gift from the gods amounted to nothing more or less than knowledge of his ignorance; both with respect to specific cases—as given by his *daimon*, and in the more general terms indicated by his interpretation of the Oracle's message. This awareness serves as a Hoplite's armor preserving him from hubris and mimetic behavior. While we earlier referred to this knowledge as a gift of the gods, Achilles' divine armor, Socrates' purpose in the *Crito* is to make this awareness available to any decent citizen, to any Hoplite.

When Crito's fortunes are compared to Socrates' from a more material perspective, Crito's substantial wealth stands in stark contrast to Socrates' manifest poverty. But this also makes it downright remarkable that Crito, despite having ample personal wealth, a liberal temperament *and* the good fortune of having been born in fortunate proximity to the best and most prudent Athenian of all, still wonders at the connection between Socrates' happiness and his practice of virtue. As we noted, this preference for the sleeping Socrates, though superficially suggestive of his unselfishness, still implies that a lifetime of observing the philosopher in action has not left Crito with the capacity to discriminate between the virtues of sleep and wakefulness. As much as Crito seeks to keep Socrates alive, he prefers his friend's sleeping body to his active soul. It seems that certain essential qualities of soul could not be transferred to other souls, not even by the gods. Socrates' explicit recognition of this stark fact could well be the truest reason for his being hated and feared so much by his enemies. It is quite scandalous to upholders of family values that virtues of the soul cannot be passed on by bodily reproduction or sacred ritual.

When Socrates replies to Crito's wonderment at his conduct by pointing out that it would be "discordant" for someone of his age to be vexed by the prospect of dying, we are reminded of Socrates' famous claim in the *Gorgias* that he would much rather prefer a situation where multitudes of men should disagree with him to one where he would be out of harmony with, and contradict, himself (482 b–c). While I have claimed, elsewhere, that this knowledge of self-consistency accounts for the quiet confidence with which Socrates faces the daunting prospect and unexplored country of death, here we must recognize the extent to which Socrates is confounded and thoroughly disconcerted by Crito's chronic inability to reconcile or harmonize the theory of philosophy with its practice. While he can rattle his chains in tune to the beat of Socrates' melody, this leads him to believe that he never need unchain himself. It is because Crito lacks the internal harmony of his friend that he fails to understand, and even wonders at, Socrates' behavior; this is why Crito has patterns of behavior more in common with the enemies of Socrates, and the generic *demos*, than his comrade. He is the opposite of impetuous Chaerephon who, despite having done much to lead Socrates out of the cave, could not behave properly in it.

The high value placed by Crito on sleep, contrasts jarringly to his friend's description of his mission to Athens in the *Apology*. Then, Socrates famously called himself a gadfly: his task was to rouse and awaken the somnambulant and self-forgetful Athenian polity (30e–31a). Crito is an emissary from the Athenian body politic to the proud soul of Socrates. His mission is to make Socrates repudiate his cherished principles and cease disturbing the Athenians. In this way, both Crito and his fellow citizens would be permitted to sleep as soundly as Socrates does. Unlike Xenophon's Socrates, who would have lulled men to sleep, Plato's hero hoped that his way of going to a long dreamless sleep (death) would have awoken Crito and the other Athenians to a better understanding of their rights and duties. It certainly is clear that Xenophon's Socrates would have been a far more soothing companion to Crito than Plato's daimonic character; one might speculate that the dialogues that Crito is supposed to have written would have had more in common with Xenophon's works. They would be more like five-finger exercises than sonatas.

We are also reminded of Socrates' ironic allusion in his *Apology* to the possibility that his death would be no more than a dreamless sleep (40 d). When Socrates described this condition as a "wondrous gain" and suggests that some men, including even the Great King himself, would envy such a sleeper, he could well be suggesting that the condition of being free of all material illusions and distractions, "dreams" as they would seem to the philosopher, would be not unpleasant in comparison to the other possibility of an unjust and deluded existence. Socrates might be gently implying

that the dead philosopher would be happier and more alive than the greatest tyrant alive. This parallel suggests that the eternally vigilant and com-
petitive condition of many cave-dwellers actually amounts to nothing more
than an uneasy state of fearful false consciousness, one that mistakes
ephemeral matters for things of substance. From this standpoint while
Socrates is already happily dead to most things of the world, Crito comes
to summon him back to the chains of shadow and illusion; it is hardly surprising that Crito, whose own dreams have been interrupted by Socrates'
eccentric and reckless activities, envies his old friend for his ability to
sleep soundly. This is not the least of Socrates' gifts; a philosopher must
find it to derive from his awareness of having done nothing unjust or
unworthy. Added to his clear conscience is something only a philosopher,
unlike a scheming genius like Themistocles, could know: Socrates has reason to believe that reality outside the cave is benevolent and just. This is
not quite the same as Odysseus's recognition that the gods were well disposed towards his resilient ways.

Yet we are told that Socrates has in fact been dreaming (44a). The state
of dreaming may be contrasted to that blissful state of dreamless sleep mentioned by Socrates in the *Apology* (40d), a state where one is only aware of
being at rest amongst one's treasured memories like Odysseus on his final
journey home; it is more akin to contemplation. May we infer from this
dream that he still has earthly concerns and bonds that hold him back? If, as
suggested, the entire dialogue could be interpreted as a dream, and if dreams
represent what we are subliminally aware of but cannot confront directly,
then there is good reason to believe that Crito would be the most appropriate "dis-easing" topic for Socrates to dream of. There is also the matter of
his body; we recall from the *Meno* that the irrational is always slumbering
in the body of a rational figure as much as the "*mathema*" or knowable
things are ever available to even a slave. Although Eumaeus stated that Zeus
takes half of a man's wits away the day he becomes a slave,[12] the fault may
be in him, rather than in his stars for letting another man, or his incorrigible
belly, make his decisions for him. Here, Socrates' body is his mnemonic
soul's slave. Yet we recall that one with cares and clients sleeps less soundly than one without. Socrates is neither disembodied nor friendless.

Crito has hastened to the prison to inform Socrates that he must shed
his chains and make his escape immediately. His mission inversely parallels that of the philosopher in the *Republic*. We recall that this enlightened
former captive courageously returns to the subterranean jail to urge its
prisoners to escape, only to be met with incredulity and contempt.[13] In a

like manner Crito, who believes himself to have been once captivated by philosophy, now wishes Socrates to abruptly repudiate his allegiance to all nebulous principles, his shadowy ideals and dreams, and face reality. Crito's words are striking; they are imperative and almost triumphant: "Think, or rather now is not the time to think but to decide" (46a). The body commands the soul! It is self-evident conventional wisdom, first proclaimed by the Thracian slave girl looking down the well,[14] and echoed by Aristophanes, that lofty philosophy must beat a hasty retreat when it is either reproachfully or scornfully confronted by the comic exigencies of the body. Both Socrates and Crito are trying to awaken the other to the truer reality. Mill's words come to mind again. Would Crito rather be a Thracian slave girl than Socrates with only one day left to live?

The question as to which of the two domains, the sphere of the body or the realm of the forms, is ultimately real and authoritative is a matter that will always divide the philosopher from the non-philosopher. Indeed, this issue also separates the practitioner of the philosophic way of life from one who merely offers lip service to its ideals; it even divides certain aspects of the same soul from others. While the philosopher finds the presence of this barrier to be tragic, the problem can only seem comic (in the rather cruel Aristophantic sense) when seen from the other side of this spiritual divide. While Crito admires Socrates for his capacity to sleep soundly, his ability to dive into the realm of dreams and ideals and bring back wonderful tales from this shadowy underworld, there is no doubt in Crito's mind that the real world is one of chains: families, money practical concerns and bodies in motion. This nagging somatic awareness inhibited Crito's ability to dwell in the realm of the ideas beside Socrates, just as practical concerns now invade his sleep.

Let us now awaken to the sober realities of Crito's world and attend to the details of the matter that he sets before his friend. As we know from the *Phaedo,* Socrates would normally have been executed almost immediately after his trial. However, owing to a religious event, an annual voyage to Crete that commemorated Theseus's slaying of the Minotaur, during which executions were not permitted to take place, many days elapsed between the trial and the death of Socrates.[15] In religious terms, this delay corresponds to the lag-time between Theseus's slaying of the Minotaur and his return to Athens to found a new regime; in real time, it is identical to the period between the trial of Socrates and his execution. Crito has now received word that the ship carrying out this mission has been sighted just outside Athens (43d). Unlike Menelaus he has been pre-warned, that his

treasured helmsman is about to abandon ship, by Apollo.[16] This meant that
Socrates' execution would occur on the next day.

The long delay between trial and execution is of considerable significance. We are reminded of the comparable 40 days between Good Friday
and the disciples' discovery that Jesus's *evangelion* or good news was
stronger than even the fear of death; it only was then that the Church or
ekklesia came into being. Just as Jesus's originally fearful disciples came
to see that their teacher's words were too real to keep to themselves, many
Athenians and foreigners were moved to wonder by the spectacle of this
condemned felon still calmly conversing about virtue and justice before
the yawning gates of Hades. Still, both Socrates' friends and enemies
hoped this fortuitous "time-out" would have given him a chance to recon-
sider his hot-blooded refusal to go into exile instead of facing death. As we
suggested, it is likely that Socrates' prosecutors never expected him to conduct his defense as aggressively he did. In all probability they only sought
to humiliate the old man and expected him to blink first. Instead, they had
a dangerous political martyrdom on their hands. Diogenes Laertius says
that the men of Athens came to feel great remorse over this act: Meletus
was executed while the other accusers were banished.[17] It is hard to imagine a doubling of the prison guard that night. It is likely that Socrates' enemies would have assured Crito that punitive measures would not be taken
against anyone who spirited him away, thus defusing a dicey situation. This
could be the service that Crito had done the guard. If such an offer were
made, Crito would not have mentioned it to Socrates.

Socrates reacts to Crito's tidings strangely. He claims that a dream he
just had suggested that his death would take place *two* days later. It was
thus opportune that Crito had not awoken him immediately. Socrates
claims to have dreamed that a beautiful woman, all dressed in white,
informed him that on the third day he would arrive in fertile Phthia
(44a–b). We must recognize that this "dream" is playfully prophetic, since
Crito has come to propose to Socrates that he escape to Thessaly (of which
Phthia is a part) the next night. Following this plan meant that Socrates
would indeed arrive in Phthia on the third day since Thessaly was a hundred miles to the north of Athens. Otherwise, by refusing to accept Crito's
advice, if we assume that the ship had been sighted just beyond Athens the
previous day, Socrates would face execution on the next (the second) day;
this arrival would be equivalent to his death.

What is the significance of this dream? Though Crito believes that this
dream is strange (*atopon*), he agrees with Socrates that its meaning is all

too clear (44b). However, he does not proceed to elaborate as to what this dream signifies in his mind. Neither does Socrates. Yet, the fact that Socrates finds nothing odd about this curious dream might cause us to suspect that he has already anticipated Crito's request and plans to deny it. He seems to have fabricated this dream to explain why he will not go AWOL or *a-topon* (out-of-place) in the face of death. Analysis of this strange dream explains Socrates' refusal to be estranged from Athens.

Any Athenian possessed of a modicum of education would immediately recognize the literary/religious allusion contained in Socrates' dream. He is alluding to Achilles' famous response to Odysseus in the *Iliad.* Achilles was asked to rejoin the Trojan War and save his comrades from disgrace. This is the very disgrace Crito will allude to later; he along with Socrates' other friends will be blamed for letting him die. In response, Achilles described himself as an honest man who hated more than the gates of Hades, a man who conceals one thing in his heart and says another. Achilles assured crafty Odysseus (who has fully repeated Agamemnon's offer of great gifts but prudently suppressed the High King's demand that Achilles accept his authority) that, far from returning to the Greek ranks, he would leave Troy the next day and set sail for home. Achilles expected to see his home "fertile Phthia" on the third day of sailing.[18]

Although the allusion seems to be straightforward enough, suggesting that Socrates' execution will be postponed for another day, there is much about Socrates' dream that is very *a-topon* in the sense of being taken out of context. We have already noted that, rather than falsely predicting the exact day of his death, Socrates' dream—which is almost certainly a playfully constructed myth and not a revelation—could just as well refer to Crito's plan that he should escape death by physically fleeing to Thessaly. Then, not just to complicate matters further, we also recall Socrates' reference in the *Apology* to the choice that Thetis presented to her son, Achilles. According to Socrates, "the son of Thetis" could either kill Hector, only to die shortly after, or live long and ingloriously as a bad man who did not avenge his dead friends. In the *Apology,* Socrates claimed that he, likewise, had to choose between death and dishonor (28c–e). Now, in the *Crito,* this choice is re-presented, albeit with a twist: Socrates must choose between dishonorable flight to fertile Phthia, and dying nobly in Athens for friends who, for the most part, do not want him to die. We wonder whether philosophy would wither away a day after Socrates' flight or death? Is this the meaning of Socrates' dream? Is his real concern for those left behind?

It is noteworthy that Crito assumes the womanly role of Thetis in this prophetic dream. Charitably suppressing, or leaving implicit, the well-founded suspicion that Crito, like Odysseus, is concealing a part of the relevant information concerning his situation, Socrates initially prefers to deal with his well-intentioned but deceitful friend in a less confrontational manner—as is his usual comic wont. According to Socrates, who takes the part of Achilles in this striking analogy, Crito is invoking bodily or maternal authority to dispatch him to Thessaly on the third day instead of posing an existential choice before his soul. As we see from the *Iliad* Thetis, though knowing her son was doomed, preferred that he set sail to Phthia, thus protecting his life at the expense of honor. Thomas West tellingly points out that "Phthia" also puns on the verb "*phthein*" meaning "waste away, decay, die."[19] The suggestion is that Socrates, like Achilles, would ingloriously dissipate his soul in rude Thessaly, instead of taking his stand in Athens and doing the right thing by his comrades. It is also noteworthy that "decadence" or "wasting away" is an effect of corruption. As we shall see, Socrates will continue to suggest that this effect is also the prime cause of the Athenian regime's corruption. Far from being the cause of corruption, as Meletus carelessly alleged, he is the only thing that protects the city from this contagion, from the fear of death that now afflicts even his oldest comrade. But we must also see that life in the cave must not be hated and despised by a would-be philosopher. His values should not be hidden away in the cave since they are not opposed to those of life, the body, or the cave—only to its chains.

We must now take into account the remarkable fact, brought out by Socrates himself in the *Lesser Hippias*, that Achilles lied when he described his plans to set sail for Phthia the next day (370b–d). In the *Crito,* Socrates playfully protects the honor of Achilles by attributing these words to a mysterious woman who is not referred to as Thetis by name, just as Odysseus omitted Agamemnon's demand for submission[20] and Crito prefers not to mention his deal with Anytus and Meletus. In all these cases the virtue of "criton" or judgment is at issue. It was suggested in the *Lesser Hippias* that Achilles, though said to be a better and more truthful man than Odysseus, was incapable of speaking the truth in this context due to his susceptibility to strong emotion (370e). Is the implication that Crito is not of sound mind in making his well-intentioned, but wrong, recommendation that Socrates abandon his honor and flee to Thessaly?[21] Or is Socrates, like Odysseus, a better deliberate liar (370e) who will lie nobly for the good of others? In other words, is Socrates moved by Crito's plight, though not to the point of altering his decision? Just as Achilles rejected his mother's advice, Socrates is using this false dream to deny Thetis' authority and divinity even as he sets things up for the apotheosis of Achilles/himself. Achilles knows that Thetis's access to Zeus's power is ultimately not going to lead to his glory; if anything, as we have seen in our reading of the *Euthyphro*, the famous "plan of Zeus" seeks his death and failure.[22] Crito's ties to political power are just as dangerous; he must not liken himself to the sacker of cities and try to corrupt Socrates' otherwise impregnable soul. While Socrates' death is certain, his *way* of dying, like Achilles', will shake Olympus and bring down the false gods of the city. Socrates will not be swayed from his destiny. Just as Achilles hated deception more than Hades, Socrates in his *Apology* said he feared injustice more than death. We see that he feared injustice more than Achilles hated deception. It is to this end that he will cultivate the muses.

Crito is yet unaware of the significance of his friend's mockingly prophetic dream, which, as we have seen, used Homeric imagery to suggest that Socrates was already aware of and unfavorably disposed towards his proposal. In the main body of this dialogue we shall see Socrates directly address his old friend's concerns. Crito must be made to see that Socrates' actions stem from a combination of political responsibility and personal integrity. The vanities and fears of the body must be educated and governed by the higher powers of the soul. In his new *persona* as a tragic hero, dying as Achilles after living like Odysseus, Socrates pauses deliberately before the very gates of Hades to show his terrified companion, this semblance of Deiphobos, that a just man's thought and deeds are consistent. His fears will not make him to go *a-topon*, to be estranged from his city and forsake his duty to enter Hades like Heracles, even at the cost of his family. Socrates reiterates his strange resemblance to Achilles, who also pretended to prepare for departure while secretly scheming to rejoin the Greeks. As noted, Socrates hopes to be indelibly enshrined in the Athenian civic pantheon by his death; he will beat the chthonic forces by joining them and then harrowing Hell itself! Like Oedipus, he will die deep within the sacred political unconscious of his polity in order to ward off the corruption now menacing Athens from within.[23]

Before undertaking the impossible task of looking directly at Socrates, and piercing the darkness that shrouds his under-worldly prison-chamber, the structure of the dialogue demands that we examine the soul of the man after whom it is named: Crito. Through deconstructing the "unstable" position defended by Socrates' interlocutor we may discern what the subtext of the dialogue suggests indirectly. Although Crito is evidently an old crony of Socrates, perhaps even his closest comrade, there seem to have been certain ironic limits that their friendship could not overcome. We should ponder Socrates' poignant words in the *Lysis*, "I'd rather have a good friend than all the gold of Darius" (212a). These words give more evidence that the fabled happiness of the Great King referred to in the *Apology* was not the subject matter of the philosopher's dreams (40d). Also worthy of mention is Crito's choice of *epitedeios* not *philos* to describe the quality of their association (44b); he'll never find someone as *useful* to him as Socrates. Even as he intends to repay Socrates for these services, the qualitative gap between utility and friendship persists.

Crito would clearly prefer Xenophon's sobriety to Plato's madness. His striking inability to understand the choices made by Socrates exposes the immense gap separating the philosopher from his comrades; this distance of pathos is even greater than that between the divine Achilles and the other Greeks; we recall that in the absence of the son of Thetis, both Diomedes and Ajax withstood Hector with no little success. It was only the direct action of Zeus, aiming ultimately to kill Achilles, that corrupted the Greeks' resolve. While the Olympians could bestow invincible might on the battlefield with arbitrary casualness, it is far more difficult to produce someone with the enduring and resourceful virtue of an Odysseus; these qualities cannot be transferred and their possessor may only be congratulated.[24] It is worth noting that Athena and Odysseus are related as chaste lover and beloved;[25] in the idiom of the *Phaedrus*, Athena recalls her true nature by seeing Odysseus's erotic potential.[26] He helps Athena evolve from the scheming nocturnal predator of the *Iliad* into a more statesmanlike force, almost Boethius's Lady Philosophy, by the *Odyssey*'s end. Socrates' relationship with the Laws of Athens follows a similarly dialectical pattern.

The abyss separating Socrates from Crito has everything to do with character. Because it is easier to move from what is more familiar to the unique, it is both useful and appropriate that Crito's commonsensical character and opinions should be used as the background against which Socrates' uncanny nature reveals itself to the readers of the dialogue—like the dawn slowly piercing the darkness that cloaks the setting of the dialogue. As my earlier readings help to bear out, Plato consistently uses this device in his dialogues. The soul of the interlocutor is revealed through his encounter with Socrates; once these psychic defects are revealed the enigmatic conduct of his interrogator suddenly makes a great deal of sense to the reader. While a dialogue's surface suggests that Socrates is continually frustrated in his efforts to gain wisdom, we are playfully urged to emulate the fanatical Apollodorus, in being critical of all but the self-deprecating Socrates (173d–e), to discover a dialogue's concealed but ever-suggestive *phusis*. Many self-proclaimed close readers of the dialogues, in their desire to distance themselves from ugly Socrates and gain the respect of the thumotic city, refuse this gift of the gods.

Although Crito appears both in Xenophon's works and other Platonic dialogues, the *Euthydemus* is easily our longest and most interesting source of information about him. Just as Euthydemus always operates in tandem with his co-sophist and brother Dionysodorus, it is not unreasonable to suppose that the *Crito* can only be understood fully when it is read in conjunction with the *Euthydemus*. The body and soul of Socrates are likewise inseparable in the *Crito*. The earlier dialogue consists of Socrates recounting to Crito details of an interesting encounter he has just had with the two sophists. Although Crito was within shouting distance of this argument, he proved either unable or unwilling to witness it at first hand; he prefers to question Socrates about it later (271a). This tells us much about Crito's general disposition towards philosophy and its tragic but necessary political implications. It is also very striking that Crito has a tin ear for irony; when Socrates announces his intention to take instruction from two thoroughly worthless charlatans, it does not even occur to Crito that is he is not serious (272b). But again many "close readers" believe that Plato desires an alliance between Socrates and Gorgias and even side with Clitophon against Socrates. Insecure thumos is just as invincible and self-defeating as ignorance.

Despite his philosophic pretensions, the tone—and attitude towards philosophy—assumed by Crito in both the *Crito* and the *Euthydemus*, is surprisingly similar to that of Callicles in the *Gorgias* (484c ff). We recall that Callicles, who claimed to be quite well disposed towards Socrates (485e), chastised him for taking philosophy far too seriously. While granting that there was something charming about young men engaging in philosophic banter, he pompously warned Socrates that it was ridiculous for an older man to occupy himself in this manner (465b). Socrates was urged to emulate those who had a livelihood and a reputation; philosophy would leave him incapable of defending himself in a court of law even against the paltriest rogue (486 b–c). Callicles would surely have held Crito's conduct in higher esteem, deeming it prudent.

Crito's reproaches to Socrates in the *Crito* are not entirely surprising to a reader of the *Euthydemus*; the latter dialogue shows that Crito is very attentive towards those who move and shake public opinion. After Socrates has recounted the details of his disputation with the brothers Euthydemus and Dionysodorus, Crito, in turn, tells of a chat he had with another observer of the encounter. This person is described as someone who "thought of himself as a man of ability" and "was proud of his cleverness in making speeches for the law courts" (304d). We note that Crito seems, always, to be quite discreet about naming the sources of his information. This is quite important to our present context; Socrates described Anytus in the *Meno* as one who believed he had an edifying influence on the polity (95a). It must also be noted that Crito is always dependent on how others framed or interpreted a human event.

Crito's companion, who as we know prides himself on his forensic ability, remarks that the dialectical struggle just concluded between Socrates and the two young sophists was a useless ado about worthless matters (304e). When Crito meekly interposed the comment that philosophy was a graceful thing, the other man repeated that it is quite worthless. Furthermore, he is sure that Crito would have been shamed at the sight of his friend (Socrates) putting himself in the hands of these powerful and dangerous men. Indeed, both the system of dialectic and the men engaged in it are contemptible and ridiculous. While Crito does not endorse this blanket condemnation of dialectic, he too feels that it was blameworthy (of Socrates) to take on such people before such a large crowd (305b). Crito is very sensitive to the contagion of shame. He feels that Socrates, through association with the likes of the brothers, has indirectly brought him into disrepute.

Crito's guarded criticism of Socrates in the *Euthydemus* anticipates his more outspoken comments in the dialogue named for him. In both cases, he is faithfully echoing the opinions expressed by men for whose opinions he has no small regard, even though he knows them to be ignorant. He is more concerned about the opinions of the ignorant than he respects the knowledge of those who are not ignorant. Crito claims that the opinions of ordinary people cannot be cavalierly disregarded on account of their ignorance (44d); perhaps their very incorrigibility, what the old Church called invincible ignorance, makes their unruly power even more dangerous. He surely believes that the physical body resembles the body politic in this respect. He does not see that Socrates' pious ignorance serves as divine armor, making his soul immune to the effects of the slings and arrows of the many. To him, Socrates' physical plight shows that these persons can cause even a virtuous man endless trouble (44d). What makes his situation even more inexplicable is that it was Socrates who showed Crito how to deal with sycophants like Meletus. As noted earlier, Xenophon tells us that Socrates advised Crito to cultivate the friendship of a man who would harass the very sycophants who extorted money from him.[27] Crito profited from this advice, but why then does Socrates prove incapable of following his own good counsel? But then, conversely, why is Crito so incapable of acting on principles that he readily gives assent to?

Socrates responds to Crito's unnamed acquaintance's condemnation of him by asking what manner of man his critic is. Socrates does not ask Crito to disclose the identity of this man; instead, he seeks to know whether this man is an orator himself or one who composes speeches. When Crito states that this man never appears in a court of law himself but instead composes clever speeches, Socrates says that men of this kind straddle the border (*methoria*) between philosophy and politics. It is fitting that this man is not named since he is neither a philosopher nor a politician. Enjoying the advantages of both fields, he stays clear of the danger and conflict that prolonged exposure to either arena would bring (305b–e). These men are hostile to true philosophy because, though believing themselves wise, and able to impress public opinion through their fine rhetoric, they are nevertheless vulnerable in informal (dialectical) conversation that would expose their true character. Little better than itinerant sophists, these "frontiersmen" are far better at dealing with the public as a mass. Since they know enough about the look of philosophy to manipulate words and appearances, they are content with the status quo and prefer puffing around clouds of opinion, to the perplexities entailed in searching after truth or virtue. Their souls and bodies are never informed by the honest *ergon* of either philosophy or politics. They are like hucksters who trade between opposed camps but never understand either position.

Socrates points out to Crito that when two things are good but not directed towards the same things, as is the case with politics and philosophy, those who stand between both these things, impeding the *daimons*, are worse than either. The implication is that these "border-men" are inferior to honest practitioners of either politics or philosophy since they apply the goods of both areas "*a-topon*" (out of context) to basely profit from the disagreements of others. Reaping where they did not sow, they are the opposite of the daimonic ones who mediate between and weave together what the parasites would keep apart. Yet Socrates adds that they must not be too critical, "we must be content with anyone who comes close to wisdom as long as he bravely acts according to what he thinks" (306c–d). The combination of courage and philosophy usually turns out well. While philosophy is aware of its un-wisdom, and must always deal courageously with uncertainty, courage—if it transcends blinds thumos and looks to the good—does not lack virtue.

Socrates' words contain a muted but powerful criticism of his friend. Crito seems to be inferior even to these dabblers in politics and philosophy since they, at least, strive to put their knowledge into practice. Crito appears in the *Euthydemus* as one who listens to the words of the philosopher, the politician, and the speechwriter with equal attention, without truly committing himself to any of these ways of praxis. As in the *Crito*, he lurks in the grey area between body and soul, theory and practice. We recall Socrates' earlier ironic assurance that studying with the brothers would not hinder him from making money (304c). This, apparently, is what precludes Crito's active involvement in either philosophy or politics. Like Meno, he believes that the company of good men is advantageous (97a); we have already noted his self-description of his relationship with Socrates. As long as he fails to live by any of the positions that he has sampled, Crito dwells at the level of appearances. He is contrasted to Socrates, who, despite the ridicule of his fellow students, is learning to cultivate the muses (60e)—he has begun harp lessons (272c).

These words hit home. Crito confesses that he is quite perplexed about the proper way to educate his sons. (306d). Yet he is not really concerned about the education of his own soul. In a sense he associates with virtue for advantage rather than experiencing the erotic benefits of giving that come from being virtuous: he would rather be the passive lover than the active beloved in the sense of being affected by the erotic encounter. Crito, the responsible parent, stands in striking contrast to Socrates, who still follows his education while disregarding the economic interests of his sons. Crito concedes that none of the other matters that he has tried to arrange for his sons, such as marriage and money, is as important as their education. He admits that he has been quite unsuccessful in finding someone to provide them with a proper tutelage in philosophy (306e–307a).[28] He is unlike Socrates, who prefers to teach his sons by silent but unforgettable example.

Meanwhile Crito has evidently been searching for the perfect tutor: one who both seemed wise and could guarantee that his sons would turn out likewise. Yet, the body of the *Euthydemus* has indicated, with clarity sufficient to our purposes, that training in philosophic dialectics only inculcates readiness or perpetual potential. It is an intellectual gymnastic, rather than a discrete body of knowledge that could be poured into a student by one such as the bath-man to whom Socrates once compared the sophist Thrasymachus.[29] In other words, philosophy is not something that a rich father can buy and transfer, like a slave or a racehorse.[30] This is another reason for Socrates' ironic suggestion that Crito and he enroll as students with the brothers; only sophists promise to provide the kind of guaranteed success that Crito desired for his sons; only they could chain down the famous statues of Daedalus[31] and treat the very gods like runaway slaves. While Socrates could protect Crito and Critobolus from the sophists, his influence evidently went no farther. Despite his contiguous association with Socrates, Crito has not adopted a philosophic way of life. Thus, since he cannot distinguish between reality and appearances, he is still vulnerable to the many pressures exerted by the few and the many. His right opinion has no *logos*[32] to protect it from socio-political *ananke*. To him the soul of Socrates resembles an unchained statue of Daedalus.

Just as clerical corruption does not prove god's non-existence, Socrates advises Crito that he must not let the abuses of any given profession discredit it in his eyes (307a–b); he will use this same argument in the *Crito* itself to show that mistakes by the state do not prove that government or law are essentially unjust and oppressive, merely that its power has been incorrectly used. A young man must be properly trained to employ the techniques of any given art in a fine way. Crito could well have used Socrates' debunking of the various professions to justify his own posture of intellectual laziness towards the discipline of learning. Yet surely anybody of judgment paying attention to the conversation recounted in the body of the *Euthydemus* would be able to distinguish between the absurd word play of the two sophists and Socrates' far more substantial, albeit informal, contributions to the discussion. Socrates knows that guarantees cannot be honestly provided in learning; since courage and practice are essential aspects of education, anyone issuing such a guarantee is evidently unaware of the fact that knowledge cannot be instilled or poured into the human soul. Crito is advised not to shop around for what is useful to his sons, but to practice a skill himself (307b–c). Crito could best help his sons by setting them an example of virtuous praxis, instead of treating education as something slavishly bought and sold.

Here Crito reflexively approaches the question of Socrates' security in a manner largely similar to that in which he approached education in the *Euthydemus*. While Crito sincerely cares for Socrates' well-being and security, to the point where he is quite willing to expend a good amount of money and even run certain political risks in exchange for the valuable advice and services he has received from Socrates, he believes that the best guarantee of Socrates' safety is secured by sending him safely over to Thessaly, at the 'boundaries' of Greece, along with the equivalent of a SUV, a credit card and a full tank of gas. Once in 'Phthia' Socrates would be a safe, non-practicing, spectator of life. Invisible in the Hades-like 'waste-land' of Thessaly, the Athenian equivalent of Las Vegas, he would enjoy a long and inglorious life of bodily comfort. He believes, too trustingly, that 'what happens in Vegas stays in Vegas.' Crito does not know what human virtue really is. Thus, for all his good intentions, he is ill suited to advise Socrates on the course to be followed. But should Socrates be responsible for the future course of Crito's life?

The *Euthydemus* shows that Crito's eponymous "judgment" is only nominal, it is not a virtue he possesses or has practiced with courage and grace. This deficiency undermines the very friendship that he believes he has with Socrates. To him friendship is amoral and non-judgmental in the sense of pertaining to the physical wellbeing rather than the moral good of his friend. These seem to be the necessity-dictated limits of friendship in a reality that is ultimately irrational and adversarial. This separation of judgment from the noble means that Crito views friendship merely in terms of the familial and the familiar. To this extent he is little better than Critias, his superior in intelligence and evil; he lacks the erotic disposition towards what is beyond the physical and familiar. This striving is based on true criticism: judgment about the intangible good rather than the same and the pleasant. True friendship thus turns out to be between good men who help bring out the best in each other, rather than being only about preserving the comfortable and private in a world gone mad. As Aristotle rightly saw, friendship represents the true basis of the polis and is qualitatively superior to the family in being chiefly concerned with the actualization of the good life,[33] as opposed to the merely feminine bringing into being and preservation of life. In the deepest sense, our trust in the goodness of the gods is founded on the experience of friendship between good men and the bold openness to the beauty of the cosmos that this erotic disposition makes possible. While the hyper-masculine associations of the likes of Alcibiades, Critias and the oligarchic clubs of the last days of Empire had discredited the erotic aspect of the polis, it is now up to Socrates to salvage what is truly manly against the shame that Crito casts on it. Since the flourishing of the polis originates in the lived experience of erotic friendship between good souls, Socrates must defend the possibility of other-directed virtue and the polis itself, before one who does not know eros, judgment or the true meaning of friendship; he must do so in the darkness of Plato's cave.

By its insights into Crito's soul the *Euthydemus* serves as an introduction and prelude to the vexing questions yet to be debated in the *Crito*. Once we see where Crito is coming from, we can better understand why Socrates does not wish to go "*a-topon*" to where Crito would send him. Now, we are ready to open our eyes and, looking at Crito with a fuller sense of what Socrates saw and did not see in him that dark morning, attend to what is said and unsaid in the *Crito*.

2. Stranger, Go Tell the Athenians

"Reader, if you seek his monument, look around you" Sir Christopher
Wren's epitaph at St. Paul's

We have already examined the significance of the dream that Socrates claimed to have seen before waking up. Socrates has compared himself to Achilles, and it is from this heroic or hubristic perspective that he expects to earn eternal glory. He will die gloriously before the walls of the city instead of fleeing ignominiously for the highlands. Yet Socrates is not Achilles. He is a fat and ugly old man who is clearly not of divine ancestry: it is as though Falstaff were to claim to be more beautiful than Henry V. Therefore, if this comparison is not to be dismissed as the most absurd hubris, we must see whether there are any plausible grounds for its assertion. Just as Falstaff appeared most ridiculous when making his physical farewell to the theatre dressed up as an old woman in *The Merry Wives of Windsor,* instead of the reported death scene so movingly reported in Henry V complete with Socratic echoes, Socrates himself would appear in a similarly absurd light if he were to escape to Thessaly, probably down a sewage pipe, disguised. Surely even Aristophanes would be reluctant to visit such a fate on his old enemy?

It should be noted that Achilles only became himself, the stuff immortal dreams are made of, by dying heroically. The reputedly blind bard, Homer, was himself surely divinely inspired to transform a short, nasty, and brutal life of someone like Billy the Kid into an ideal of undying appeal. It seems that Socrates' death had the same effect on Plato, although Socrates' life was certainly not lacking in inherent moral virtue. Nevertheless, just as Achilles' death overthrew the hegemony of Zeus and substituted tragic human striving in its place, the Platonic account of Socrates' death (occurring after the collapse of the gloriously short-lived Athenian Empire) undermined the hegemony of tragedy and promulgated a humanistic ideal of goodness. This encounter with Crito, the Last Temptation of Socrates, will test and prove our hero's divine armor of virtue before his heroic death in the *Phaedo*. Clearly, Achilles' greatest ordeal was not his ugly vendetta against Hector, it was the battle against his own mortality. This is beautifully captured by the image of Hector, clad in Achilles' armor, being pursued by Achilles around the walls of Troy.[34] Likewise, just has he refused to speak as anyone other than himself in court (17c), Socrates' virtue must protect his soul against the pleadings of his body to disguise itself in a peasant's leather cloak, perhaps even supplied by Anytus the tanner, and flee Athens (53d). If Hector embodied Achilles' mortality, Crito stands for Socrates' body in the duel that is to follow. But this opposition must not be too extreme. Socrates can only vindicate his soul through his body, by taking command of it. If not we only have sterile life-negating dualism. It is only *after* asserting the soul's rule over the body-soul continuum that Socrates can pass beyond the physical.

Crito's first weapon, the first spear he "hectoringly" casts against the tested integrity of Socrates is shame. Crito shamelessly claims that Socrates has exposed him to great shame by allowing the uninformed many to suppose that he (Crito) could have saved Socrates had he been willing to spend more money (44c). This theme is carried over from the *Euthydemus*. There, Socrates was critical of Crito's own willingness to be ruled by popular opinion instead of investigating the truth of matters. Socrates repeats this assertion in the *Crito,* saying that only the opinion of the reasonable people is worth considering. When Crito responds by telling Socrates that he should show more regard for the opinion of the many, those who have shown their power by sentencing him to death, Socrates reiterates his belief that these people—selected by lottery—act at random, with no great capacity for either good or evil (44c–d). Of course we have seen that there are good reasons for supposing that Crito also appears on behalf of the politically influential few, those worthies who claim to be more reasonable than either the many or the philosopher.

Unlike Crito, who genuinely believes that the many have power to do great harm to the good man, we shall suggest that Socrates is more concerned with the daunting task of improving these many. While Crito's actions towards the many are motivated by fear, Socrates is moved by erotic generosity towards those "who know not what they do"—he does care for the opinions of the many but only with a view to improving them. He cannot do so directly but is able to remove the false knowledge impeding their access to what is beyond the cave. Socrates certainly does not fear their capacity to do him harm but the fact remains that the many exert great influence over most of those who wish him well; there is ample reason to believe that Crito himself may be counted among the ranks of the many for all intents and purposes; it is clear enough that Socrates' old crony shares many demotic attitudes and fears. Crito also wants the *demos* to think well of him; to him shame is more external and bodily than internal and spiritual.[35] Given these presuppositions, it may be inferred that Crito is "prejudiced" towards Socrates for "reasons" that have less to do with virtue and principles than we might unthinkingly suppose to be the case. His "judgment" or decision to support Socrates is irrational; it is at variance with many of the principles that govern his life were they to be regarded as rational precepts rather than as being anything more than old habits or accustomed ways of being. In short, Crito himself is his own best argument for why Socrates should show greater respect for the opinions of the many. If the *demos* possess the power to corrupt most of Socrates' friends, in the sense of infecting them with their "ruling passions" and fears, then they will indeed possess the power to hurt Socrates, at least if a version of Aristotle's claim that our happiness can be affected posthumously by the fortunes of our loved ones is to be taken seriously.[36] Also, leaving these personal considerations aside, the Socratic legacy would be blemished by the very argument that Socrates used against the Athenian statesmen of yore;[37] Socrates' inability to bring about lasting improvement of the moral quality of his associates must militate strongly against his desire to leave behind a living legacy. As Thetis' son, he must leave his tent once more to fight for the polity/city wall that his friends hide behind.

All of this does not gainsay the fact that Crito is loyally disposed towards Socrates; my only point is that the "bonds" that tie him to the philosopher are more chthonic than philosophic. Socrates' reasons for being intimate with Crito may be said to be of a different quality, although we do not choose to examine them at this point, they are certainly no less sincere and heartfelt. If, as we have suggested, this entire conversation is a dream, Socrates' inability to enjoy the sound dreamless sleep he described so glowingly in the *Apology* has to do with his concern for Crito and his ilk. Socrates will strain every intellectual resource at his disposal to fight to rescue Crito's soul from the power and prejudices of the many. Conversely, Crito's body and emotions will fight hard to save his old friend from death; this being the case he will deploy every rhetorical device to achieve what he sincerely believes to be best for every fiber of Socrates' body.

While Crito is concerned with saving Socrates' body, Socrates wishes to use his last days and hours of life to make Crito see that philosophy is not simply life-denying necrophilia; it is a way of erotic life that must serve as the basis for the restoration of the polis as a place where humans will once again be able to bring erotic words and courageous deeds together. The dour doctrines of the *Phaedo* merely preserve the idea of the rational soul for export; they do not truly depict the soul's erotic motion in life. We must also see that it is through his friends in Athens, rather than by a few metaphysicians in Megara, that philosophy will be saved. Friendship is more essential to Socrates' legacy than literalized myths that can be passed on as doctrines easily turned into dogma. This also means that Crito's reduction of friendship to physical comradeship, family ties, and economic convenience presents a real, if banal and insidious, threat to philosophy.

It is in this spirit that when Socrates counters that the many, who are ruled by chance, lack the power to do good or evil (44c), Crito tries to turn his own words against him. Crito accuses Socrates of playing into the hands of the contemptible *demos* and bringing about what they could not accomplish: his utter ruination (45c). Now adding the force of family to shame and fear of death in making his second assault on Socrates' soul, Crito claims that he is guilty of great cowardice in deserting his sons instead of taking care of their education; this is inconsistent with Socrates' claim to have made virtue his goal through his life. There were three points when the whole sorry affair could have been settled had not Socrates been both hot-headed and cowardly, Crito is not sure which is worse (45e–46a); it seems that Socrates has un-tethered all of his secure definitions and certainties. Crito has unthinkingly joined body to soul and now finds his thoughts ruled by his body; so, when the time comes for his life-long association with Socrates—the soul of their friendship—to dissolve, Socrates must show him a better way of ruling his body and finding his soul. If not, Crito will have contempt for his soul and even corrupt Socrates' sons by default. Socrates does not want to be *the* one, and he cannot let Crito regress back to the many.

It is very likely that the three points at which Socrates could have backed down are consecutively reported in the *Euthyphro*, the *Apology*, and the *Crito* respectively. Socrates (a) came to court when it wasn't necessary, (b) conducted his defense the way he did, and (c) refuses to save himself by going into exile. This pattern indicates the tragic-comic theme unifying and animating the three dialogues in question. But, to Crito the story is far from being a tragic trilogy, its overarching theme is one of flagrant irresponsibility. Crito suggests that Socrates' opponents did not seek to kill him; rather, his reckless cowardice has been his own worst enemy at all three junctures in the process. In baseball terms, the *Crito* is about a possible "third strike" but also an easy way for Socrates to get on base; while he's swung wildly at two pitches well outside the strike zone, it's still not too late for him to take an intentional walk to Thessaly. Crito—the judge or umpire—knows that the pitcher's intention is to walk Socrates.

Crito's passionate accusation of hubristic cowardice only makes sense if we assume with him that Socrates' seeming stubbornness is sustained by a fear of being humbled before public opinion. Even though Crito does not acknowledge that Socrates' position has any ontological grounding,[38] he has little difficulty in believing that shame in the eyes of the many is real. He'd rather be their slave than a day laborer/released prisoner. Crito believes that justice is clearly on the side of public opinion, and his politician-friends; the positive law condemned Socrates, and now sound judgment demands that he goes into exile. While he readily accepts that one must do what is right, this has very little to do with internalized ethical principles. The natural rights to life, liberty and the pursuit of happiness trump any obligation to follow the law or act virtuously. Perhaps Socrates is to blame for this state of affairs. His denial of certain knowledge concerning justice and virtue seems to have placed persons like Crito at the mercy of the sycophantic forces of shame, custom and habit. Now that Socrates had exercised his moral freedom in his own way, surely they are equally free to make their own choices, especially after having seen the ruinous results of his behavior. Isn't this the very human wisdom we are left with after Socrates has freed us from the gods? The opinion of society is, after all, the basis of the laws, which dictate procedures. But this opinion also extends to the ultimate particular, as prudence. Socrates failed to see that justice is no more than a process or a language game. Now he has played the game and lost, he is expected to leave the table and plead bankruptcy. He must not wager the lives of his family and the honor of his friends over something as silly as a game of chance, played with the rabble making up the jury. Both the idealistic and demotic elements have had their say and now the sensible men must intervene. This critique *by* practical reason can neither see the ideas above nor the moral law within.

Socrates responds by trying to remind Crito of the various moral precepts that they had agreed on over the years. He gains assent to the idea that one should do what is right and not mindlessly follow the opinions of the uninformed many (47a). Consistent with his *persona* as a heroic athlete maintained at public expense at the Prytaneum, Socrates, the publicly housed prisoner, speaks of himself as though he were an athlete in training for his pending encounter with death. As such an athlete, Socrates claims that he must disregard Crito's views, since he may only follow the advice of a qualified doctor or trainer (47b). In the *Apology,* Socrates spoke authoritatively, as a brave veteran, noting that a man who could outrun death would succumb to injustice, which ran faster than death (39a–b). By contrast, Meletus's father, fearing death, became complicit in the murder of Leon of Salamis ordered by the Thirty. The lot of a short-lived man, who stood his ground and died nobly like Achilles, was far preferable to a longer life – an ignoble tenure on earth spent fleeing death and being exposed to injustice. We know from other dialogues that Socrates had behaved with distinction during retreats undertaken by the Athenian army in the early days of the Peloponnesian War.[39] Here too, like famously fleet-footed Achilles, Socrates could outrun death, by ignobly abandoning his shield of virtue and fleeing to Phthia, but he wouldn't obey his body. By occupying the moral high ground, he uses his courage and power of thought to try to rally his fellow Athenians and urge them to flee evil rather than death. As he noted in the *Phaedo*, if his sinews and bones had their way, he would have been in Megara or Boeotia long ago (99a); the self-possessed veteran still remains in control of his body.

The moral convictions of Socrates remain unchanged over the daunting ordeals he faced over his last days; though several tactical decisions had to be taken, his principles were not in the least affected by the accidental fact of the position of a certain ship in relation to Athens; the real question was how he could best exercise his spiritual responsibilities as a man and citizen. He would not allow his fear of the unknown to overwhelm him. While Socrates tries to remind Crito that damage done to the soul is far worse than physical debility, it is evident that the fear of losing Socrates, coupled with the respect that he feels for the opinions of their enemies, has caused Crito to forget the importance of tending his soul. Though Socrates is still quite capable of securing Crito's assent to various moral doctrines, as he has done before, the fears of Crito's body are stronger than the convictions of his mind. They will cause him to lose his self-possession and merely drag these ideas behind him in flight. If Crito's conduct gives any indication of how Socrates' other associates would behave after his death, then all Socrates has tried to do during his divinely mandated mission to Athens, could be of similar impermanence. Even if his friends showed the courage that the Greeks displayed fighting over the body of Patroclus, in fighting to save his *body*, they would not have understood why he rashly risked his life and their dishonor.

Socrates starts to reassert the authority of reasoned argument against opinion, what he describes as Crito's eagerness (46b), by asking whether some opinions are better than others (47a). While Crito has demanded that he acknowledge the power of the opinions of the many, Socrates cares more for their spiritual potential than their raw power. Crito must in turn accept that since there are many opinions, some are worthier than others. To this Crito, who has already stated that Socrates should choose what a good and brave man would choose, raises no objection. Socrates next replaces the good opinion of the *Aner*, the brave and good man, with the prudent man. Again Crito, who surely believes himself to be more prudent than brave, cannot contest the view that the opinions of such a man, as opposed to those that are idly speculative or foolish, are what should count. Now, using an argument that takes fuller form in the *Gorgias*,[40] Socrates secures his agreement that the physician and gymnastic trainer have authority in matters to do with the body (47b). Disobeying them, and heeding the opinions of the many, only brings harm to the body. Socrates does not say that a perfectly healthy body can also be destroyed by the moral diseases of the many, however unjustly. As noted, this problem is even more acute without a proper authority in respect to moral matters. Though Socrates famously claimed to be the only living practitioner of the true political art,[41] most Athenians were obviously not of this opinion. Also, without a consensus that the moral plane was more important than the physical, the true political art could still be overruled by the violent authority of the body, or by a false political art.

Socrates' response parallels his claim that the unexamined life is not worth living. He claims that if the authority of the one who understands these matters, *if* there is such a person (47d), is disregarded, we damage that part of us which is made better by justice and harmed by injustice (47d). It follows that since living with a seriously damaged body is worthless, and since the part of us to which justice and injustice pertain is better than the body, living with that part of us damaged is not worthwhile (47e) since what's important is not living, and finding happiness in sleeping thoughtlessly, but living well (48b). Here while it probably seems to him that living without Socrates—that part of him that supplies pure reason and good conversation—is not truly living well, practical Crito feels that living without Socrates is preferable to his not living at all.

Meanwhile Socrates' argument is presupposing what he may only truly convince Crito's practical reason and desires of by his heroic death, that he is the man who knows the aspect of us that is improved or harmed by justice and injustice. While Crito seems to agree, he could contest Socrates' claim that these matters are more vital than life itself. But as to the point that life with this part of us damaged is worthless, which Crito agreed to, we must question whether Socrates would damage this part of him, the very part that Crito once regarded as his own artificial mind, and become evil by flying to Thessaly. Socrates' own moral authority rests on this claim. Though the mind is not damaged by evil the soul is. Some would even find this view morally corrosive to the extent that it could lead to men becoming beautiful souls, fearing to wage war for the city on the grounds that this would damage their *souls*. This kind of view of philosophy, reified by Neo-Platonic and Christian readings of the *Phaedo*, actually did much to fatally undermine the city. So even if Socrates does convince Crito that the soul is worth more than the body, Crito can still harm his soul by acting un-erotically and pusillanimously. Philosophy is not just about thinking.

Yet Socrates makes no such argument here. His position is its contrary: a good soul cannot be separated from a just life. The respective responsibilities of a good man and a good citizen are not distinct. Now this claim, amounting to saying that man is a political animal, is also hard for Crito to disagree with since he has been trying to persuade Socrates that he should pay attention to the opinions of the many. Socrates uses it as the basis for his view that he should not try to escape without persuading the Athenians. The question now is whether the damage that the Athenians could inflict on his body is less injurious than the injustice he would visit on himself and Athens by fleeing his polity: we note that "that which is damaged by injustice" could be either the soul or the city, especially since "what's important is living well" and the city is about the truly *good* life. Socrates might be saying that while his death will only directly harm one man physically, and affect his family, by doing injustice he would do greater damage to many more: the citizenry of Athens. Yet if he is indispensable to the moral wellbeing of the Athenians surely he did them injustice by not accepting a lesser penalty that would have let him live alongside them? The fact that Crito remains unaffected by his words suggests that Socrates could only truly begin to teach the thick-skinned Athenians by the "rare example" of his death. The horsefly had to draw blood, his own, and the Athenians—like the dead in Hades—would only understand after they drank of it. They had to see that Socrates was more and less than a rare example; he was a model or paradigm of real virtue, a good life within the capacity of everyman and the heirloom of nobody. But only by his death could this paradigm penetrate the thick skin of sleep-loving Hellas.

It seems that Socrates, like Crito, is affirming a strong connection between one just man and the many. While Crito has warned Socrates of the power of the many to harm the one, Socrates, who had said in his *Apology* that divine law (*themis*) dictates that a good man cannot be harmed by the injustice of one worse than he (30d), now says that a good man can harm many, including himself, by injustice. While he must not sin against the gods by abandoning the foolish Athenians, he also sees that he must not corrupt them by living/dying as if he valued the purity of intellectual virtue over the daily dilemmas of moral life and the grubby obligations of citizenship.

Crito had earlier witnessed Socrates' ability to control his body and sleep well, even in the face of his imminent death; he will now see the eponymous "enduring power" of Socrates, like Tiresias the one man possessed of his wits in the bat cave of Hades. His friend will amazingly stand his ground and fight for the general good of Athens even in death, like Oedipus and the other heroes. As during the trial of the admirals after Arginusae, he will do so before the raging fury of the majority.[42] Once again, he will demonstrate the power and priority of the soul over the body; more importantly, he will strive to defend and argue for the rights of divine law (*themis*), the very law that dictates that bad men could not hurt the good, over human positive law which sets out to protect the body, property and honor of the good (or successful) from the bad. Yet, unlike Antigone, he will not merely oppose sacred fury to human *hubris*; the issue is quite more complex. He looks to a new *logos* that reconciles four powers: the sacred furies, the *demos*, the good of Athens and truly divine law. This union anticipates the great account of the four cosmic principles in the *Gorgias*: Earth, man, gods and Sky (508a). Transcending both the fatalism of Sophocles and the sophists' belief in chance, he also unties Crito's bonds of physical and familial identity. Socrates must protect the free city from the sacred necessities of body and family.

By his linking of virtue to justice, Socrates once more takes on the aristocratic *arête* of the *kaloi kagathoi*, the best and brightest, and its ethic of helping friends and harming enemies. In many ways the fine life consisted more in plundering and pillaging, as practiced in Homeric times or the glory days of Pericles' Empire, than in the productive tasks of making and cultivating. This is why the just life of the *Republic* seems to depend on the activity of punishing injustice before it has anything to show for itself; virtue itself is defined as living a short supposedly glorious life of egotistical self-actualization, excellence defined as exceeding all others in excess. Yet Socrates often attacked this predator's morality, pointing out in the *Republic* that defining justice as the advantage of the stronger is the opinion of a rich man with an exaggerated opinion of his own worth (336a). The *Republic* depicts the perfected end of such a life: a tyrant who is murderously paranoid, utterly bereft of friends and no better than a wolf with a taste for human flesh.[43] As we noted in the context of the *Euthyphro*, this model of justice is based on a dangerously literal emulation of the Homeric gods, itself tautologically derived from the selfish traits of the rulers of the Bronze Age; at this time there was no shame in answering the question whether one was a pirate in the affirmative.[44] Conversely, Socratic piety steers Euthyphro towards a non-adversarial view of ultimate reality. The *Apology* likewise starts with holy ignorance about the strife-ridden gods of Homer and yields a harmonious model of the soul, once it's purged of these false gods. Now the *Crito* yields a model of an erotic political life that mediates between the microcosmic temperate soul of the *Apology* and the macrocosmic benevolent gods of the *Euthyphro*.

It is this way of living that Socrates is anxious to pass on as his legacy. This is why he must persuade Crito's will. His crony is comfortable playing the language game of philosophy, as in the *Euthydemus*, from the baseline; as soon as any existential issues are involved Crito defaults to practicing the adversarial ethic of the *demos* he was so quick to criticize. This is why Socrates must persuade Crito in a way that affects his deeds. While Crito all too comfortably believes that *ananke* or necessity rules the realm of action, Socrates wants to free his friend's soul from these insidious chains of bad faith. The mystery of the freed prisoner's return to the cave is deepened further by his quixotic refusal to stop trying to free others, even when menaced with death.

This unchaining amounts to convincing Crito that he must not be ruled by the political theology of Athens; the worship of money, pride, violence, jealousy etc. all derive from a crass view of reality that sees the soul as a mere function of the body, irresistibly governed by psychic, physical and social necessities that tempt us to manipulate each other and degrade our own selves. Socrates has devoted his life to replacing these fungible physical, social and psychological vices with virtues that cannot be owned or transferred but rather make us limit and know ourselves. Crito must see that Socrates is not a miracle or "gift of the gods" given him as a rare trustworthy friend in times of unprecedented depravity and deprivation. These virtues and the resultant happiness are within the capacity of every human. They are not violently given against our will or stolen from the jealous gods, but rather emerge from a life of thoughtful speech and deeds. Such a life is as beautiful to the divine as it is good for the soul. The only real liberation from half-witted voluntary slavery comes by the power of deliberation. This art in turn presupposes that reality has a rational order and structure, one that the mind can discern and the soul can participate in. That is why the look or idea of the beauty of the cosmos is more than sufficient. Actual technical knowledge of the inner structure of reality gives too much destructive power to the slavish and craving aspects of the mind. Any willfully demented mortal could then destroy the possibility of this rational structure abiding over time. This is why old and ugly Socrates is perfectly suited to serve as the mortal paradigm of this beauty. He will also reveal its invulnerability to physical evil.

It is not sufficient, and actually morally dangerous, to accept a principle in theory and violate it in practice. Lamely saying "some God made me do it" ultimately destroys the very possibility of a city and compromises the integrity of a soul; not merely because the belief in capricious gods or divinized vices seems to suggest that reality itself is adversarial and flawed, but also since it denies the possibility of virtue. A city is impossible without a core group of self-ruling citizens, friend, lovers and guardians capable of making and keeping promises, pledging their sacred honor—to each other and themselves. While Aristotle saw that politics, the art of the city, rules through the beautiful and just,[45] the political equivalents of the gods of the *Iliad*—the older powers of violence, money, jealousy and pride—are determined to tear the city apart. These a-cosmic powers are deeply opposed to the integrity of the soul and bonds of friendship that are the true walls of a city. Socrates is inspired by Apollo to replace these wanton gods with civic virtues and ideas that inspire and form the soul. Like the 300 at Thermopylae, his death will seal the walls of his city and soul against the barbaric energies threatening to tear civilization apart.

Those who learn the theory of politics but fail to en-soul its practice, preferring to possess it as a weapon or power in service of their desires, are like the immature and incontinent persons on whom Aristotle famously said that this study was wasted.[46] This is why Socrates now asks Crito if they too are no better than children in being ruled by desire and thus unable to put words and deeds together (49a–b).[47] This question: whether the principle that injustice should never be returned for injustice should never be violated, whatever the circumstances, has everything to do with the essence of Socrates; the bull-like look that he maintained before death's labyrinth[48] suggests that he grapples successfully with the body's fear of death that is externalized in Crito, even as he speaks. The power of the soul to keep its word: to hate the practice of saying one thing and doing another, even before the mouth of Hades—which by definition causes us to forget who we are by threatening to reduce essence to non-being—testifies that evil can be resisted through the "enduring power" of the soul. The soul's brave actions speak louder than its unspoken fears. Even if Socrates' body feared death, his love for friends and city mattered far more to him and animated his desire to leave behind a rare example of an erotic soul's power to rule the body.

This idea that one should never deliberately do what is unjust amounts to simply defining injustice as evil. Apart from rejecting the sweet pleasure given by Ares, the money changer in lives[49] as he gains infinite toxic energy by splitting the moral atom of our soul and melting many men into a fury-like plasma of rage,[50] the promise to never do injustice, even in the face of perceived dishonor or injustice, also forms the very basis of a just city—regardless of the specific order the regime assumes. This also means that a city can never be united as a tribe or band of thieves,[51] mutually pledged to help each other and harm enemies; it follows from Socrates' definition of injustice as evil that deeds of injustice—however justified as revenge or *dike*—release furious energies that pollute the soul and city of its agents. Just like a virtuous soul, a true city is held together by erotic memories and reasoned persuasion. Neither demagogic rhetoric nor sacred violence is an acceptable substitute; both warp memories, corrupt mores and disintegrate souls.

This is why Socrates' seemingly hyperbolic words to Crito about there being no common basis for deliberation between those few who believe that injustice is evil and all the others who do not (49d), must be taken literally; we are reminded of the *Crito*'s leitmotif of body and soul, as well as Callicles' complaint that Socrates has described a world turned upside down.[52] Only those who renounce the alluring temptation of injustice can be part of a true city; this basic distinction between cave and city is at least as firm as that separating the City of God from the City of Man. From his bat-like perch Crito may not be able to act fully on this belief, but at the very least he must pledge himself to it. He duly does so but yet seems unable to grasp the implications of this view when asked if it would be unjust to leave the city/cave without persuading its denizens (49e–50a) of this basic tenet of virtue, that injustice is evil. This is why Socrates cannot leave the cave and must die within it; he can only transcend or overcome the cave by being resurrected within it.

There seems to be little practical difference between those sybarites who lived for the sake of pleasure, and professedly prudent men like Crito who try to minimize their inconvenience and only *use* philosophy to advance this purpose. Even Crito's professed willingness to spend his last obol to rescue Socrates must be seen in this light; though this would be the correct thing to do, Crito like Meno[53] wants virtue to be profitable; for how else could he recognize it? Thus he has no hesitation about making pragmatic arrangements that would save his money and Socrates' body whilst allowing Anytus to "tan" his friend's reputation. The real question is whether the virtue of the soul or the gratification of the body served as the ruling maxim by which one's actions were conducted. The respective ways men lead their lives will eventually separate those belonging to the City of Virtue from the denizens of the overheated City of Pleasure; feelings of envy or compassion for each other become irrelevant. Habits of vice make the soul opaque to *sophrosune* as surely as practiced virtue grants it immunity from the contagion of peer pressure.

When Crito said earlier that he hoped that Socrates wasn't worrying about the material effects that arranging his escape would have on his friends, Socrates said that he had other *greater* worries on his mind (45a). These, as we have suggested, presumably pertained to the spiritual welfare of his friends and fellow-citizens. These worries are best expressed in his own words: "If I leave Athens without persuading the City, don't I do evil to those I should least hurt?" (50a). As noted earlier, Socrates' personal integrity, the quality of his soul was inextricably connected to the unredeemed moral condition of the Athenians. Socrates had earlier expressed this commitment in the form of a divinely imposed mission towards the Athenians; here, in the skeptical, but deeply personal context of the *Crito,* he will express this obligation in more primal terms. He has to convince his fellow-citizens because he could not take his property and leave Athens. His property consisted precisely and exclusively of his virtue and way of life. Just like Themistocles, Socrates could not have become himself anywhere but in Athens, the only legacy he could leave his sons was the improved moral condition of the Athenians. Since this was also the criterion he used against the most renowned statesmen of his polity,[54] this self-styled "only true practitioner of the art of politics" (521d) has to stand or fall by his own ability to leave a lasting positive posthumous impression on the souls of his friends and fellow Athenians as a divinely sent paradigm of virtue. This also meant that even without escaping, and dying in prison without giving a good *logos* for his actions, he would yet corrupt his friends if he caused them to despair of justice, despise law, hate Athens and betray the true meaning of philosophy. To this extent, Crito had a very good point.

Socrates' words suggest that there is an implicit agreement that one should stand by, a Hoplite line that cannot be broken, between all those who are truly part of a city. Unlike Crito, who sees the city as a larger commercial association that one uses to advance his own personal and economic ends, in the very spirit Socrates chastised the Athenians for valuing wealth, honor and reputation over virtue and truth (29b), Socrates' view of politics is derived from his post-Homeric model of the soul. He knows that the unrivaled opportunities that Athens offered for amassing these goods could be greatly deleterious to the soul. While Crito finds it natural that a city be as strife-ridden as Euthyphro's Olympus or the American Wild West, the *Crito* suggests that this crassness must lead Socrates to show Crito that *a good* life could not be purely apolitical.

This rehabilitation of politics begins with Socrates denouncing the practice of being ruled by a majority "that would readily put a man to death and just as swiftly bring him back to life without thought" (48c).[55] Rather than contesting the effects of this procedure as Crito urges him, Socrates is more interested in overturning this understanding of justice as an act of revenge. We note that his attitude fuelled endless cycles of revenge, an evil that the *Orestiea* tried to warn Athens against, and reinforced the view of reality as a zero-sum game. In effect, much of the reward of winning came from the divine pleasure of witnessing the pain of the loser. The *Iliad*'s idea of a short glorious life had everything to do with dying at the right time, before the furies of nemesis hunted one down; the shade forgets his own evil while his polity is corrupted by it—even as it must preserve his glory. We have already seen how Socrates sought to change this ethic to an equally fearless struggle *against* injustice, but a purely negative stance inevitably becomes bitter.

Socrates refuses to do injustice but what is justice? While we cannot define this idea in a way that would render it makeable, and violate the integrity of the soul by turning politics into a *techne*, we can give a good account of its erotic look and suggest how this virtue could do more than simply cleanse a community. The *Republic's* eventual view of justice as psychic friendship[56] unites Socrates' theology and moral teachings; he rejects the Homeric literalism of the many on the grounds that the gods did not cause everything but only brought about good things and were not responsible for the bad.[57] He also defines human evil as *in*justice. This means that the power of anger or injustice must not animate our actions, nor should it be the key to decoding ultimate reality. As with the *Euthyphro*, we make a second sailing from deducing the implications of a reality that is just and beautiful, like the non-coercive forces holding the polis together. Here, the paradox of a friend who did not know friendship helps us to see what Crito could not behold.

Based on his model of a temperate soul that saw the deified passions become enlightened virtues under the rule of reason, Socrates looks to the shining idea of a polis ruled by the principle that the true ends of citizens were not inherently opposed. This blinding vision moved him, Tiresias-like, to give birth to its image, in the cave's darkness. Since they do not compete over limited economic goods and the inherently adversarial stuff of honor, one soul's virtue does not compete with another's. By making the stable soul-based state of *Eudaimonia* its goal, rather than living off faction-creating/craving *thumos,* the city can look to the general good of its citizens, rather than viewing politics as a glorious and sacred blood sport. The vertical dimension of reality outside the cave transcends the zero-sum conflicts over economic goods, honor, and the battles royal –hardly *pagkalon ergon*- staged to flatter decadent gods. It is worth noting that Socrates' model of aristocratic rule in the *Republic*, for all its weird details, is based on the idea that the rulers of a city could not be ruled by family values or the *ananke* of economic need or greed.[58]

While Socrates does not define the general good here, because this ultimately has to do with values conducive to the self-realization of individual souls, he is anxious that Crito see its legitimacy as a core political principle. Like Churchill in 1940 he is fighting alone but not for himself. The alternative is a false realism, held in common by both Anytus and Crito, a view that finds nothing wrong in treason or betrayal; the body's pagan sanctification of life becomes a vain struggle against the inevitable injustice of death and only causes us to conclude that ultimate reality is unjust. This stance leads to the denial of temperance and the practical abolition of man. Since we are incapable of respecting each other when we cannot hope to trust ourselves, we huddle together as families and friends and exploit strangers because the gods make us do it; we are but natural slaves of divinized desires. Since all men are equally wanton in being bought, sold and ruled by desire, democratic equality is justified. Even the gods merely maintain order by their own cycles of strife. As the cynical rich and greedy many strive vainly and violently to emulate these divinized passions, the virtue of temperance was found impossible and even impious, as Sophocles' *Ajax* and Euripides' *Hippolytus* reveal. This is why men like Aristides the Just who were too good for politics as usual were ostracized.[59] Socrates' denial of Homer's gods changes everything. Denying that the gods were moral monsters, reaping what they did not sow, he urges us to realize our buried talents/potential and be equal to ourselves. Once this view of the gods is rejected, virtue is no longer a matter of calculation: the science of how to flatter and appease the gods; instead, our epistemic ignorance of the gods' vices makes conscience—knowing with—possible. We learn about what it is to be human along with the inspired poets and rational laws.

Socrates must also explain how one is to live as an adult once the accusing voice, literally the *Satan*, of the furies—demanding satisfaction for ancient resentments—has been rebuked and silenced. As we have seen, this "spirit of gravity" is strong enough to prevent individual transcendence; it even warps religion itself. By splitting the psyche, this power gains the energy to stoke an ever-burning Gehenna, a soul-consuming unholy ground that is the origin of Homer's Hades and Plato's Cave. Plato's Socrates leads the human spirit out of the false piety of shared fury and guilt, towards a vision of a city ruled by law and devoted to the education of the soul and proper care of the gods—in all their erotic otherness—and this enterprise begins here. But many doubts remain: Are friendship and concord strong enough to hold a city together without relying on the furies of Aeschylus and the lies of Aristophanes? Aren't we born and bred in a chthonic womb, body and cave? Are reason and speech adequate measures and masters of the irrational matter of daily reality? Can we hope to oppose divine grace to the primal way of sacred violence? Armed with the divine gift of Socratic ignorance, which seemed to show that humans were both foolish and impious in projecting their own vices on the gods, Plato expands the political rule of rational speech, and denies the primacy of the unknowable and thus unspeakable chthonic gods.

Yet Crito is aghast at Socrates' hubristic refusal to accept the ultimate authority of the flesh, the family, and fury-stoked public opinion. To him the claims of philosophy are self-evidently superseded by these embodied values. This is why Socrates must first respond to Crito's reproach that he not abandon his sons, leaving them fatherless and penniless (45d). His response suggests that politics and common sense must take their true bearings from transcendent rather than chthonic standards; clinging to sacred blood ties out of a mistaken sense of loyalty imprisons a soul in an underworld of bitter regret, blind spite and blasphemous rationalization. As with Athens, he could claim that what he has not bequeathed them is more valuable; he has not left them an Oedipal blood-inheritance of self-doubt, guilt and fury. Since he would not probably have lived long enough to see them as adults, his death is a legacy of virtue and heroism; a name honored and respected throughout Athens is more valuable than the memory of a poverty-stricken man being nagged to death by his wife. We may as well blame Jesus for courting death and not taking care of Mary.[60] Socrates entrusts Xanthippe and his children to his beloved disciple, Crito.

By emphasizing the formal role played by the regime in shaping the genetic matter mixed together by his parents (50d–e), Socrates also counter-claims that, far from betraying his children, he refuses to deny the true parents of both himself and his sons, the Laws, in their hour of greatest peril. As with Jesus, his true family is those who follow his words. It is as though the political Crito plays Creon and tries to kidnap Socrates/Oedipus from his chosen resting place of Athens.[61] Like Oedipus, the blind but authoritative Laws depend on their children to faithfully interpret their spirit in unfamiliar times and circumstances. Socrates also goes beyond the intransigent ways of Antigone, who set up a fatal opposition between piety and politics. In other words, it is essential to follow the strategy described in our reading of the *Euthyphro:* one must redeem the past by respectfully learning from its ancient sorrows and realizing the meaning of its blindly expressed yearnings in the future. By claiming to be chosen or exceptional and refusing to learn from the past we condemn ourselves to blindly repeat its errors. This is why the parties of Fury and Forethought, blind loyalty and foolish hope, must be reconciled under the banner of virtue.

But virtue cannot occur apart from ties of true friendship, in isolation from the erotic act of giving of oneself—*qua* fully actualized human being—to others. Such an act clearly has political implications. Also, as we noted, Aristotle saw that true *eudaimonia* is about giving rather than receiving.[62] We must then fear death only because we live as in Hades, where we cannot give of ourselves, indeed having no idea of who we are;

conversely, one who lives well does not fear death because he is aware of his soul's invulnerability to all but wickedness. But this good life, which Socrates opposed to merely living (48b), can only take place in a virtuous polis or be experienced through the activity of bringing virtue to a polity. This is why, as we have suggested, even Socrates fears death to the extent that he fears for the souls of his comrades. For this reason Aristotle paradoxically said that the courageous person has the most to lose through death; unlike one who is rash because he hates his life,[63] such a man enjoys a good life. A good death is thus the ultimate actual feat of self-actualization; it is surely accompanied by self-knowledge of the sort that Socrates experienced when he let his *daimon* speak through him to the jury. Such an act necessarily seems to point beyond itself: it is performed before the polis and even captivates the Olympian gods: the ideal spectators of the best actualizations of powers that the immortals only represent in a frozen iconic manner. As suggested, this is why Athena depended on Odysseus as much as Apollo seems to need Socrates here. The gods are the highest judges of whether Socrates deserves the Olympic honors he claimed from the Athenians. But that is because heroic caring actions change our view of the gods. Even Euthyphro can see that this is the ultimate act of piety.

While Socrates will only explicitly speak of his recognition that he should have learned to cultivate the muses in the *Phaedo*—an almost unique positive revelation—it is highly significant that the first reference made to his belated decision to take music lessons occurs during the course of a conversation with Crito. This means that Socrates sees, through Crito's massive obtuseness in the *Euthydemus*, undeniable evidence that he should learn to appeal to the desires of his friends; only in this way could he bridge the yawning abyss between theory and practice. If not, he would forever be in the Sisyphean situation of continually repeating the same futile activity of animating their minds and failing to inform their bodies. There was little pleasure in being the only man to retain his wits amongst a swarm of dead souls (100a) suffering from Alzheimer's. Although his listeners would obligingly answer "yes" or "no" to his painstaking questions, their souls would remain fast asleep. Various fears and jealousies held his friends back, both from their true selves as well as each other. The implicit political doctrines of the *Crito* seem to represent Socrates' final heroic effort at overcoming these insecurities by articulating the outline of a common goal and good. Just as true reverence had to be born out of the potential wasted in fear, philosophy had to actualize the power of poetry so that beauty could save the world.

Plato's aim is that Crito, who represents everyman, must somehow be made aware of the meaning, and highest potential of the Athenian political experiment; the "School of Hellas" could not be corrupted by the "nudge, nudge; wink, wink" wisdom of the cynical few that philosophy was only a childish language game; once school was out, it was every man for himself and the devil took the hindmost.[64] In other words, while it is necessary for Socrates to demonstrate by his deeds the possibility of ruling his body, and dethroning the falsely deified vices from his soul, this is not sufficient. A new understanding of the polis had to be revealed to protect the soul from backsliding towards ennui or using its newly found power to oppress others, just as the Athenian polity—after expelling its tyrants—fell victim to anarchic and/or autocratic pressures. Otherwise put, the soul-body continuum had to be ruled by an account of virtue conducive to the general good that pointed towards a benevolent ultimate reality. This way of life also had to be capable of being passed on through or over the generations in the confidence that it would command the assent of any reasonable man of good will. While a city cannot survive without trust in tradition, the power of law and our power to obey it, this belief must be reinforced by a complementary confidence in the community's ability to learn from what was originally foreign and strange; this is part of Odysseus's resilience that Socrates incorporates into his persona and psyche: as both an ignorant man seeking wisdom from all and a sacker of many impious cities and vain souls. The Socratic polity would "gladly learn and teach" but it would refute all the false gods it encounters.

The human potential "to rule and be ruled in turn" that Aristotle celebrated at the horizontal political level[65] first had to realized on the vertical axis: the soul had to rule the body by reason and music whilst being itself ruled by the erotic authority of the eternal ideas. Cultivation of the muses had to be conducted so as to realize the fullest potential of the Homeric muse and the Athenian polity. A literal take on Homer had to be replaced by a reading that understood the movement from *Iliad* to *Odyssey* and traced the self-discovery of the soul's power for resilient virtue and interpretive self-knowledge. We have seen that the *Euthyphro* could be read in this way. Likewise, Pericles' Athens was an unprecedented beginning, the first true experience of political freedom, but it would have been no more than the political equivalent of Achilles' short glorious life without a great poet like Homer or Plato to bring out its true essence. Here Socrates' ignorance must replace Homer's blindness; he must be to Pericles what Odysseus was to Achilles. The vengeful fury of Achilles could not be allowed to haunt the polis and negate its own deeds: the dead must not kill the living. The dead truly die in vain when the backward-looking, effectively suicidal, law of revenge replaces the erotic power of the quest for goodness, truth and beauty. This blind commitment to sacred but bitter memory betrays the future. While the chthonic powers are necessarily present at the origin of a polis, and provide the energy that it needs to overcome the gravity of nature they can never be allowed to stifle its destiny. The true muses must cultivate the blood-sodden soil of a polis, helping it transcend the incestuous desire to endlessly relive its past that blights its future. While Aristotle said that justice and beauty rule the polis, we cannot ignore the power of interpretation: the gift of the gods that saves the erotic polis from imploding under the deadweight of thumos. This drug saves us from viewing all men as swine; it gives us the power to reverse the Circe-like encircling charms that both enslave the many and corrupt the few left unenslaved by filling them with tasty misanthropic disgust.

The basis for cultivating the muses must be the principle of judgment; so it is fitting that aptly named Crito should be the interlocutor. We have already seen that Crito, like any slave boy from Phthia, can recognize self-evident moral principles when they are presented to him. The problem is that he is too enslaved by his desires, whether physical or social, to be able to act on them. Even if Crito comes to believe that it is good to rule over his desires and go to his death like Socrates, and even sees that this is possible, he still needs to be convinced that this would be to his advantage. Since Socrates did not have the time to convince his jurors individually (37a–b), this chat with clueless Crito—which sums up the existential import of many prior conversations that his oldest crony had been privy to—must replace this personal encounter for those like ourselves who can only hear his speeches without actually knowing him in the flesh. Those who see by the inner light of their souls are surely better and happier than one who sees by the eyes of the flesh but cannot believe. The gods of Socrates and the logos are nothing if not just and fair.

At the deepest level, Socrates' response to Crito began with an appeal for rational (self) consistency. Much is presupposed in accepting with Crito that what is correct should be valid in any time or place (46c). It means that philosophy is not a language game played in some other utopia or virtual reality constructed in speech; it is rather a way of life with authority throughout reality. This position holds that reality is not held together by violence; if this were the case, speech itself would be impossible or meaningless—consisting in the latter case of a series of mutually exclusive emotive ejaculations. The very dignity of being human is founded on our capacity to recognize and speak the truth, a power that only adults fully realize. It was for this reason that slaves were interrogated under torture;[66] only adults could be trusted to testify under oath. Being an adult was not a matter of reproductive maturity, it meant that one was capable of making and keeping promises: even to oneself. Such a promise could even override the body's biological drive to stay alive by any means possible. It meant that an adult could retain his integrity and remain able to see or act in a way consistent with the better angels of his nature.

This ability to keep one's word also implies that ultimate reality is amenable to keeping promises of the kind that an adult would make; the basic features of reality—both supernatural and natural—will prevail unchanged so that heroic actions and winged words from many millennia past still have meaning today. Even if Crito were to counter by saying that reality isn't this way, that it is society that creates enclaves where people can put words and deeds in common, this is precisely where Socrates is being asked to remove himself from. As we're reminded in the *Phaedo*, Socrates only ceases to be himself when he stops talking.[67] But even going beyond this claim that we only believe in man because we still believe in language, the logos and logic, for one who does not have need of language is either an irrational god or a beast, Socrates is also appealing to every soul's capacity to recognize truth. While we can argue that these lofty but humanly recognized self-evident truths do not exist on earth, where there's no such thing as a perfect circle, we yet admit that every human mind still participates in a realm higher than that of flux and change, even by our use of speech. Though the fact value distinction seems to deny the objectivity of moral truth and virtue, the standard of rationality should not be an inverted Turing Test that makes all that calculators and computers cannot understand meaningless. Socrates' argument only makes sense when we're not trying to be machines but speak to each other as men. Though promises are broken all the time, we still know that we should try to stand by our word. Our current bankruptcy of language is chillingly consistent with the corrosive consumerism that has made post-modern man incapable of keeping his word to others or himself. As the Cretan paradox shows, language itself cannot allow us to say with any consistency that we are liars, hence also the protection that the Fifth Amendment offers against the related mental torture of self-incrimination. It could even be said that it is harder to admit that one is a murderer than to commit an act of homicide; Caesar testified as much when (after crossing the Rubicon) he disarmed the magistrate who tried to stop him from seizing the treasury, even after being menaced with death, by saying that it was harder for Caesar to threaten to kill someone than it had been for him to actually kill without words, as he was used to doing over many years as a general.[68] When we re-enter the polis we participate in a world of eternal values, changing facts and evocative speech.

But even if we grant that human virtue is pleasing to heaven, is it possible for it to endure for any significant time on earth, against the strong imperatives of the body, family and society? Hobbes argued that sovereign violence was always necessary for preserving a state since no man could be persuaded to give himself up to be killed.[69] The translator of Thucydides defended the self-evident *ananke* or necessity of the body's drive for self-preservation, claiming that it trumped all other values. Yet Socrates, who unlike the historian survived this war, both physically and morally, emerged from this experience with a totally opposed take on morality and reality; the *Gorgias* even seems to blame this very morality of strife for the chaos of the war. We could see Socrates' very deflation of Olympian religion, an extension of the monster-killing exploits of Heracles and Theseus, as part of his mission to bring chthonic influences and psychic powers under the rule of moderation; powers once held to be unspeakably holy had be dragged before the bar of reason and made to explain themselves. Even if such an account could not reveal the essence of the quality in question, it at least brings it under the rule of the good. The *Euthyphro*'s affirmation of god's non-tautological goodness is complemented by the *Apology*'s affirmation of the soul's integrity and the *Crito*'s obligation to discuss the common good in a cleansed polis.

If one man is able to rule himself by preserving his integrity and staying within his limits, ironically if not comically defying these supposedly soul-splitting forces of necessity, it proves that the furious powers are not divine; belief in these "gods" is based on their making human virtue impossible or short-lived. Socrates thus confounds the so-called tragic "wisdom of Silenus" that it is best for mortals is to never have lived at all.[70] The *Crito* corrects the impression left by the *Apology* and *Phaedo* that Socrates takes leave of the ugliness of politics and the body with relief, shaking the human dust off his beautiful soul. The *Crito* sees him return to the cave to take full control over his body and die demonstrating in the most eloquent way possible, the power of the virtuous soul over bodily vice and social necessity. While not denying the gods, Socrates sees their influence as being indirectly exerted on the individual soul by the grace of mediating *daimons*. The god he serves is benevolent and rational; this idea of the divine is thus absolutely opposed to the irrational and fearful piety of the cave. Political theology lives off the "managed fear" that the many feel when they are confronted by Sophocles' "many mad masters"[71]—the irrational brew of mutually incompatible chthonic, psychic and societal powers that constitute their sacred ethos.

Socrates' feat is of no little significance in our own day. All the monsters he vanquished have returned Hydra-like in the post-Christian polytheism of our 21st century global society. While Socrates' life of virtue showed that these old gods were psychological and not ontological, this distinction is moot in the face of postmodern man's inability to withstand temptation, coupled with religion's self-serving denial of the power of temperance—power to know and rule oneself—in favor of an omniscient god who knows us better than we know ourselves. Today, Thomas's brave affirmation of divine rationality in the face of Augustine's pessimism is frequently denied in the name of an Ockhamist-Lutheran voluntarism that ultimately amounts to an absolute Islamic submission to the Divine Will; ironically, the irreligious Post-Modern consumer submits to the deified market in much the same fashion. The self-contempt spawned by religious anti-humanism once joined with the infinite desires of atheistic science had lethal results: their combination leads to the denial of virtue, a re-deification of the passions, and the deposition of *sophrosune* by purely quantitative and end-less calculation. If we are not forced to choose between Fraud, Freud and Fundamentalism, our reason must be shown to be more than a brain in a vat, a calculating device easily superseded by faster artificial processes; as our present plight shows, the power of judgment cannot be delegated to artificial intelligence; computers cannot account for those intangible non-quantifiable qualitative factors that make human thought both slower and incalculably richer. As these ideas cannot be measured or mastered they may only be beheld or discussed in speech, by men unashamed of being human.

For these reasons, both ancient and post-modern, just as Prospero cannot leave his island without recognizing his part in Caliban, Socrates' return to the cave and body—as a benign ruler and viable role model—cannot succeed without Crito. While Crito stands for the bodily aspect of Socrates, his name reminds us of qualities of judgment and prudence pertaining to the ultimate particular or the individual entity, and his affection for Socrates represents the many friendships and conversations without which the polis cannot survive; these matters cannot be grasped by the mind apart from the body or society. Just as Crito without Socrates is reduced to shrewdness and calculation, Phaedo's Socrates will be eternally alienated in clouds of abstraction without the bonds of non-intellectual affection and bodily solidarity that Crito represents. Though it is clear that Socrates' mind should rule Crito's body, this authority could not be meaningfully used by a disembodied mind. It is fitting that Crito and Socrates wrestle in the boundary area between principle and practice where judgment lurks. It is here that the city must be re-founded in speech.

The broader point is even more vital. If the ideas of law and the state are to be actualized following the principles disclosed in the *Apology*, any human must be expected to have the power to be both ruled by universal principles and exercise prudential judgment towards particular cases: to be capable of leaving the cave and returning to it. The true meaning of human equality seems to be closely related to the capacity we possess to learn from each other and interpret past and present together. Thinking for the general good of all, the precondition for the soul's self-actualization and happiness, is futile if all those who are "thought for" cannot be addressed as logos-bearing humans, with the potential of beholding and giving assent to the same common ideas. The state exists because many are not naturally aware of their potential for the examined life; they find that human life is good by thinking privately and deliberating together; this truth cannot be conveyed collectively, by explicit or cognitive violence, whether silent or sophistic. The fact that the words of a Homer or Socrates still have meaning after many millennia suggests that reality has a rational structure formed by the adequacy of the mortal mind to timeless truth.

This trust in language is essential to the ongoing task of refuting the falsely deified passions of the body; while their reality—as elemental powers—cannot be denied, they become false gods or warping heresies when their *ananke* occludes the fullness of human experience. While comic trust in the ultimate irrepressible goodness of reality can never defeat our tragic awareness of the ever-present possibility of evil, the properly cultivated individual soul can always contain vice and refuse it divinization or admiration. While evil is real and cannot be ignored, it is best refuted by comedy, even within the soul of one who must confront it; it only becomes a contagious force once it is given ontological status and treated as a power co-extensive with the good, to be fought by all means available. Since evil is more tangible than the good, we often mistakenly suppose that using violent means to fight evil is sufficient to make us good; the tragic result is the welcoming of this contagion into our own soul. Though evil tastes like honey, and infuses us with great energy, we recall that this power comes from splitting the psyche, which then comes under strife's furious rule. So flawed a soul, a house divided against itself, lacks the "enduring power" of Socrates. It becomes addicted or enslaved to Ares, the sacred violence underlying every evil it fights. As befitting a symbol of eternity, Ares' serpent will continually sink its teeth into the human spirit and harvest new generations of fighting men to blindly butcher each other in the name of their gods.

Socrates refutes the hegemony of this adversarial view of reality through his comic interrogations of false wisdom or so-called realism; he goes beyond merely exposing the ontological groundlessness of these claims to also living in a way that revealed to himself and many others that the gods would not allow a good man to be harmed by those worse than he.[72] Since his happiness in life existentially refuted the pessimistic "wisdom" of the poets, it only remains for his way of death to "seal the deal" by showing that his gods did not forsake him. Socrates has told Crito that one should heed the advice of the experts and ignore the opinions of the many (48a), those ruled by Furies and Clouds. While he countered Crito's objection that the ignorant can still do harm by proving that his foes could not shake the integrity of his soul, he has neither explained how souls with less self-knowledge can be protected nor identified the genuine experts or authorities who should be heeded. Who or what replaces the Homeric gods, the kings, the furies, and the opinions of the many? While we have already seen why human wisdom should replace stories about violent gods, just as we would have it take the place of the quantitative artificial intelligence regnant today, it remains to be seen how this non-violent authority could acquire the ordering force of law in the face of the benign indifference of gods who protect the soul while exposing the body to absurdity and violence. Even as we reject both the efforts of fundamentalism to make man into a mindless beast and the delusory divinity that addictive consumerism promises, we still need a principle that rules mind, body and society. How do we rule and protect ourselves without coercive violence, whether divine, chthonic or social? We need a criterion, a measure of personal virtue and limit on violent excess, a norm that has the authority to bring out the best in man and contain our ever-present potential for violence.

The criterion or standard that Socrates places before injudicious Crito is the idea of law. To the extent that Socrates himself has established that his virtue, contrary to the tragic poets, cannot be violated by their gods, he is similar to Achilles in the manner discussed earlier: even Zeus could not violate his integrity against his will, even in death. This reveals that the poets have inaccurately described the gods. They have divinized merely human passions that can be brought under the control of reason and virtue but just as importantly are never capable of being ruled by purely material necessity without a symbolic narrative or logos. As Socrates has shown, the divinely infused poets are not their own best exegetes; their esoteric wisdom only emerges through criticism, often posthumously in the literal sense of being taken out of the cave or womb that gave it birth. Law itself should then become paradigmatic rather than being punitive, negative and violent. *Themis* is not sacred irrational fury; like the Olympians, Laws can be edified and persuaded by action at a distance: beautiful feats of valor and virtue, but they must only be enacted by the divine gift of honest human speech aided by the comforting divine gift, or Hermes-given holy spirit of interpretation. Rather than punishing out of a fear of disorder, we can affirm an order of justice based on our awareness of analogous structures in soul, city and the cosmos itself. It follows that ultimate reality is non-adversarial and not irrational. We must also remember that the very capacity for judgment presupposes a rational structure to our reality that is compatible with the mind's powers of reason and critical judgment; while the mind can see the highest knowable things: the ideas or *mathema*, the body has access to the ultimate particulars: individual living beings and purely physical objects. Acting through the body, the soul can bring these ultimate particulars under the authority of the universal ideas by persuading the laws and reforming the political ethos of a city.

While Socrates did not have the time to convince his jurors that they had the power to rule themselves, and overcome the forces of fury that diseased their consciousness, Plato seems to be hinting that Crito—his last judge—must earn the right to his name by gaining self-knowledge. Unlike Euthyphro, who lacked insight, and Meletus, who did not care, Crito must recognize that he has the power to think and act for the common good, both with regard to his psychic economy, thus overriding the many incontinent desires, currently ruling it like Penelope's suitors, and the greater transpersonal orders—political and cosmic—that his intellect allowed him to participate in.

Crito must see that the meaning of the city and the idea of law are not refuted by the bad judgment shown by one jury, especially since it was seduced by Socrates into seeing the weak arguments of Meletus as stronger than they truly were. Serving as a divinely appointed midwife, even to the very end of his life, Socrates is seeking to remind Athens of the truest possibilities of their democratic experiment. This vision is co-extensive with his Delphic revelation; since none could claim divine wisdom, all are compelled to collectively seek and recollect human wisdom. It even follows that the greatness of Athens was not exceptional or sacramental but is paradigmatic, like the wisdom of Socrates. Just as it should be seen that the extraordinary cultural resilience of the Jewish people is at least as much hermeneutic as it is hereditary, representing the post-Second Temple shift from a legalistic and sacrificial cultic religion to ethical concerns and prudential interpretations of both ancient text and contemporary context, it could be said that the continual activity of interpreting the inspired works of Homer and Hesiod (since the two powers could not inhere in the same person) constituted the spiritual backbone of the city of Athens. By reading Homer and Hesiod via the Socratic insight that all the wisdom available to us is of human things, we see how much Greek culture had gained, and stood to profit, through wrestling with these humanistic humanizing texts. This gift of the gods, the divine spirit sustaining the logos, is at the heart of Hellenization: the cosmopolitan horizon that made it possible for the Christian revelation—that God is Love—to spread throughout the Roman Empire.

The shift away from tragic culture, based on the belief of the tragic hero that the jealous gods were hostile to his apotheosis, to the humanistic polis, predicated on the revelation via the logos that the divine is well disposed towards human virtue, is epitomized in the movement from Achilles through Odysseus to Socrates. Though, in keeping with the separation of inspiration from interpretation, it took a while for the best of the newly literate Achaeans to see that Achilles ultimately portrays the mindset that led to the destruction of the Heroic Age, it is even harder—even for our times—to see that the *Odyssey* also represents a progression towards a place where while virtuous men like Eumaeus the swineherd and the cowherd will be seen as the equals of Telemachus,[73] Odysseus, the last hero, must go on a long journey of purification. In other words, and to cut to the chase, neither Odysseus nor Socrates is a truly autonomous hero, a person qualitatively superior to and independent of all other men. While Odysseus's narrative and a certain view of the divine philosopher support this illusion, close reading of the *Odyssey* gives ample support to the claim that Odysseus has the blood of about 729 victims on his hands;[74] according to the *Republic* this is the exact ratio by which the life of a virtuous man is better than that of a tyrannical ruler.[75] The meaning of the tale told by this self-confessed liar will only emerge before a jury of fearless critics who will probe it from all angles, as thoroughly as Odysseus roasted the paunch stuffed with innards over the fire. Likewise Socrates takes pains to tell the Athenians that he is given to them by the god as a paradigm of *poros* and *penia*, human wisdom and divine ignorance. He must inspire the polis to become a community of interpretation, a democratic jury that all poets and exegetes must convince as they strive to grow and share human wisdom. As Euthyphro was shown, grooming our myths is co-extensive with caring for our souls.

His refusal to leave Athens shows that Socrates' moral and intellectual integrity depends very much on his continual interaction with others; even though he does not gain wisdom in divine things, there is no doubt that it would be hard to find his equal in human wisdom. Yet, what good is human wisdom without other men? Even Socrates' Delphic mission to exchange false divine wisdom for honest human ignorance consists in a process of moral purification that helps the city to perform its real tasks: the activities of fostering individual virtue, continually renewing its laws and caring for its cultural heritage. While the dedication of Pericles' Athens to the beautiful[76] must be internalized, using Socrates' resilient soul as its new paradigm, Socrates will deconstruct any effort to make him into an exceptional figure; he refuses to be a savior or scapegoat by whom other souls are relieved of the duty to practice virtue. This frustrates men like Alcibiades or Crito who hoped to gain wisdom through him. Just as Nietzsche argued that God could not exist for otherwise he could not bear not being God,[77] the *Symposium* reveals how Alcibiades turns Socrates into a god to overcome his frustration at not being able to emulate him.

Socrates thus serves as an example or paradigm in two ways: first by commanding his body to withstand and refute the powers of the divinized passions, and second by maintaining friendly conversations both with and about the laws of Athens, even as they condemned him to death. Socrates is steadfast in his desire to fully discharge the debt of gratitude he owes his city. He could not have become Socrates anywhere else and he wants his fellow citizens to realize that he has not enjoyed any special divine privilege beyond knowledge of his ignorance. Otherwise put, anyone could be as happy as Socrates. The only task remaining is for him to make the Athenians understand and follow his way of seeing the laws and interpreting the works of the poets. The way Socrates views reality, while none are born wise and some have ignorance thrust upon them, all are capable of loving wisdom and seeing its beauty. But since wisdom doesn't play favorites, the polis must frame laws that help all its citizens to see and discuss the beauty and order, physical and eidetic, surrounding their cave. This is the best a father can do for his sons: to leave behind the ideal of a regime where all have a fair chance to realize their potential for virtue.

Socrates' conversation with the laws suggests that they can neither enslave us—as the old gods and tyrants would—nor give the unconditional license promised by Dionysus and the democratic demagogues; both slavery and anarchy are incompatible with the nature of law. The very fact that these laws speak to him and demand that he try to persuade them (52a) before accepting their decision suggests that their authority is noncoercive; they require our reasoned consent and only forbid us the "right" to regress to the state of Circe's swine in the cave. This idea of combining laws with a reasoned account or logos plays a central role in Plato's *Laws*; here too rulers and ruled must never separate laws from rational speech.[78] Yet both the religious Right and the emotive Left would object to this view; they hold in common that reality is ultimately absurd and they will join forces to kill the Logos in the name of an imperator: either God or Caesar.

Crito who unknowingly represents the soul's eponymous ability to see, judge and even act rightly, overriding the false necessities of the physical and mimetic orders when faced with the authority of what is just and beautiful, seems to have been only convinced by Socrates' heroic death. This suggests that the chained prisoner is only persuaded to leave the cave by the heroic death of the escaped prisoner who returns to bear witness to the light. Indeed the tenuous arguments of the *Phaedo* in support of the generic soul's immortality pale in comparison before Socrates' bold existential proof of his own eponymous enduring power. We know that Crito wrote dialogues[79] and even if these were written more after the style of Xenophon than Plato, they are evidence that he overcame the power of sleep; he is no longer a guardian dog that did not bark in the night! Once this power is rooted in this own body, he will be a glowworm, if not a gadfly. Crito will come to see that he can no more deny the existence of earth and water, the tribute his body pays to the sovereign power of life, than he can doubt the reality of speech and the ideas. These are the presuppositions of human association, the true basis for his friendship with Socrates and the possibility for continued talk about the best way to live, even after his friend's death. These erotic inquiries acknowledge the existence and authority of these ruling beginnings of human actions, as they remind us of the impossibility of supplanting or claiming to go beyond them. They define and delimit the field for our common strivings and mortal wisdom. Even if he may never grasp philosophy, Crito will no longer live like a shade in Hades, believing that only Socrates can give fleeting self-knowledge to his otherwise clouded soul. At this point, I can best defend my speculations by explicitly connecting them to a Platonic "proof text"—the *Republic*.

By questioning Crito about these matters, Socrates encourages his comrade to exercise his own soul's access to a supernatural order of truth and goodness that transcends the selfish fury of the cave or city. No longer would the exceptional feats and tragic fates of heroes be used to deter men from disobeying the reified powers of the cave. The way out of all existent or possible caves leads to this common structure of archetypal ideas that human souls can apprehend and are bound to by the power of speech and the necessity of conversation. As Socrates said in the *Apology*, "it is a very great good for a human being to have conversations every day about virtue" (38a). This insight leads to his celebrated claim that the unexamined life is not worth living (38a) and dovetails with his assertion in the *Crito* that the most important thing is not living but living well (48b). The irresistible conclusion is that the best life cannot be separated from discussions about living well; these deliberations bring men together, calling them out of their different caves or economic origins to come under a common horizon of metaphysical morality. This is like the prisoner leaving the cave, leaving behind imperfect images of the gods that claim to supersede thinking but only occlude his awareness of the erotic light and ideas that make thought necessary.

Since these ideas have authority over us—both organizing our experience and demanding to be realized in everyday reality—humans, incomplete by nature, then return to their caves and try to form or reform societies where images of these ideas unite and complete their chthonic aspects. Like the gods of the *Euthyphro*,[80] or the prisoners in *Republic*'s cave, men tend to disagree over the adequacy of images to the ideas, prone by nurture to confuse their cave's gods with original paradigms, especially if they have never cognitively met the idea itself. There is usually fierce resistance offered to those who, once having left the cave to see the ideas in their purity and are then impregnated by the vision, are sent back to the cave to talk and give birth to new images of what they have seen. Their opponents are both those who hold their forefathers' images to be sacred, as well others who cynically make images reflecting demotic desire to gain power over others.

As it is impossible for any man to dwell outside the cave, the basis for the battle between philosophy and poetry/politics has to do with the sacralized status of the images. While poets and politicians treat the image as a domesticated actualization of a dangerous titanic force that cannot be dragged into the cave but can only be appeased and flattered, in the spirit that gave birth to tragedy as an attempt to keep Dionysus out of the city, the philosopher deplores the vile corruption ensuing from the reduction of what is transcendent and divine to base proportions. He demands that the images be ruled by and admit to their elusive transcendent origins, instead of being venerated as sacred originals. The destiny of the polis must involve talk about fashioning increasingly adequate laws or images of these ideas, adjudged appropriate to its specific cultural context. While we may not know the origin or essence of these ideas, we cannot dispense with them or deny their authority. Since the ideas do not violate the soul's freedom, but rather cooperate with its integrity, their power is authoritative but non-coercive. As noted before, not even the gods can change a soul's moral quality against its will. Our freedom is not denied by grace.

Socrates' questions refute those who claimed to "know" an idea in the sense of believing themselves able to make the godly quality in question conform to their will or fury. To know the essence of these forms is to lay exclusive claim to power over them; as we noted, this technical knowledge effectively destroys their universal authority since human plurality would lead different men to bend these ideas to their own wills. Instead we only know them as transcendent looks or ideas. As his take-down of Euthyphro showed, Socrates did not doubt the existence of the ideal or god itself; he only refuted any claim to define them that let the diviner usurp the authority of the divine. Such an activity was obviously deeply repugnant to those politicians, poets and artisans—the makers of gods—who affirm or believe in a sacred covenant between their god(s) and the chthonic order that gave their own community privileged status under heaven; they continue to show Earth's desire to subdue the sky or jealous Hera's wish to rule Zeus. Socrates by contrast seems to view all "gods" or ideas as aspects of the Good, a principle beyond being that could not be represented or known other than by its benevolence. This meant that while the poet-priests and politicians affirm the centripetal power of the womblike cave, philosophy "midwifes" the power of the soul to climb out beyond the cave and see the originals of the sacred images in the high places; when the soul returns to its origins, the erotic authority of the meeting inspire it to talk with others about, and refine, the images by which the ideas are represented communally. This clash between the erotic returnee and the thumotic defenders of the old ways of sacred representation is inevitable since we need both secure origins and erotic individualization.

While the forces of thumos are more interested in defending the sacredness of the ways of the cave, and the inviolability of its laws, the erotic party wants these laws to point beyond themselves to their origin: the sublime and unrepresentable vision of a benevolent cosmic order. This also means that while every cave ritually proclaims its exceptionalism, condemns the bad infinite beyond its holy limits, and affirms maternal chthonic values with boyish spiritedness, the champions of the good question the value of this Mediterranean union of male violence and female favoritism; they remind us of the impersonal benevolence of the universal transcendent principles whilst warning against the blind jealousy of the chthonic mother-gods. While a soul must be born within a womblike cave, every cave, community or church tends to see itself as our tainted nature's solitary hope and denies the possibility of salvation outside its sacramental order. As befitting his ancestor, Socrates looks towards laws that move like the statues of Daedalus and give an account/logos that summons each generation into conversation about its origins and *telos*.

One particularly interesting aspect of this struggle between the values of the cave and the philosopher has to do with the idea of justice. While the cave understands *dike* in terms of the furies and revenge, philosophical justice according to Socrates has more to do with being equal or just towards one's own soul.[81] The cave pulverizes this possibility of psychic individuation while angrily claiming exceptional treatment for its own brood, which it prefers to keep blind and bereft of self-knowledge; it is thus diametrically opposed to philosophy which affirms natural grace, shining like the sun on the good, the bad and ugly, while acknowledging the uniqueness of the individual soul. This means that while the womb is the source of individuation, only the sun of the good can nurture it. While all men are brothers under the sun, the cave limits the rights of unconditional fraternity to those born inside its confines whilst denying recognition to friends within and strangers beyond its confines. Since the claims of universal brotherhood are as abstract as the obligations of blood loyalty are stifling, the ideal synthesis must be found in a polity where the uniqueness of each soul is nurtured in a community both large and small enough to make genuine recognition and realization possible. While the *Euthyphro* suggests that divine law is impartial, offering all an equal opportunity to flourish, this law's spirit can only be realized in a small polity, a place where the specific qualities of everyone can be known and cultivated, albeit at the expense of the material economies of scale that have caused even the nation to wither away.

The *Euthyphro's* insight that the gods do not give special privileges or knowledge of them to any person leads us to conclude that the true interests of different mortals do not conflict; happiness is not gained by a short glorious career of violence towards others in a fractious reality. This is only possible if these interests are ultimately non-physical and self-limiting in so far as they pertain to material things. These deductions are co-extensive with certain conclusions about the human condition that can be drawn from the life of Socrates; there was nothing exceptional about his birth or fortune.[82] His life is exemplary because of his self-contained *eudaimonia*, both in life and manner of death. As we have seen, the crucial ingredient to this flourishing was his denial that any humans could possess divine wisdom. From extrapolation of the meta-revelation of Apollo that no one was wiser than Socrates, we have deduced that no person had or could have knowledge that would provide them with godly power over their own life or those of others. This suggests that the gods are just and non-adversarial; far from deriving pleasure from our fear or discomfiture, they used Socrates to deliver mankind from false ideas about them that caused so much impiety and injustice. These falsely attributed vices should be neither imitated nor feared.

The new purpose of law then is to foster the emergence of virtuous individual souls, men like Socrates. We do not become virtuous through him but by living lives like his. While this telos is within the capacity of all, it may never be realized collectively by the many, as a mob. Socrates serves the city as a kind of *daimon*, warning it against the false gods of wealth, honor and power. Freed from false knowledge about jealous irrational gods, Socrates' life flourished and we have reason to believe that most communities could still profit greatly from these tidings.

But is this revelation sufficient to explain widespread human suffering? We have seen how Socratic education sets out to exorcise the soul's inherited origins of thumos that seems to be the truest cause of evil and suffering. Just as festering lilies smell worse than weeds,[83] parents' unrealized erotic capacities, especially those frustrated by false accounts of the gods, seem to be passed on in a mutated thumotic form to their children; their errors are often, if not inevitably, tragically reproduced and sanctified. Crito's all-too-human beliefs in divine omnipotence and chthonic necessity, both cause and effect of this suffering, must be prevented from leading his sons astray. While the gods do not play favorites, and all minds have access to the erotic grace of the ideas, some are too damaged by internalized chthonic fury to give birth to their souls. As Socrates said in the *Republic*, the gods do not cause bad things.[84] The fault lies in our brutish souls, misused freedom and deified passions rather than the gods. Sunlight cannot enter the cave.

Following this logic we can infer that while the non-good are not hated by the gods, they are born turned away from the light of the good by their flawed origins. This condition lasts as long as they languish chained in the womb-like cave to toxic religious beliefs and self-negating family values by the Platonic version of original sin. This is compatible with Socrates' discovery that even the gods cannot have power sufficient to violate any soul's nature and/or grant the prize of *Eudaimonia*. We learn from the *Euthyphro* that this soul-negating power cannot exist in heaven or on earth; it is incompatible with divine justice and the integrity of the soul. Plato's gods rule by beauty and inspiration; they are not envious, violent or direct. They only influence us through the justice of *daimons* and by inspiring beauty. While a *daimon* will jealously destroy the false ideas that corrupt or disintegrate the soul, intimations of beauty will remind us of true happiness.

Since happiness cannot come from external sources, because it cannot be given or taken, then it must come from within the soul—although the soul's flourishing depends on a benevolent transcendent order that summons it out of the cave and body before sending it back. As Aristotle saw, randomly given happiness violates the order and beauty of the cosmos.[85] *Eudaimonia* is not gained passively or stolen from jealous gods; it comes from the virtuous deed of turning inherited Thumos into Eros. This view of happiness co-exists with the idea that true human interests do not conflict with each other or the gods' will. To Socrates divine benevolence is not a private good or secret teaching; it is cosmic law. Plato sees it as a demand that the polis dedicate itself to teaching all men of their potential for virtue and happiness; false gods must not crush the human spirit.

Applied to the law and its goal of the general good, this line of thought also reinforces the Platonic view of justice as rehabilitative rather than retributive;[86] self-knowledge and awareness of the truth about happiness must replace holy vengeance: an adversarial and thumotic idea derived from toxic theology. While human freedom necessitates that wickedness be confined and ignorance exposed, the insidious desire to gain pleasure and cheap virtue from punishing vice is one of the chief ways evil spreads.

Socratic pedagogy combines both punishment and education. Gently leading a corrupt man to see himself, Socrates lets him see that he was only damaging his own soul and so catalyzed a recognition that would otherwise occur at a point where its effects were irreversible.[87] Genuine lasting happiness only comes *after* justice, through friendship and politics; their essence is a civic civil conversation interpreting law and vindicating tradition.

Just as his discussion with the laws represents his refusal to leave the city and desert the realm of articulate speech, a loyalty he maintained by his conduct until his very moment of death, Socrates passes to the underworld to refute/uproot the chthonic fear of death. This is the meaning of the Laws' claim that their brothers, the Laws of Hades would not receive him well if he were to destroy them, the Laws of Athens (54c). This suggests that even the dark chthonic powers are open to enlightenment, at least in how they are viewed, and confirms our claim that they are tied to the positive laws of the polity. Otherwise put, Socrates also seeks to deliver body and *oikos* from the contagion of fury, the curse of irrationality and the fear of death. Unlike the deadly head of the Gorgon, his gentle maieutic queries will melt long-frozen stone tablets of law and reveal the true causes and fears underlying their draconian mandates. By the logos of conversation and speech, the spirit of interpretation or the divine gift of Hermes reveals parallels between fathers and sons. By this triad of divine law, logos and exegesis, the past redeems the future. Like the child Jesus in the doomed Temple, the Logos must do his Father's business by discussing Law.[88]

By demonstrating the soul's power of integrity, Socrates hopes to educate the polis to its fullest possibilities and also reveal that ultimate reality is erotic and non-adversarial. Here we are reminded of his statement in the *Apology* that instead of killing those who oppose us we should instead equip ourselves to be as good as we can be (39d); this statement also has deep theological resonances. While his life teaches the polis that the unfamiliar is not necessarily hostile, its deeper significance is that the gods are not envious of human virtue but glory in and are glorified by it. While not the least part of the beauty of the cosmos lies in the non-mechanistic freedom with which every monadic aspect has the freedom and power to mirror the ideal harmony of the whole—both within the soul and in the city— to the greater glory of reality, the complementary attribute of justice requires that the gods will not give any soul or monad an ugly or literally unfair advantage over another. These divine laws conflict with chthonic *dike* with respect to blood loyalty and the related notion that virtues and other essential qualities are necessarily transmitted from parent to child. As we saw, this insight angered self-made men like Anytus who, not having given birth to their souls, wished to pass their diseased arête on to their sons.[89] Perhaps only the self-righteous rage of *thumos* is inherited; true virtue arises from the soul's erotic motion out of the cave of the familiar and towards the light of the Good. Our origins must be redeemed, not venerated.

Yet Socrates realizes all too well that the young, or not yet good, are all too susceptible to corruption by those who falsely—even if sincerely—believe themselves to be wise. His assertion that he could not be harmed by his enemies, since a good man cannot be harmed by those worse than he, allows for the possibility of the non-good first harming themselves and then each other. This position accounts for human evil in the soul and polis while denying the necessity of belief in unfriendly gods. Human eros and divine grace must struggle against doctrines of unjust gods and the contagion of souls corrupted by psychic furies that they can neither understand nor control. Just as Socrates' speeches and deeds informed the laws of the Athenians, persuading them to bring their *nomos* into better conformity with the non-adversarial order of the cosmos, his death will exert a similar influence on the political unconscious of Athens. Only here, by the way of his death, will his career as gadfly and *daimon* be rooted and be seen to have divine sanction.

It cannot be said too often that Socrates did not have secret knowledge about his soul's fate. Likewise his death was exemplary and heroic, but not contagiously sacramental. Refuting the power of Hades, the fear of death, which seemed to trump all of his words and deeds to Crito, Socrates' exceptionally peaceful way of dying will existentially prove that the gods are well disposed to one who chooses justice over blasphemous piety. The cock Crito would dedicate to Asclepius, the god of healing in the *Phaedo* (118a), not only shows that the *fear* of death, represented by Crito and his body, was overcome by Socrates, it also suggests that death itself has no sting and that ultimate reality is non-adversarial. These tidings heal sick Plato[90] and inspire him to write dialogues testifying to the vitality of Socrates' spirit. While the eros of Socrates is not easily communicated, even unerotic Aristotle was convinced that the gods were not jealous.[91]

Socrates' way of facing death is not his resurrection; it merely compels the attention of those too fearful or passion-ridden to attend to the virtues he embodied. Though we are neither "saved" through his dying nor converted by his proofs of the soul's immortality, his way of living—if it is emulated and not imitated—seems to carry with it its own reward. Plato suggests that only by living as Socrates did can we enjoy comparable happiness. Like Paul, who was perhaps not unaware of his Classical predecessor, Socrates poured out the dregs of his life like a libation and ran a good race.[92] By his valiant avoidance of evil and his whole-hearted dedication to dispelling vice he has set an example of intellectual probity and virtue that still shines through twenty-four intervening centuries of dead dogma, draconian despotism, and dull domesticity. Crito went down to visit Socrates in his cave-like prison, hoping to convince him of the truth of Achilles' rueful words that he would rather live as a landless day laborer than reign as prince among all the dead. Now he, Crito, must attest that Socrates would far rather rule over the vast memory chamber of Hellas than be reduced to another shameless political refugee in Thessaly.

To reach Thessaly from Attica, the traveler must pass through Thermopylae. Here Leonidas's three hundred Spartans, by their seemingly suicidal but truly heroic resistance, inspired all Hellas to repel the Persian juggernaut and gained immortality. Likewise, Socrates refuses to leave his station before the Gates of Hades and fly to the fleshpots of fertile Phthia, even though stalked by certain death. It is not inappropriate that the surface rhetoric of the *Crito*, Socrates' last testament to dying Athens, seems to echo Simonides' epitaph to the immortal three hundred.

Go tell the Athenians, citizen passing by, that obedient to your laws, Socrates here lies.

But perhaps Socrates' example could also provide the inspiration needed to revive the soul of his beloved Athens in our own times and help us to avoid the Scylla of technology and the Charybdis of fundamentalism. Then the West would be able to give voice to an even more heroic message:

Go, tell Socrates that here, persuaded by his example, the human spirit yet endures.

Endnotes

The Euthyphro

1   See Ranasinghe, *The Soul of Socrates* Cornell U.P. 2000, chapter 3.
2   "Platonic Political Philosophy" valorizes the atheistic realism of Callicles and Clitophon.
3   In the *Theaetetus* Meletus is mentioned as the only accuser.
4   See Robin Waterfield, *Why Socrates Died*, W. W. Norton, 2009, pp. 7–8.
5   Xenophon, *Memorabilia*, II.9.
6   Xenophon, *Apology of Socrates*, 5–9.
7   Xenophon, *Apology of Socrates*, 4.
8   Strauss, *On the Euthyphron* in *The Rebirth of Classical Political Rationalism*, Univ. of Chicago Press, 1989 pp. 190–91.
9   Ibid. p. 191.
10 Homer, *Odyssey* XXI. 258–59.
11 Diogenes Laertius, *Lives of the Philosophers*, II 29.
12 Xenophon, *Memorabilia* III. 6. 1.
13 *Cratylus* 396d.
14 Homer, Odyssey XVIII. 1–13.
15 Emily Watson, *The Death of Socrates*, Harvard Univ. Press, 2007, p. 78.
16 *Plutarch's Lives*, *Life of Caesar*, Modern Library, N.A. p. 856.
17 See entry on Aristophanes in *Oxford Classical Dictionary*, 3rd Ed. Oxford 1996, p. 164.
18 See entry on Sophocles in *OCD*, p. 1423.
19 Aristotle, *Poetics* 1447 b 10.
20 Nails, Debra *The People of Plato*, Hackett, 2002, p. 56.
21 *Theaetetus* 174a.
22 Here he is like Thrasymachus and Gorgias who also want to be called wise for possessing powers they exert by a combination of opportunism and chance.

23   See *Apology* 37a.
24   See Thomas and Grace West, *Four Texts on Socrates*, Cornell University Press, 1984, p. 44.
25   Hegel, *Lectures on the Philosophy of World History* trans. Nisbet, Cambridge Univ. Press, 1981, p. 54.
26   See Waterfield, p. 126–28.
27   See Waterfield, p. 132–34.
28   See Aristophanes, The *Clouds*, 1311–27, 1437–50.
29   See *Meno* 93c-95a.
30   See Nails, p. 56.
31   Hesiod, *Theogony*, 459–90.
32   Homer, *Odyssey*, XI. 489–91.
33   Aeschylus, *Agamemnon*, 1497–1504.
34   Aeschylus, *Agamemnon*, 1567–76.
35   Aristotle, *Nicomachean Ethics*, 1149 b 10 ff.
36   This point is made convincingly by R.E. Allen in *Plato's Euthyphro and the Earlier Theory of Forms*, New York, Humanities Press, 1970, p. 21. Allen says that Euthyphro's father acted with "unusual scrupulousness;" he would have been well within his rights in immediately executing Euthyphro's man.
37   Aeschylus, *Eumenides*, 984–87.
38   *Apology* 27b-e.
39   Euripides, *Bacchae*, 39–43.
40   Hesiod, *Theogony*, 159ff, 626ff. Gaia even resurrects monsters from below the earth to aid these efforts.
41   Aristophanes, *Clouds*, 1443–46.
42   Machiavelli, *Prince* XXV.
43   Thucydides. *Peloponnesian War*, I. 70.
44   Ibid, I.1.
45   Ibid, 3.82–84 and 5.84–111.
46   Aristotle, *Nicomachean Ethics*, 1100 b 12–18.
47   *Job* 2.9.
48   Thucydides 1.5.2, also see Nestor in *Odyssey* iii. 71–74.
49   While this is explicitly done in his *Ekklesiazusae*, and *Lysistrata*, the theme runs through his corpus.
50   See Ranasinghe, *Soul of Socrates* Chapter 1.
51   Herodotus, *Histories*, 7.161.3.
52   Aeschylus, *Agamemnon*, 1489–96.
53   Girard, *Deceit, Desire and the Novel*, Johns Hopkins University Press, 1976, pp. 1–52.
54   This point is explicitly stated in *Sophist* 246a.
55   *Republic* II, 383c.
56   *Republic* III, 391e.
57   See *Republic* VIII 568a-c.
58   Homer, *Iliad*, VIII. 18–27.
59   Nietzsche, *The Genealogy of Morals*, III, 11, 15, 17–22.

60　See *Gorgias* 453a-b.

61　See Proclus's abstract of the *Cypria* in *Hesiod, the Homeric Hymns and Homerica*, edit. & trans. Hugh Evelyn White, Loeb Classical Library, 1977, p. 491.

62　Perhaps the closest Socrates comes to saying this directly is in *Republic* IV 444a, where he links ignorance to what destroys the harmony of the soul. The converse position, connecting the activity of virtue with moral knowledge, rather than intellectual knowledge/wisdom, is a central tenet of Socratic philosophy.

63　Homer, *Iliad* XIV 231–56.

64　See *Meno* 82b–86b.

65　This is the effective meaning of Thrasymachus's rejection of Clitophon's positivistic definition of justice in *Republic* (340 a-c). Thrasymachus makes it clear that injustice is a science practiced by an expert (340d).

66　Strauss, *Rebirth of Classical Political Rationalism*, p. 198.

67　Thucydides, *Peloponnesian War*, II. 43.

68　In Karl Marx: *Selected Works*, vol. 2 (1942). Paraphrase of the opening sentences of The Eighteenth Brumaire of Louis Bonaparte (1852). The actual words were: "Hegel remarks somewhere that all great, world-historical facts and personages occur, as it were, twice. He has forgotten to add: the first time as tragedy, the second as farce."

69　Thomas and Grace West, *Four Texts on Socrates*, 1984, pp. 13–14.

70　This corresponds to Aristotle's position in the *Nicomachean Ethics* that happiness cannot be added to 1097b15. Likewise the most godlike cannot be praised or honored but simply congratulated 1101b25.

71　As Joseph Cropsey puts it, "Euthyphro pleads other business and flees. Socrates sends him on his way in a cloud of ceremonious contempt...." *Plato's World*, (Chicago, 1995) p. 67.

72　Homer, *Odyssey* VIII. 89–99.

73　C.H. Kahn *The Art and Thought of Heraclitus* Cambridge UP 1979 fragment 94.

74　Aeschylus, *Prometheus Bound*, 753ff, 907ff.

75　*Republic* 425 d-e, *Laws* 628 c-d.

76　*Genesis* 22.

77　William Faulkner, *Absalom, Absalom*, Vintage.

78　Aristotle, *Nicomachean Ethics*, 1095a 5–7.

79　*Symposium* 212a.

80　*Gorgias* 468c, 472e.

81　See entry on Tantalus in *Oxford Classical Dictionary*, p. 1473.

82　Strauss, *Rebirth of Classical Political Rationalism* p. 200.

83　*Gorgias* 508a.

84　Hesiod, *Works and Days* 42.

85　Hesiod, *Works and Days* 210–11.

86　*Symposium*, 189c-193e.

87　See Ranasinghe, *"Nature, Nurture and Nietzsche"* in *Faith in Reasons and Reason's Faith*, ed. Wayne Cristaudo, University Press of America, 2011, pp. 93–110.

88　Homer, *Iliad* VII. 58–59.

89 See Pindar, *Isthmian Ode* viii 34–54.
90 Hesiod *Works and Days* 109.
91 See Ranasinghe, *"Trojan Horse or Troilus' Whore?"* in *Shakespeare and the Body Politic*, ed. Bernard Dobski, Lexington Books, 2012.
92 Homer, *Iliad* I. 407–12.
93 Homer, *Iliad* VIII 1–31.
94 Homer, *Iliad* XVI 512–48.
95 Homer, *Iliad* I.590–660. We must bear in mind that Eris hurled the golden apple at the scene of Zeus's great triumph: the marriage of Thetis, who was fated to bear his successor, to a mortal, Peleus. See also note 76 re: Prometheus's prophecies, and note Aristophanes' curious comment that Peleus, the reputed sire of Achilles, was impotent: *Clouds* 1063–69. While Thetis herself makes this confession to Hephaestus, himself the impotent husband of lusty Aphrodite about her aged spouse: *Iliad* XVII. 433–34, it could very well be that the reason for her secret hold over Zeus is that Achilles is truly his son.
96 See David Malouf, *Ransom*, Pantheon, 2010.
97 See Wendy Doniger, *Other People's Myths: the Cave of Echoes*, Univ. of Chicago Press, p. 105.
98 See *Soul of Socrates*, Chapter 2.
99 See *Phaedrus* 249d.
100 Compare this to Machiavelli's gleefully told anecdote about Caterina Sforza exposing her ability to bear more offspring when her children were held hostage: *Discourses on Livy*, Oxford Classics. 2009, p. 272.
101 See Homer, *Odyssey*, VIII. 161–65, XVII, 473–74.
102 Hesiod, *Works and Days* 11–24.
103 Nicomachean Ethics, 1103a5.
104 See Pascal's *Memorial*, in *Pensees*, Oxford University Press 2008, p. 178.

Plato's Apology of Socrates

1   See Zuckert, *Plato's Philosophers*, Univ. of Chicago Press, 2009, p. 4 footnote 8
2   As we shall see, he uses the *Euthyphro* to speculate about the implications of Socrates' deeds while letting Socrates himself reveal his accusers' true motives in the *Apology*.
3   Matthew 22. 11–14.
4   Plato, *Second Letter*, 314c.
5   Aeschylus, *Libation Bearers*, 886.
6   Homer, *Iliad* XVIII. 110.
7   Homer, *Odyssey* IX. 216ff.
8   Thucydides, *Peloponnesian War*, 2.52.
9   Plato, *Meno*, 100a.
10 Plato, *Republic*, 488a–489a, *Gorgias* 521d.
11 Homer, *Odyssey*, XII. 185–91.
12 Matthew 12. 43–45.
13 Xenophon's *Apology* 4.

14 Martin Heidegger, *What is Called Thinking*, Harper, pp. 17–18.

15 Homer, *Iliad*, IX. 415.

16 Aristotle, *Nicomachean Ethics* 1126b11–12.

17 *Life of Solon in Plutarch's Lives* Modern Library, pp. 108–9.

18 Aeschylus, *Eumenides*, 94ff.

19 Strauss, *On the Euthyphron* in *The Rebirth of Classical Political Philosophy*, pp. 187–206.

20 Homer, *Iliad*, IX.363.

21 Thucydides, *Peloponnesian War*, II.53.

22 See Plato, *Republic*, 475b ff.

23 See Aristophanes, *Clouds* 142ff.

24 This phenomenon is most memorably described in Aristophanes' *Wasps*.

25 Pseudo-Aristotle, *Melissus, Xenophanes and Gorgias*, 979a10.

26 I Samuel 8 5–8.

27 Ranasinghe, *Soul of Socrates*, chapter 5.

28 C.H. Kahn *The Art and Thought of Heraclitus* Cambridge UP 1979 fragment 114, p 81.

29 Kierkegaard, *Concluding Unscientific Postscript*, Princeton Univ. Press, 1992, pp. 248–49.

30 Cicero, *Tusculan Disputations*, V.10.

31 Plato, *Alcibiades I*. 119c ff.

32 Descartes, *Meditation #4*.

33 Plato, *Gorgias* 521d.

34 Xenophon, *Anabasis*, III. i.4–5.

35 Aeschylus, *Eumenides* 1–19.

36 Aristotle, *Nicomachean Ethics*, 1100b10.

37 See C.D. C. Reeve, *Socrates in the Apology*, Hackett, 1989, p. 29.

38 Plato, *Charmides*, 166e ff.

39 See Hannah Arendt, *The Concept of History* in *The Portable Hannah Arendt*, Viking Penguin, 2003 pp. 280–81.

40 Hegel, *Phenomenology of Spirit*, 665.

41 Rousseau, *Second Discourse*, Note XV.

42 See Plato, *Lesser Hippias*.

43 Herodotus, *Histories*, VII.228.

44 Over a half-century of activity as a playwright Euripides won first prize on only three occasions (and a fourth posthumously). This compares unfavorably to the thirteen and eighteen victories garnered by Aeschylus and Sophocles respectively. *Oxford Classical Dictionary* p. 571.

45 See his *Philoctetes and Ajax*. In each case Odysseus is presented as the villainous betrayer of a tragic hero.

46 Matthew 13 24–30.

47 Strikingly Jesus says "my word is not my own, it is the word of the one who sent me ... the Paraclete, the Holy Spirit . . . will teach you everything and remind you of all I said to you" (John 14 24–26). Here too, the Word or Logos does not or cannot interpret itself.

48 Aristotle, *Nicomachean Ethics*, 1159b25.
49 Lessing, *Philosophical and Theological Writings*, trans. H. B. Nesbit, Cambridge Univ. Press, 2005 p. 95.
50 Bloom, Allan *An Interpretation of Plato's Ion* in *The Roots of Political Philosophy*, edited by Thomas Pangle, Cornell University Press, 1987 pp. 383–84.
51 Feuerbach, *The Essence of Christianity*, trans. George Elliot, Harper Torchbooks, 1989, p. 25.
52 Plato, *Republic X*, 611d.
53 Plato, *Gorgias*, 519a.54 Homer, *Odyssey*, X. 286ff.
55 Aeschylus, *Eumenides* 864–65.
56 Xenophon, *Apology of Socrates*, 3.
57 Benardete, Seth G. *The Bow and the Lyre*, Rowman and Littlefield, 2008, pp. 95–97.
58 Sophocles, *Oedipus at Colonus*, 1224ff.
59 Diogenes Laertius II.40.
60 Xenophon, *Apology*, 10.
61 This is the effective result of his reframing of the charges at 24b. See West, *Four Texts*, p.73. #38.
62 Akenson, Donald Harman *Surpassing Wonder: The Invention of the Bible and the Talmud* University of Chicago Press, 1998 p. 295.
63 See Hesiod, *Theogony*, 535ff.
64 Aristotle, *Nicomachean Ethics*, 1099b15.
65 *"Repentance and Self-Limitation"* in *The Solzhenitsyn Reader*, ISI Books, 2005, pp. 527–554.
66 Matthew 25 14–30.
67 George Anastaplo, *Human Being and Citizen*, Swallow Press, 1985 p. 24.
68 Homer, *Odyssey*, XI.576–600.
69 Socrates sets out to refute this position in *Republic* I. Its origins in Odyssey VI. 180–185 must be governed by the moderate conclusion of the *Odyssey*.
70 *Republic* 375d– 376b.
71 *Gorgias*, 481c.
72 Homer, *Odyssey* XXI. 205–16.
73 *Gorgias* 518c–519b.
74 Nietzsche, *Zarathustra II* in *The Portable Nietzsche*, trans. Walter Kaufmann, Viking Penguin, p.225.
75 This is the basis for Socrates' refutation of Polemarchus's spirited definition of justice as helping friends and hurting enemies: *Republic* 334b–c.
76 Homer, *Odyssey* X. 236–244.
77 Xenophon, *Apology* 18. While these words do not appear in Plato's *Apology*, they are certainly not untypical of Socrates.
78 Plato, *Republic* VI. 493b–c.
79 '*In Memory of W. B. Yeats*' in '*Another Time*' Random House, 1940.
80 Nails, *The People of Plato*, Hackett, 2002, pp. 199-202.
81 *Phaedo* 60e.

82 Socrates' *logos* of the afterlife at the conclusion of the *Gorgias* is consistent with this, the main goal of the *Republic*. In the *Gorgias* he administers this-worldly medicinal punishment.

83 Homer. *Odyssey* XXIII.266–67.

84 See Rene Girard, *The Scapegoat*, Johns Hopkins Univ. Press, 1989, pp 25–26.

85 *Crito* 43d–e also see Homer, *Odyssey*, XI. 134–35.

86 DK 12 in *Early Greek Political Thought from Homer to the Sophists*, editors Gagarin and Woodruff, Cambridge Univ. Press, 1995.

87 Homer, *Iliad* XXII. 324–26.

88 Aristophanes, *Clouds*, 1490 ff.

89 Herodotus, *Histories*, I.32.7.

90 Bettany Hughes, *The Hemlock Cup*, Jonathan Cape, 2010. p. 336.

91 *Constitution of Athens* 27.5, Siculus 13.64–66.

92 Diogenes Laertius, II.43.

93 *Euthyphro* 6c.

94 Homer, *Odyssey*, X.31.

95 Homer, *Odyssey*, VIII.523.

96 Homer, *Odyssey*, IX.366–67.

97 See Sartre, *No Exit and Three Other Plays*, Vintage, 1989, p. 12.

98 Xenophon, *Anabasis*, V.1.2.

99 Homer, *Odyssey*, X.493–95.

100 Eva Brann, *Homeric Moments*, Paul Dry Books, 2002 p. 205.

101 *Gorgias* 524a.

102 Homer, *Odyssey*, X.306.

103 Homer, *Odyssey*, I.32–34.

104 Aristotle, *Nicomachean Ethics*, 1099b20ff.

105 Homer, *Odyssey*, XXIV. 351.

106 Diogenes Laertius, 11.26.

107 Aristotle, *Nicomachean Ethics*, 1100a20ff, 1100a22ff.

108 See West, *Four Texts*, p. 97. #85.

109 Homer, *Iliad*, XVI 431–60.

Crito: Or What Must Be Done

1 Aphorism for Book Five of Nietzsche's *The Gay Science* trans. Walter Kaufmann, Vintage Books, 1974, p. 277.

2 For succinct accounts of their careers, see Emily Wilson, *The Death of Socrates*, pp. 82–88.

3 Homer, *Iliad* IX. 410–16. Achilles falsely tells Odysseus that his mother has told him that he has this choice.

4 Liddell and Scott, *Greek English Lexicon* Oxford University Press, 9th Edition, 1996, p. 997.

5 Strauss, *Persecution and the Art of Writing*, University of Chicago Press, 1988 p. 155.

6 *Meno* 80a.

7   Diogenes Laertius, *Lives of the Philosophers* II.121.

8   Leo Strauss, *Studies in Platonic Political Philosophy*, University of Chicago Press, 1983, p. 58.

9   Roslyn Weiss points out that it is Crito who, in the *Phaedo*, accompanies Xanthippe home. *Socrates Dissatisfied*, Oxford University Press, 1998 p. 45.

10 Matthew 27.58–60, Luke 23.50 53.

11 *Republic* VII 514a ff.

12 Homer, *Odyssey*, XVII.322–23.

13 *Republic* VII 517a.

14 *Theaetetus* 174a.

15 *Phaedo* 58a–c.

16 Homer, *Odyssey* III. 278–81.

17 Diogenes Laertius, II.43.

18 Homer, *Iliad*, IX, 357–63.

19 Thomas and Grace West, *Four Texts on Socrates*, 1984, p. 101.

20 Homer, *Iliad. IX* 160–61.

21 George Anastapolo points out that Crito "does not know what would be truly faithful to his friend." *Human Being and Citizen*, Chicago, Swallow Press, 1975, p. 209.

22 See also Scholia on *Iliad* I. 5 quoting the Cypria in *Hesiod, the Homeric Hymns and Homerica*, edit. & trans. Hugh Evelyn White, Loeb Classical Library, 1977, p. 497.

23 Sophocles, *Oedipus at Colonus*, 1765.

24 Aristotle, *Nicomachean Ethics*, 1101b20.

25 See Homer, *Odyssey* XIV 339–40. Athena's strange words to Odysseus, "Never did I have any doubt, but in my heart I always knew you would come home," are far more about trust in virtue than divine omnipotence. They are the ultimate answer to the Euthyphro question as to whether the gods recognize or create virtue.

26 *Phaedrus* 251a.

27 Xenophon, *Memorabilia*, II.9.

28 Weiss proves that Crito does not have any idea of what philosophy is. *Socrates Dissatisfied*, pp. 48–49.

29 *Republic* 344d.

30 See Socrates' short exchange with Callias. *Apology* 20a–b.

31 *Meno* 97d–e.

32 *Theaetetus*, 201d.

33 Aristotle, *Nicomachean Ethics*, 1160a20.

34 Homer, *Iliad* XXII.135 ff especially 199–201.

35 See *Socrates in the Underworld*, Ch. 2.

36 Aristotle, *Nicomachean Ethics*, 1101a20.

37 See *Gorgias* 515a ff.

38 Weiss says that had Crito not known Socrates, he'd have voted for his execution. p. 56.

39 *Apology* 28e.

40 *Gorgias* 464b ff.

41   *Gorgias* 521d.
42   *Apology* 32b–c.
43   *Republic* 576a ff.
44   Thucydides, *Peloponnesian War*, I.5.2.
45   Aristotle, *Nicomachean Ethics*, 1094b15.
46   Aristotle, *Nicomachean Ethics*, 1095a.
47   Aristotle, *Nicomachean Ethics*, 1226b15.
48   *Phaedo* 117b.
49   Aeschylus, *Agamemnon* 437–38.
50   For a parallel account see Nietzsche, *The Birth of Tragedy* 7–8.
51   *Republic* 351c.
52   *Gorgias*, 481c.
53   See *Meno* 96e.
54   *Gorgias* 519a.
55   Here we recall Thucydides' account of the mercurial humor of the Athenians regarding their decision to kill the entire male population of Mytilene: *Peloponnesian War* 3.36–50.
56   *Republic* 592b.
57   *Republic* 379b–c.
58   This was why members of the "mother of parliaments" only began to receive salaries exactly a century ago, and the holding of an office of profit under the crown was automatically grounds for exclusion from the legislature.
59   Plutarch, *Life of Aristides*, Modern Library, pp. 395–96.
60   John 19:26–27.
61   See Sophocles, *Oedipus at Colonus* 728ff. Here Creon would also act in the name of Socrates'/Oedipus' sons.
62   Aristotle, *Nicomachean Ethics*, 1159b25.
63   Aristotle, *Nicomachean Ethics*, 1117b10.
64   This is notoriously the position of Callicles (*Gorgias* 482c ff) and other "realists" who defend Clitophon's position in *Republic* I that justice is whatever seems to be to the advantage of the stronger (340b).
65   Aristotle, *Politics*, 1277b7.
66   For a suggestively casual reference to this practice see *Frogs* p. 44 trans. Richmond Lattimore in *Aristophanes Four Comedies*, Ann Arbor Paperbacks, 1994.
67   *Phaedo* 63d–e.
68   Plutarch's Life of Caesar in *Plutarch's Lives*, Modern Library, p. 876. Caesar significantly does not speak of this incident in his own *Civil Wars*.
69   Hobbes, Leviathan, XIV 19, XXI 9 ff.
70   Sophocles, *Oedipus at Colonus* 1224.
71   *Republic* 329d.
72   *Apology* 30c.
73   Homer, *Odyssey* XXI.214–16.
74   Here we add to the 600 (50 men in 12 ships) who sailed back with Odysseus, the 108 suitors, their 6 servants, the 12 maids, the goatherd, the priest and Eupeithes— the father of Antinous.

75 *Republic* 587e.
76 Thucydides, *Peloponnesian War*, 2.43.
77 Nietzsche, *Thus Spake Zarathustra*, PN p. 198.
78 *Laws* 722b–723c.
79 Diogenes Laertius II.121.
80 *Euthyphro* 8d–e.
81 While the *Republic* offers the most memorable indirect proof of this claim, the paradoxes of the *Gorgias* (472d, 480c ff) argue more explicitly in its favor.
82 We are reminded of Plato's myth of Er in *Republic X* where Odysseus about to be reborn chooses the life of a private citizen who minded his own business (620c–d).
83 Shakespeare, *Sonnet XCIV.*
84 *Republic* 379c.
85 Aristotle, *Nicomachean Ethics*, 1099b20.
86 *Gorgias* 478a ff.
87 See *Gorgias* 525b–c. These souls can only serve as a negative example for others. This is also the theme of such works as Wilde's *Portrait of Dorian Grey* and Sartre's *No Exit*.
88 Luke 2.46–50.
89 *Meno* 93c–94e.
90 See *Phaedo* 59b.
91 Aristotle, *Metaphysics*, 983a.
92 2 Timothy 4.6–8.

Index